ELLEN AND EDY

■ **Joy Melville** is a writer and freelance journalist. From 1971 to 1982, she was an assistant editor at *New Society*. Her other books include *Phobias and Obsessions* (1977), *How to Survive Unemployment* (1981) and *The Tranquilliser Trap* (1984). Joy Melville has lived and worked in Canada, the USA, Italy and Greece. She now lives in London.

Pandora Press
LIFE AND TIMES

Already published:

Woman of Letters
A Life of Virginia Woolf
Phyllis Rose

Jane and May Morris
A Biographical Story 1839-1938
Jan Marsh

For further details, see back of book.

ELLEN AND EDY

A BIOGRAPHY OF ELLEN TERRY AND HER DAUGHTER, EDITH CRAIG, 1847 – 1947

Joy Melville

London and New York

First published in 1987 by Pandora Press
(Routledge & Kegan Paul Ltd)
11 New Fetter Lane, London EC4P 4EE

Published in the USA by
Routledge & Kegan Paul Inc.
in association with Methuen Inc.
29 West 35th Street, New York, NY 10001

Set in Sabon 10/11pt
by Columns of Reading
and printed in the British Isles
by The Guernsey Press Co Ltd
Guernsey, Channel Islands

Library of Congress Cataloging in Publication Data
Melville, Joy.
    Ellen and Edy: a biography of Ellen Terry and her
daughter Edith Craig, 1847-1947.

    (Pandora Press life and times)
    Bibliography: p.
    Includes index.
    1. Terry, Ellen, Dame, 1847-1928.   2. Craig, Edith,
1869-1947.   3. Actors – Great Britain – Biography.
4. Theatrical producers and directors – Great Britain –
Biography.   5. Costume designers – Great Britain –
Biography.   6. Mothers and daughters – Great Britain –
Biography.   I. Title.   II. Series.

British Library CIP Data also available
ISBN 0-86358-252-4 (c)
      0-86358-078-5 (p)

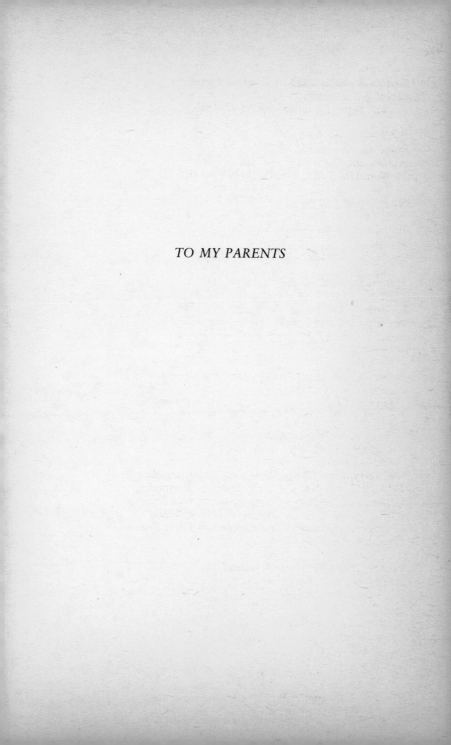

TO MY PARENTS

CONTENTS

ILLUSTRATIONS

PREFACE

The Victorian era was one of proclaimed moral respectability. Yet Ellen Terry, who reached the heights of the acting profession, had three husbands, a lover, two illegitimate children and a remarkably close stage relationship with her acting partner, Henry Irving. How did she get away with it?

Researching her life for the answers was exhilarating, because her gaiety came through so strongly and unexpectedly. Looking through the books in her library, for instance, I was taken aback to read, after a passage by Stephen Coleridge about the sanctity of wedded love, her scrawled comment, 'Really Stephen – you *cannot* mean what you say!'

But it was the enigma of Ellen herself that proved so absorbing. Although she wrote her own memoirs, so many diaries and letters were burnt, by Ellen, by her daughter, and then by the woman with whom her daughter lived, that proof about much of her private life is hard to find. The more I investigated, the more I came up with questions and not answers. What was the real reason for the break up of her first marriage to the painter G.F. Watts? Why did her lover, Edward Godwin the architect, leave her? Did she really have a love affair with Henry Irving?

As an actress, too, she had two sides. One was the talented professional, whose partnership with Henry Irving at the Lyceum Theatre from the 1870s to 1890s is now legendary, and who would study twenty-five reference books to get the character of the part right; write meticulous notes in her prompt copy; endlessly rehearse (Irving used to stand at the side of the stage and drop a handkerchief if she shouted too loudly); and advise actors to use the three 'I's': imagination, industry and intelligence.

But there was another, frivolous, side to Ellen Terry. She had a habit of collapsing with laughter on stage; she was so unpunctual that callboys would call her well in advance; she once saved time and startled Irving by sliding down the bannisters; in later years she forgot her words and had to pin her script up on the back of the stage furniture; and once she grabbed some rising scenery and, until spotted by a shocked property man, was carried some feet above the stage.

As a further complication, the actress in her warred with the woman. She always claimed to have no ambition and said that the greatest happiness in life came from 'absolute devotion to another human being.' And she left the stage without hesitation to spend years in the country with her lover, Edward Godwin, where she lived an entirely domestic life, cooking, cleaning, looking after the babies. Only the need for money made her return to acting.

Yet when she played at being a dutiful Victorian wife, unconventionality kept bursting through: on one post-marital social visit she took it into her head to roll over and over down a sloping lawn, looking, to her hostess's distress, like a long brown cigar.

At the Lyceum Theatre she earned more than any other woman in England, but, coming from an acting family, took self-sufficiency and freedom of choice so much for granted that she was almost puzzled by the suffragette movement. She would have sat uneasily on a platform with the militants, preferring suffragettes to be feminine rather than feminist, and believing that a 'wobbler' like her would only do mischief if she voted.

But her daughter, Edy Craig – Ellen impulsively bestowed the surname Craig on both her children after glimpsing the famous Scottish rock, Ailsa Craig – was an ardent suffragette. And as I began to research this book on Ellen, I became increasingly interested in her daughter and the inter-dependence between the two of them, which was quick to turn to a jealous possessiveness over each other's relationships. Ellen twice stepped in to block a love affair Edy was having, for instance, and Edy, in turn, locked the garden gate between their two adjacent houses when Ellen made a late, third marriage. Edy had two failed love affairs with men, then formed a lasting and happy relationship with a woman. Ellen disliked this at first, but became reconciled to it. After Ellen's death, Edy, perhaps unconsciously, began to resemble her more and more. She would even feel her way through doorways, in Ellen's half-blind manner, though her sight was all right.

Edy was a highly original costumier, the founder and producer of the Pioneer Players, a theatre society, and the organiser and producer of a great many pageants and plays staged around the country. Yet she is a shadowy figure, and I could get glimpses of her early days only through the memoirs and letters of her mother and her brother, who mentioned her in passing. Unlike them, she wrote nothing about herself and throughout her life can only be seen through others' eyes. Her manner could be brusque, in complete contrast to Ellen's effortless charm: Lilian Baylis refused to have her work at the Old Vic, on the grounds that she would upset the staff. But her friends and colleagues, after her death, wrote a commemorative collection of essays in which they praised her underlying generosity, her creativity, her fierce striving for perfectionism.

I have deliberately given Edy's brother Ted, known as Gordon Craig, a lesser place in the book. As an influential and talented theatrical pioneer, his life and work have been well documented. Instead, I have concentrated on the story of Ellen and Edy, their lives, off and on stage, and the ultimate strength of their relationship.

ACKNOWLEDGMENTS

My principal thanks are to Margaret Weare, Curator of the Ellen Terry Memorial Museum in Smallhythe, Kent, and her husband Tony, for their enthusiastic and generous help to me while I was researching this book.

A great many other people have helped me in different ways. I would especially like to thank Edward Craig, grandson of Ellen Terry, who gave me valuable information about both Ellen Terry and her daughter Edy, and read the manuscript; and Robert Craig, another grandson, who also gave me material assistance. I would also like to thank David Doughan of the Fawcett Library; David Goddard for additional research and indexing; Tony Gould; Richard Jefferies, Curator of the G.F. Watts Gallery, Compton in Surrey; David Loshak, for information on G.F. Watts; Ken Mahood and Pauline Melville.

The Ellen Terry Memorial Museum is the property of the National Trust and I would like to thank the Trust for its cooperation; and also all those who helped me at the Bibliothèque Nationale in Paris; the Theatre Museum, while housed at the Victoria and Albert Museum; the Enthoven Collection, Victoria and Albert; the Museum of London; the British Film Institute, for the private showing of an Ellen Terry film; and the British Theatre Association.

I would finally like to thank Philippa Brewster, my editor at Pandora, for her help and support.

All the photographs in this book are reproduced by kind permission of the National Trust, apart from the photograph of G.F. Watts in 1864 (by kind permission of the owners, Margaret and Tony Weare); the drawing of Ellen Terry by Violet, Duchess of Rutland, 1879 (by kind permission of the Watts Gallery); the photograph of G.F. Watts in 1858 (by kind permission of the National Portrait Gallery); and the cartoon by Bernard Partridge of Ellen Terry's jubilee (by kind permission of Punch Publications).

I am grateful to the following for permission to reprint material: Mr W. D'Arcy Hart of Gilbert Samuel & Co., literary executors for Ellen Terry, for the extracts from unpublished letters by Ellen Terry; to Robert Craig for permission to quote from unpublished letters from Ellen Terry to Edward Gordon Craig in the Bibliothèque Nationale; to the Society of Authors for the quotations from *A Correspondence* by Ellen Terry and Bernard Shaw; to Century Hutchinson for the quotations from *Ellen Terry and Her Secret Self* by Edward Gordon Craig; *To Tell My Story* by Irene Vanbrugh and *Mrs J. Comyns Carr's Reminiscences*; to Faber & Faber for the quotations from *The Laurel and the Thorn* by Ronald Chapman; to Laurence Irving for the quotations from *Henry Irving*; to Victor Gollancz for the quotation from Blanche Patch's *Thirty Years with G.B.S.*; to Hamish Hamilton for the quotations from *England's Michelangelo* by Wilfred Blunt, *Letters from Graham Robertson*, *Time Was* by Graham Robertson and *Our Three Selves: a life of Radclyffe Hall* by Michael Baker; to Punch Publications for the quotation from Henry Silver's diary; to Latimer House for the quotations from *The Conscious Stone* by Dudley Harbron; to Hulton Press for the quotations from *Index to the Story of My Days* by Edward Gordon Craig; to John Johnson Ltd for the quotations from *The Same Only Different* by Margaret Webster; to Edward Craig for the quotations from his book, *Gordon Craig*; to the Hogarth Press for quotations from *Between the Acts*; to Penguin for quotations from *Vita* by Victoria Glendinning; to A.M. Heath for quotations from *A Pride of Terrys* by Marguerite Steen; to the Victoria and Albert Museum for unpublished letters from Ellen Terry; and to Hodder & Stoughton for quotations from *Laughter in the Second Act* by Donald Sinden and *Dare To Be Wise* by Violet Vanbrugh.

Every effort has been made to trace owners of copyright for material used in this book. We will be happy to make any further acknowledgments in future editions.

GROWING UP: 'THE SPIRIT OF THE MUSTARD POT'

Ellen Terry had an endearing habit of thrusting her long hands into the air, as if she was catching moths. Yet, as a very young girl, she was so ashamed of her large hands she kept them tucked up under her arms – making one French theatre manager shout, 'Take down your hands! *Mon Dieu!* It is like an ugly young *poulet* going to roost!' But only the few found fault, and even then it was mainly over minor things: the way she always fiddled with her bag or her hair; her untidiness and unpunctuality; her lack of interest in her personal appearance; her frivolity. The rest bowed down to the queen of the theatre: her striking beauty; her deep, husky 'Terry' voice with its perfect enunciation; her light, graceful movements; her irrepressible gaiety and vitality; her naturalness on stage and the enormous pathos she was able to bring to her parts; her intimate, sympathetic and poetic way of acting; and her extraordinary charm that captivated her audiences.

She was born in Coventry on 27 February 1847 – despite her own lifelong belief (her birth certificate had been misfiled) that she was born a year later. The confusion extended to which theatrical lodging house she was born in; for years, a haberdasher's shop on one side of a narrow street bore the inscription, 'Birthplace of Ellen Terry,' while a tripe shop on the other side declared it was 'the original birthplace.' The argument ended when both were demolished in World War II.

The street itself was just round the corner from the old Coventry Theatre, pulled down in 1913, where Ellen's father, actor Ben Terry, was appearing on stage at the time of her birth. Both Ben and his wife Sarah were strolling players, the romanticised name for members of the circuit companies that toured the provinces. But Sarah took only small roles over the years – such as the part of the fourth singing witch, Hecate, in *Macbeth*, at the Theatre Royal, Glasgow, in the year that Ellen was born.

A tall, elegant woman, with her fair hair coiled around her head and an attractively deep speaking voice which her descendants inherited, Sarah's stage appearances were limited to brief periods between pregnancies and miscarriages. Since her marriage in 1838 she had given birth to four children before Ellen; Benjamin, born in 1839, two more who had died in infancy, and Kate, born in 1844. She was twenty seven when Ellen was born in 1847 and George, Marion, Florence, Charles, Tom and Fred were still to come.

Although Ben was to become a successful circuit actor, neither he nor Sarah came from theatrical backgrounds. Both were born and brought up in Portsmouth. Sarah's mother came from a rather respectable Scottish family, one of whose members had been John Singleton Copley, the painter and Royal Academician, while her father, Peter Ballard, was a builder and a Wesleyan lay preacher. Neither was exactly ecstatic over Sarah's choice of Ben Terry, an attractive swashbuckler in peg-top trousers, with easy Irish charm. Although Ben's parents – his father was an Irish publican – were good Wesleyans, like the Ballards, Ben had never settled into a steady job and had become infatuated with the theatre.

The Theatre Royal, Portsmouth, closed in 1836 after 'unseemly and improper conduct' on its premises. But the decision to reopen it the following year saw eighteen-year-old Ben Terry constantly hanging around backstage during the rehearsals. He gained an invaluable insight into the theatrical trade, and a grounding in acting techniques, just by watching the new manager, William Shalders – caricatured as Vincent Crummles by Charles Dickens in *Nicholas Nickleby*.

Shalders, anxious to make the new theatre a success, was a one-man whirlwind. He painted scenery, made the props, ran the box office, and even wrote pirated versions of London dramas, in which he and his wife and daughter acted the minor roles, and visiting actors the lead parts. Actor-managers like Shalders ran the provincial theatres in the nineteenth century, financing and organising their own stock company of actors and actresses. Shalders was paternal and tyrannical in turns towards his company of actors. Their job was to support the visiting actors who, if well known, usually had a low opinion of them. There is a story of Edmund Kean arriving at a small provincial town and being greeted by the manager of the stock company there, who asked him when he would like to rehearse. 'Rehearse!' said the great actor. 'I'm not going to rehearse. I'm going to sleep!' The manager asked if he had any instructions for the waiting company. 'Tell 'em to keep a long arm's length away from me and do their damned worst,' was Kean's reputed reply.[1]

In common with all stock companies, the Theatre Royal Portsmouth filled out its bill with burlesque and farce. Bernard Shaw recalled that on his first visit to the theatre in Dublin he saw a three act drama, followed by a complete Christmas pantomime, with a couple of farces as an hors d'oeuvre. Each actor would be typecast into a certain role: the Leading Man, the Leading Lady, the Ingenue, the Heavy Father, the Low Comedian and the Walking [On] Ladies and Gentlemen. Ben, who by persistence had managed to get the job of fiddler in the orchestra of the Portsmouth theatre, was able to watch these actors night after night, and be paid a few shillings for doing so. It only fuelled his passion to act – which hardly encouraged his courtship in the eyes of Sarah's parents. Actors had a low social status: they were thought of as rogues and vagabonds. Sarah would be demeaning herself.

However Sarah, with the resolution she continued to show throughout years of near poverty in theatrical lodgings, believed in Ben and was undaunted by the life he wanted to lead of a touring actor, with its constant travelling around the country and starvation wages. On 1 September 1838, when she was twenty one, she arranged to marry Ben at St Mary's, Portsea. Neither told their parents. Ben lied about his age – he was two weeks short of twenty one at the time – and, in the marriage register, cheekily put down his profession as 'gentleman.'

They left Portsmouth immediately, to start the circuit life. Circuit players travelled round in companies from town to town and village to village, taking supporting or even leading roles with the resident stock company. It could at times be a happy, casual life, but only devoted actors would put up with the constant, tedious journeys, the frequently poor business,

Ben Terry, Ellen's father, the first actor in the great theatrical family of Terrys.

and the bad theatrical accommodation – though in Ben and Sarah Terry's time it had at least improved since the days of the actor John Kemble (1757-1823), who at some of the towns and villages he visited was threatened with the stocks and with being whipped at the cart's tail.

John Coleman, biographer of the dramatist, Charles Reade, met Sarah and Ben on the Worcester circuit and recalled that Ben was 'a handsome, fine-looking, brown-haired man, and the wife as a tall, graceful creature, with an abundance of fair hair, and with big blue eyes set in a charming face.'[2] Although Sarah had no acting experience, she took the name Miss Yerret (an approximation of Terry spelt backwards) and was cast as a 'Walking Lady' – which meant appearing in crowd scenes, elegantly decorating the stage when needed, and helping backstage. Her work only brought in a few shillings, but with Ben earning, on average, about £1 a week, her money was crucial if they were to manage, particularly once the babies started coming.

Ellen later praised the way her mother had raised them all in such circumstances:

> She worked hard at her profession and yet found it possible not to *drag* up her children, to live or die as it might happen, but to *bring* them up to be healthy, happy, and wise – theatre-wise, at any rate. When her babies were too small to be left at the lodgings (which she and my father took in each town they visited as near to the theatre as possible), she would bundle them up in a shawl and put them to sleep in her dressing-room.[3]

The eldest boy, Benjamin, had nothing of the artist in him. Despite Sarah's care he grew up so undisciplined and troublesome that he was barely out of his teens before he relieved his family of his presence by working his passage to Australia. But no other future was thought of for Kate and Ellen apart from the stage.

They were fortunate in being born at a time when the theatre, and the scope it gave to actors, was radically changing. Until the mid nineteenth century, there had been remarkably little change since the time of Charles II in what the theatre offered its audiences. It was a thin enough fare. During the years before Charles's restoration to the throne in 1660, the

Puritans had tried to suppress drama entirely by outlawing theatre performances. In 1737, under the Licensing Act, the right to put on plays was reserved, but in a strangely tortuous manner by the issuing of patents – or licences – to two London theatres only, the Theatre Royal Drury Lane and the Theatre Royal, Covent Garden. Only these two licensed theatres could put on serious drama and all new plays had to be submitted for approval to the Lord Chamberlain. Other theatres had to be licensed by magistrates for the performance of *burletta* (burlesques).

It was a confused situation. The law was less severely enforced in the provinces; and in London the burlesques gradually moved closer to the 'legitimate drama' shown at the two great patent theatres. In 1830, an official examiner of plays complained that the minor theatres

> made their Recitative appear like Prose, by the actor running one line into another, and slurring over the rhyme; soon after, a harpsichord was touch'd *now and then*, as an accompaniment to the actor; sometimes once in a minute; then once in five minutes; at last – not at all.

In 1843, an Act for Regulating the Theatres was passed and the patent system ended. But the theatre was by now in a poor state: audiences were so rowdy that the middle and upper classes no longer went and, apart from burlesque, there was little opportunity for actors.

It was into this theatrical world that Ellen Terry was born; and had the outstanding actor managers of the time, like Sir Squire and Lady Bancroft, Charles Kean and Henry Irving, not made the theatre a respectable entertainment, offering serious drama, Ellen could well have spent her life playing the parts of boys in burlesques.

Ellen's first stage part was to have been the Spirit of the Mustard Pot. She seemed ideal – having pale yellow hair and being tiny enough to fit into the property mustard pot – but she screamed when they tried to squeeze her in. It was all very unprofessional and her father told her reproachfully that she would never make an actress.

Indeed, it was Kate, Ellen's elder sister, who became the success of the family. In 1852, aged eight, she played Prince Arthur so well during a stock season at Edinburgh, that critics recommended her to Charles Kean when he was casting his production of *King John* that year at the Princess's Theatre in Oxford Street. She was called up to London for an audition and, to her parents' delight, was again chosen for Prince Arthur. They realised it was her chance to break away from the provincial circuits and become known to London audiences and they were right. Kean was so pleased with Kate's acting that he retained her to be in all his plays, until he gave up management in 1859.

At that time, Ben had an acting engagement in Liverpool, but as Kate could not stay in London alone, Sarah joined her with young Ben and the new baby, George. Five year old Ellen was left in her father's care, but instead of him looking after her, she looked after him – even cooking his breakfast each day. Despite her domestic duties, Ellen delighted in spending her days in the company of her spirited father. Her temperament was similar to his: they were both impulsive and sunny-tempered.

She learned nothing scholastic from him, but in her memoirs recalled that,

He never ceased teaching me to be useful, alert, and quick. Sometimes he hastened my perceptive powers with a slipper, and always he corrected me if I pronounced any word in a slipshod fashion. He himself was a beautiful elocutionist, and if I now speak my language well, it is in no small degree due to my early training.

Looking back on her early days, Ellen often regretted her lack of formal school education. Yet in mid-Victorian England, most girls, like Ellen, were taught at home by their mother or an older sister; the three R's when they were small and housewifery skills when they grew older. Only the upper middle class and upper class could afford governesses and these usually concentrated on teaching genteel accomplishments like music, drawing, needlework and a smattering of French. Because of the Shakespearian and other classical parts Kate and Ellen learned early on, they were more literate than many other middle class girls of their age. Girls' education was inadequate then because it was regarded as inessential. Their only achievement could be marriage and children. As education for both boys and girls did not become compulsory until 1876,

Ellen in her first part as Mamillius in *A Winter's Tale*, with Charles Kean, 28 April 1856, at the Princess's Theatre.

only boys were sent off to school, with a career in mind. Education was not free then and to afford to send Benjy, the eldest, to school, Sarah had to earn extra shillings from walking-on parts or sometimes by taking on the job of Wardrobe Woman.

Ben and Ellen were not separated from the rest of the family for long. Within a year, to Ben's delight, Kean asked him to return to London and join his company and he remained with Kean for the next six years.

In 1856, Kean put on an elaborate revival of *The Winter's Tale*, with Ben as An Attendant, and Kate as Servant to the Old Shepherd. Ellen, or Nelly as she was always called, was auditioned and because of her clear articulation was given the part of Mamillius, the small son of King Leontes of Sicilia. She was then nine years old. Rehearsals for a child of that age were a lesson in fortitude. There were no breaks for lunch, and performances began at seven a.m. and lasted until midnight, including Sundays. Ellen was often found asleep in the green room. To make rehearsals even more of an ordeal, Charles Kean would sit in the stalls with a big dinner bell by his side, which he rang ferociously when anything went wrong. Mrs Kean would then rush on stage to put it right.

The play opened on 28 April. It was with this production that Charles Kean started the tradition, continued and elaborated by Henry Irving, that the historical detail of both scenery and costume should be accurate. As Mamillius, Nelly wore a little red and silver dress, pink tights and sausage curls. She had to pull a go-cart around the stage and the first night she did so with such enthusiasm that she tripped over the handle and crashed over. The audience laughed and Nelly, weeping, felt it was her 'first dramatic failure' and that her 'career as an actress was ruined for ever.' But the critics praised her. *The Times* declared that she had played her part with vivacious precocity and said she was a worthy relation of her sister. And the Reverend Charles Dodgson (Lewis Carroll) commented that he 'especially admired the acting of the little Mamillius, Ellen Terry, a beautiful little creature, who played with remarkable ease and spirit.'[4] Nelly herself showed her first professionalism: the play ran for 102 nights and she never once gave her understudy a chance of standing in.

Kean's next play, *A Midsummer Night's Dream*, tested her

professionalism again. Nelly was cast as Puck, and one night came up through a trap door as usual to give her final speech. However, the trap door jammed and caught her toe. Kate, who was Titania, banged her foot on the stage as a signal to release the door — but the stage-hand, misinterpreting this, ignored Kate's signal. As in a Victorian melodrama, Mrs Kean ran on and promised the screaming Nelly that her salary would be doubled if she would finish the play. Nelly tearfully finished her speech and her salary went up from fifteen to thirty shillings a week.

A Midsummer Night's Dream ran for a phenomenal 250 nights. Nelly was called a 'delightful little fairy,' though she said herself that she was very gawky, not to say ugly. 'My hair had been cut short, and my red cheeks stuck out too much. I was a sight!' She loved playing Puck, however, as it was an imaginative role and her performance was praised for the 'hearty appreciation of the mischief she was causing.' She caused more mischief than usual one night. Puck, told to put a girdle round the earth in forty minutes, had to run from the stage, and was to be replaced by a dummy, whirling through the air. Unfortunately the dummy fell to the ground and Nelly, anxious for its safety, ran on stage, picked it up and ran off again, to roars of laughter from the audience.

Nelly remembered the incident with shame, though she was always to behave unpredictably on stage. Mrs Kean told her off, but despite her sharp tongue, she gave Nelly a grounding in acting which lasted her all her life. She showed Nelly how to draw in her breath through the nose and begin a laugh; and gave indefatigable instructions on enunciation — cautioning Nelly not to mix up her vowels like a pudding, to say river, not riv*ah*, her not *har*, God not *Gud*, remo*n*strance, not rem*un*strance. She also advised her to use her arms from the shoulder, not from the elbow, to stop her standing like a statue.[5]

The ballet master at the theatre helped too, by pinning a blanket on each player, which trailed down front and back, and then teaching them how to walk with dignity. Long narrow planks were placed some feet above the stage and actors had to walk across these faster and faster until they could do so without swerving or looking down at their feet.

In the mid-nineteenth century, the London and main provincial theatres closed for summer from July to September each year, giving actors an annual break. In the summer of 1857, after *A Midsummer Night's Dream* had ended, Ben Terry couldn't afford to take his ever-expanding family – the seventh child, Charles, was born that year – on holiday. Ellen remembered the long walk home from the theatre each night with her father and Kate (her father would wrap his enormous cloak around them both and, because they then couldn't see, pretend they were passing shops near to their home) and, on arrival, finding her mother sewing away by the light of one candle, just to keep her and Kate neatly dressed. Ellen, for many years, thought herself lucky to get a few pence a week for pocket money. The rest of her salary, like all the family earners, went towards living expenses.

So, for cheapness, Ben took them all down to Ryde, on a busman's holiday. He leased the theatre there and put on several farces that had been successful in London. Kate and Ellen naturally took part in these and Ellen was described by one critic as 'a perfect little heap of talent.' She was honest enough to admit that 'a perfect little heap of vanity' would have been more to the point.

On returning to the Princess's in October 1857, Nelly auditioned for the bad fairy Dragonetta in the Christmas pantomime, *White Cat*. With a praised summer season behind her she was shocked to be rejected and given the minor part of the maudlin good fairy, Goldenstar. By working hard, however, she got the part of fairy Dragonetta, and her own children later remembered her giving them the shivers with her blood-thirsty rendering of Dragonetta's 'I'll have them broiled for tea,' speech.

The pantomime, *White Cat*, often ran as a double bill with *A Midsummer Night's Dream*, working ten year old Nelly so hard she continued to rush to the green room to sleep whenever she could. The next year, 1858, she was given the part of Prince Arthur, in *King John*, Kate's much-praised role. But she couldn't do anything right in the early rehearsals. At one point, Mrs Kean stormed at her and slapped her and she started to cry with mortification – inadvertently getting the exact expression in her voice that Mrs Kean wanted. She was immediately told to remember what she did with her voice and reproduce it.

As Prince Arthur, Nelly, who had always thought acting fun, but disliked its grind, began to take it more seriously: 'I used to get up in the middle of the night and watch my gestures in the glass. I used to try my voice and bring it down and up in the right places. And all vanity fell away from me.'[6]

At the end of the 1859 season, the Keans gave up the management of the Princess's Theatre and went off to America, leaving Kate, Ellen and Ben Terry out of work. Ben, inspired by the success of the Ryde season, and knowing that Kate and Ellen were now a draw, decided to stage his own theatricals under the guise of a *Drawing-Room Entertainment*.

It consisted of two plays, *Home for the Holidays* and *Distant Relations* and Kate and Ellen played all the parts in each piece, doing quick changes worthy of Houdini. The production was staged at the Royal Colosseum, Regent's Park, with its weird, imitation stalactite caverns. More than 30,000 people came to see it. Its success assured a tour throughout the provinces, as well as Dublin and Belfast and the Isle of Wight. Ben Terry acted as stage manager, and did the work of an army of carpenters. For two years he and Sarah, Nelly and Kate and a musician, travelled around Britain, usually by getting lifts on wagons, as despite rapid rail development, there were not railways everywhere. Once they tramped from Bristol to Exeter. It gave Ellen her lifelong love of the countryside: 'I should like to run wild in a wood for ever,' she said. They went to a new place every day, making about £10 or £15 a performance – which helped to pay for the younger children's school fees.

When the tour ended in 1861, Nelly returned to London with her father to find work. She was engaged by the Royalty Theatre, a small Soho playhouse managed by a Madame Albina de Rhona, an attractive, petite Parisienne. Nelly was to say of her: 'Despair entered my soul when I looked at my own big limbs and thought how long and gaunt I was, and how dainty and pretty she!'[7]

It was an understandable reaction of the times. Victorian women were conditioned into being preoccupied with their appearance, and delicacy was all – right down to wearing boned corsets to give themselves a fourteen inch waist. Nelly was very conscious that her size did not conform to the Victorian ideal.

The first play she was in at the Royalty was a sensational melodrama called *Attar-Gull*, in which the cast were slowly

Kate Terry, Ellen's older sister, who initially outshone Ellen as a young actress on stage, 1860.

killed off and Nelly was required to give a series of blood curdling screams while a python strangled her. She wrote in her memoirs:

> Looking back at it now, I know perfectly well why I, a mere child of thirteen, was able to give such a realistic display of horror. I had the emotional instinct to start with, no doubt, but if I did it well, it was because I was able to imagine what would be *real* in such a situation. . . . Imagination, industry, and intelligence – 'the three I's' – are all indispensable to the actress, but of these three the greatest is, without any doubt, imagination.

Nelly stayed under Madame de Rhona's management for some months, doing a fast succession of parts as the Frenchwoman unerringly chose plays that failed to attract audiences. In one of the productions, for the first time, Nelly got stage fright and 'dried' on stage. She put it down to having five new parts to study between 21 November and 26 December. But her memory was never good; in later years she pinned up her lines everywhere – on the chairbacks, stage window, lampshades and curtains.

In February 1862, Nelly left the Royalty and along with the rest of the family went off to join Kate who, at the end of their tour the year before, had gone to Bristol and become the principal lady in Mr J.H. Chute's stock company there.

But Nelly wasn't Kate and there was no question of being given a lead, or even a suitable, part: every member of the company had to take what they were given. The work was hard, with one-act farces and burlesques mixed in, as usual, with tragedies and comedies. They rehearsed by day and acted at night. The first time Nelly was cast to play in a burlesque, she pointed out that she could neither sing nor dance. 'I was told that I *had* to! and I did, in a way – it was a funny way – but it was the best thing that could happen to me, for it took the self-consciousness out of me, and after a while I thought it great fun.'[8] She was applauded, though the Bristol audiences were shocked by her short tunic.

Unlike the Princess's Theatre, where rehearsals had been exhaustingly long, in Bristol there was hardly any preparation. Nevertheless, Nelly enjoyed herself. A watcher at rehearsals described her as being 'brimful of merriment, taking nothing gravely – a gay, mercurial child, exuberant, *insouciante*, irrepressibly mirthful.'

Other young actresses must have envied her. Mr Chute, who had married Macready's half sister, was running one of the most powerful stock companies in England at the time – among its members were Marie Wilton (later Lady Bancroft, the actress manager), and Madge Robertson (Mrs Kendal) – and both Kate and Nelly were lucky to get the chance of acting very varied parts, ranging from Shakespeare to the broadest farce. But they were by no means passengers. Both got constantly good reviews. The *Bristol Daily Post*, for instance, said

> We regard Miss Kate Terry as an actress whose mental qualifications are beyond her age. . . . Miss Ellen Terry, for so young an *artiste*, is also charming, and she possesses a natural flow of spirits which must make her a favourite wherever she appears.

Another appreciative critic in Bristol, who had also singled out and praised Ellen's performance as Puck in London the previous year, was Edward Godwin, a highly successful young architect, with wide-ranging interests. He collected rare books; played the organ – even building one into his house; he was such a Shakespeare enthusiast that he held readings; went constantly to the theatre with his wife; and wrote reviews of the plays, despite being horsewhipped by an angry actor he had criticised.

Godwin was married to the former Miss Sarah Yonge and they were then living in Portland Square, a fashionable area of Bristol. As the Theatre Royal company was performing Shakespeare, and Godwin had previously met Sarah and Ben Terry on one of their visits to Bristol, he received their permission to invite Kate and Ellen to take part in one of the regular Shakespeare readings held at his house.

Ellen at the time was an impressionable fifteen-year-old. After a life spent in sleazy theatrical lodgings, the house at Portman Square amazed her – as indeed it did Godwin's neighbours, for in style it was in total contrast to the clutter and upholstered comfort the Victorians loved. Godwin had painted the walls of the rooms in plain colours; hung oriental woodcuts and Japanese prints – rare in England – on the walls;

and covered the bare floors with Persian rugs. He had carefully selected antique furniture to match.

This sense of design, in every detail, was a revelation to Ellen. She was to say:

> At the theatre, I was living in an atmosphere which was developing my powers as an actress and teaching me what work meant, but my mind had begun to grasp dimly and almost unconsciously that I must do something for myself — something that all the education and training I was receiving in my profession could not do for me. . . . I now felt that I had never really lived at all before. For the first time I began to appreciate beauty, to observe, to feel the splendour of things, to *aspire*.[9]

She and Kate went to several of Godwin's play readings, with Ellen's admiration for him growing when she found out that he was the author of the theatrical *Jottings* in the local paper, a column she thought was 'very clever, most amusing — and generally right.' In fact, she regarded Godwin and his wife as 'a very wonderful family,' and architects and archaeologists and other professional people she met at their play readings were, to her, as memorable as the house. Much more exuberant than her calmer sister, she found the whole experience enthralling.

When, in the March of 1863, Mr Chute's stock company did a performance of *A Midsummer Night's Dream* at the Theatre Royal in Bath, Nelly was cast as Titania and Godwin designed her dress. He showed her how to damp the material and twist it while it was wet — tying it up in a similar way to the tie and dye process, so that it was crinkled and clinging. Nelly had never heard of such a process; but as far as she was concerned it 'was the first lovely dress that I ever wore.'

Godwin liked both the sisters; so did a host of local young admirers, who hung around the streets in the daytime in the hope of seeing them go out shopping; and patiently waited outside their lodgings in Queen Square to escort them to the theatre and back again. However, Sarah and Ben Terry were strict chaperones and one or other always accompanied the girls on their walk to and from the theatre.

In the same month as *A Midsummer Night's Dream*, J.B. Buckstone ('Old Bucky'), actor manager of the Haymarket

Ellen's mother Sarah Terry, née Ballard, in August 1883, at the age of sixty six.

Theatre in London, was casting for a new production of *The Little Treasure*, an adaptation of a French comedy, and heard that Ellen Terry's Bristol performance of the little treasure, Gertrude, had been excellent. She was asked to re-create the part, and opened at the Haymarket on 19 March, playing opposite Edward Sothern as Captain Maydenblush. She may have been only sixteen, but by now she was an experienced actress: the bills outside the theatre described her as 'late of the New Theatre Royal, Bath.'

Her success was immediate: *The Times* review called her 'one of the happiest specimens of what the French call the *ingénue* that have been seen on any stage.' Ellen admitted she was fond of larking around, but hated being laughed at. A particular tormentor was the hugely popular Edward Sothern, who had a mania for practical jokes. 'I could see no humour in Mr Sothern's jokes at my expense,' Ellen was to say. 'He played my lover in *The Little Treasure*, and he was always teasing me – pulling my hair, making me forget my part and look like an idiot.'[10]

She still went on larking around herself, however. The critic Clement Scott thought her a madcap and recalled seeing her

> sit on the stage in a serious play and literally cry with laughing, the audience mistaking her fun for deep emotion; and actors have told me that in most pathetic scenes she has suddenly been attracted by the humorous side of the situation and almost made them 'dry up'.[11]

In another instance, Ellen, still at the Haymarket, was playing the part of Britannia. At one stage she was surrounded by the Knights of the Round Table who were pretending they couldn't lift a particular 'property' stone, meant to be too heavy for a mortal to move. Ellen walked forward, took the mock boulder in her hands, threw it in the air, and cried out, 'Why, a child could toss it!'

Although Ellen was quite happy with the way she played her next part, Hero in *Much Ado about Nothing*, which she thought she did 'beautifully,' she nevertheless looked back on her time at the Haymarket with regret. In her memoirs she wrote:

Never at any time in my life have I been ambitious, but at the

Haymarket I was not even passionately anxious to do my best with every part that came my way – a quality which with me has been a good substitute for ambition. I was just dreaming of and aspiring after another world, a world full of pictures and music and gentle, artistic people with quiet voices and elegant manners. The reality of such a world was Little Holland House, the home of Mr Watts.

CHAPTER 2

G.F. WATTS:
'THE ATRABILIOUS
BRIDEGROOM'

When Ellen first met George Frederic Watts, the distinguished allegorical painter, she was sixteen and he forty six – a 'middle-aged, lukewarm gentleman,' according to Bernard Shaw. Their meeting came about by chance, through both Watts and the Terry family knowing Tom Taylor and his wife, Laura. Tom Taylor was an enthusiastic amateur actor, as well as a playwright, author, dramatic and art critic for *The Times* – and editor of *Punch*. He and Laura were a gregarious couple, their home in Lavender Sweep, Wandsworth, being, Ellen recalled in her memoirs, 'a sort of house of call for everyone of note' and 'one of the most softening and culturing influences of my early life.'

Taylor, always doing good turns for his friends, could see that the sisters' careers would be further enhanced by having their portrait painted by the celebrated Watts. However, Kate by this time was the toast of the town, so Watts may have asked Taylor for the introduction himself. Versions differ. The actor Johnston Forbes-Robertson for instance, said that Tom Taylor told him that Watts wanted to pay his addresses to Kate, and had asked Taylor to introduce him to the family – only to have Kate reject his advances. Watts then turned to Ellen.

Even if Watts did initially prefer Kate, it is clear from his portrait of the two of them, called 'The Sisters,' for which they sat at his studio in Little Holland House, that it was Ellen who now attracted him. She dominates the painting – leaning against Kate's shoulder, looking joyously full of life. He, in turn, attracted Ellen intellectually, though probably not physically. Ruskin wrote of him that he was 'very pale . . . thin – long faced – rather bony and skinny in structure of face features ... the thinness being evidently caused by suffering both of mind and body.'[1]

The suffering was true enough. Since childhood, Watts had been susceptible to asthma, melancholia and migraine. Born on 23 February 1817, in a dilapidated house near Bryanston Square in London, his early years were over-shadowed by poverty. His father, a piano manufacturer, was discontented with his work and put all his energy, time and money into inventing an instrument that combined wind and string. Failing, he was forced to make a living as a piano tuner.

A sickly child – the only survivor of four children – George Watts was rarely well enough to go to school. Instead he spent much of his time alone, reading what G.K. Chesterton called 'large legendary literature,' and drawing. He saw little of his mother, a bedridden consumptive, who died when he was nine. Instead his father – both depressed and obsessed – dominated his days, as he looked to his son to realise his own failed ambitions and hopes.

Watts showed early talent in his drawing and spent much of his boyhood in the workshop of the sculptor, William Behnes. By sixteen, he was earning five shillings a time for doing portraits in pencil or chalk. But conscious of his father's ambitions for him, he despaired, when only in his teens, that he 'had lived so long and achieved nothing.'

It looked as if his self-assessment was right. When his father asked the President of the Royal Academy, Sir Martin Archer Shee, for an opinion of his son's work, Shee replied: 'I can see *no* reason why your son should take up the profession of art.' Watts ignored this: often self-deprecating and even humble about his work, he nevertheless had great confidence in himself. At eighteen, he joined the Royal Academy Schools and by the time he was twenty had had three pictures accepted for the summer exhibition and was receiving a steady number of commissions to do portraits.

In 1843, aged twenty six, he entered a competition for a painting for the new Houses of Parliament and won a prize of £300. He used the money to go to Italy, a long-cherished wish. In Florence he met the British Minister and his wife, Lord and Lady Holland, and stayed with them while he painted Lady Holland, who greatly admired his work – and probably the young artist, too. Although he was a priggish young man, with no humour, he was then quite handsome.

Liking life with the Hollands, Watts showed no signs of going. Lord Holland's early approval began to wear thin, and he wrote of him as being 'terribly dilatory and indolent . . . I have worried him into painting portraits.'[2] When Watts turned to landscape painting and, despite poverty, high-mindedly refused portrait commissions as being unworthy of a true artist, Holland criticised him for being foolish, saying, 'I suspect he is just now in the fervour of historical painting, and will not be so unreasonable when the fit of glory and the visions of Michael Angelo shall subside a little.' The glory and the vision were, in fact, to remain with Watts all his life as he tried to keep alive the tradition of grand historical art.

Watts finally returned to England in 1847, but only because his friends urged him to enter another public competition – this time a painting was needed to decorate the House of Lords. He again won a prize, with his painting of 'Alfred Inciting the Saxons to Resist the Landings of the Danes.' Thus began, as Chesterton later observed, 'his great custom of offering his pictures as gifts worthy of a great nation.' But it led to no further commissions. To keep up his standard of living, Watts had to swallow his high-minded principles and continue portrait painting.

One of the portraits he painted was of an attractive woman called Virginia Pattle, later Lady Somers, who came accompanied by two of her sisters (there were seven Pattle sisters altogether), the dumpy, but energetic Mrs Sarah Prinsep and Julia Margaret Cameron, the photographer; the three of them being nicknamed 'Beauty, Dash and Talent.' It was a casual meeting, but Mrs Prinsep, like Lady Holland before her, was to become another of the masterful women in Watts' life – and, for a short time, in Ellen's, too.

Married to the genial Thoby Prinsep, a retired Indian civil servant, Sarah Prinsep had one ambition: to establish her house as a literary and artistic salon. Watts – in her eyes (and his) a neglected genius, with the added cachet of having a circle of artistic and social contacts through Lord and Lady Holland – seemed to her a perfect focal point for such a salon. Watts became a constant visitor to the house in Chesterfield Street, in London.

Needing a larger, less commonplace house for her purpose,

G.F. Watts, photographed by James Soane in 1858, six years before he married Ellen.

Mrs Prinsep heard from Watts that Lord Holland was prepared to rent out Little Holland House in Kensington. It was a large, rambling farmhouse, surrounded by long green lawns and meadows, and the Prinseps snapped it up.

Watts, now in his early thirties, was not acting as any kind of focal point, having become sunk in melancholia. 'I often think very seriously of prussic acid,' he wrote to a friend. In the years since returning from Italy, he had encountered indifference to his desire to do mural paintings. His mood was reflected in his work: he portrayed the poverty and social evils around him in melancholic paintings like 'Found Drowned' (body of a young suicide) and 'Under a Dry Arch' (a starving woman). His work showed a preoccupation with Satan.

Wilfrid Blunt, in his biography of Watts, wrote of him then: 'He was not only disillusioned and often physically ill; he was also emotionally unstable, sexually frustrated, and probably sexually ignorant.'[3] He expressed some of his sexual feelings in a number of erotic paintings, including a near-pornographic one called 'Satan and Sin.'

Watts wrote at the time: 'often I sit among the ruins of my aspirations, watching the tide of time.' In Sarah Prinsep's eyes, there was only one way to restore his spirits: Watts was persuaded to come and stay at Little Holland House. She was to say afterwards, rather like the Hollands, 'he came to stay three days, he stayed thirty years' – though in fact it was not as long as that. But once at Little Holland House, where he was looked upon with pride, called 'Signor' because of the Italian connection, tempted with special dishes, and relieved of all domestic and financial pressures, he began to paint with renewed vigour. As a precaution, Sarah Prinsep got her oldest son to act as watchdog and redirect Watts's steps to his studio, if he strayed.

However, Watts was still prey to melancholy and wrote to a friend, Mrs Nassau Senior, the sister of Tom Hughes, author of *Tom Brown's Schooldays*, that he was

> not at all well, always headache, headache, headache, I am out of tune with everything . . . sick of life, and desire to rest. Yet some lingering ambition, perhaps I should say vanity, makes me grieve to think of departing without taking a place amongst the names that will be loved and admired.[4]

Mrs Prinsep was both mother and agent to Watts, cosseting him in ill health, proudly showing him off as her pet genius at her Bohemian tea parties which acted as meeting points for celebrated guests like Dickens, Disraeli, Browning, Tennyson, Burne Jones, Rossetti, Millais, Ruskin and Thackeray. Writing of these parties, George du Maurier said that tea was handed out by Mrs Prinsep and his sisters 'almost kneeling' and that 'Watts, who is a grand fellow, is their painter in ordinary; the best part of the house has been turned into his studio, and he lives there and is worshipped till his manliness hath almost departed, I should fancy.' Another visitor, Lady Constance Leslie, wrote that 'Signor was the whole object of adoration and care in that house. He seemed to sanctify Little Holland House.'[5]

When Ellen first entered Little Holland House, she was captivated by the spacious rooms, the series of wall frescoes by Watts on 'Peace and War' and 'Greece in the Lap of Egypt,' and the shrine – approached through a red baize door – of Watts's great studio, filled with vast canvasses. Writing of it later in her memoirs, she said: 'It seemed to me a paradise, where only beautiful things were allowed to come. All the women were graceful, and all the men were gifted.' The surroundings brought back memories of the Godwins' house in Bristol. She responded rapturously to the beauty and culture around her, the artistic interior of the house and its attractive grounds. She regarded Watts himself with near reverence and he in turn was dazzled by her youth and beauty.

Roddam Spencer Stanhope, the Pre-Raphaelite painter and a former pupil of Watts, claimed that Watts told a friend he was thinking of adopting Ellen Terry and asked what he thought. 'I think she is too old,' came the reply. When Watts returned to the subject later on, saying he had thought over the advice and was now thinking of marrying Ellen Terry, he got the reply, 'I think she is too young.'[6]

Watts, however, had decided by this time that he needed a wife and was as near infatuated as someone of his reserved character could be. He was also inspired by Ellen as a model. The very qualities that were later to provoke him, now attracted him: her bubbling high spirits, impulsiveness, lack of sophistication and unpredictability. He felt her character was still unformed and it was his wish – indeed, his duty – to mould

it into shape. Soon he was to write to his friend Lady
Constance Leslie:

> Knowing how much you are interested in the Miss Terrys, I
> am going to tell you a thing that will perhaps surprise you.
> I have determined to remove the younger girl from the
> temptations & abominations of the stage, giving her a [sic]
> education & if she continues to have the affection she now
> feels for me, marry her. There is a great difference between
> her age and mine & I should not think of putting any
> pressure upon her inclinations, but I think whatever the
> future brings, I can hardly regret taking the poor child out of
> her present life and fitting her for a better.
>
> I hope in what I had undertaking [sic] to do, I shall have
> the countenance of my friends, for it is no light matter from
> any point of view, even the expense will be considerable as I
> shall have to compensate her family for loss of her services.
> . . . I should be v. glad if you would tell Mrs Prinsep and
> her family so, for you know the prejudice there is against the
> stage (I share it myself). Miss Terry is very young & I do not
> see the future at all distinctly, but give her a chance of
> qualifying herself for a good position in society. I do not
> think I ought to be thought ill of. . . . To make the poor
> Child what I wish her to be, will take a lot of time & most
> likely cost a great deal of trouble & I shall want the
> sympathy and aid of all my friends so I hope none will look
> coldly on my endeavours.[7]

Graham Robertson, the artist and writer, was later to write
to a friend: 'If Watts thought he could mould that vital and
radiant creature into what he wished her to be, he did not show
much intelligence.'[8] But Watts' request to Lady Constance that
she, and not he, tell Sarah Prinsep and her family about his
intentions, implies that he was expecting criticism. It was, after
all, an unexpected choice and raised a few eyebrows. George du
Maurier wrote to the painter Tom Armstrong in February 1864
to say,

> What do you think for a piece of news – Watts is going to
> be married on the 20th to Ellen Terry, sister of the lovely
> Kate of that Ilk. I saw E. Terry at St James's and was not
> particularly struck; but am told she is charming.[9]

The subject came up at a *Punch* dinner and Henry Silver, a staff member, wrote in his diary that 'apropos of Old Watts marrying Miss Ellen Terry – who really loves him. She received as a Valentine the ashes of her photographs, burned by an admirer – "Bly fool!" bursts out Shirley [Brooks].'[10] Brooks was later to edit the magazine.

Some of the nonsensical gossip of the time was later retold by Violet Hunt, the novelist:

Old Mrs Prinsep [was] the real demon of the piece . . . she first got the great Watts (Signor) to share her roof and shine on her with reflected glory, then . . . [to] *keep him* she conceived the idea of marrying him off to Nelly Terry, a rather simple little innocent flirt whom Tom T. had brought to the house . . . but my mother always said that Kate went to him [Watts] and said that he had made her 'poor little sister dead in love with him' and Nelly was awed and impressed by the magnificence of being Mrs Watts. She did not realise that Mrs Prinsep meant to keep him and did.[11]

The only true comment in this highly coloured and invented account was that Ellen, impressed by Watts' paintings was undoubtedly thrilled by the prospect of becoming his wife and living at Little Holland House. 'I was delighted, and my parents were delighted,' she wrote in her memoirs, 'although the disparity of age between my husband and me was very great . . . I was happy, because my face was the type which the great artist who had married me loved to paint.'

Ellen never said that she was in love with Watts: both of them would have thought that was presumptuous. Nineteenth century women were taught from childhood to revere the male. 'Love in the heart of a wife,' instructed an etiquette book of the time, 'should partake largely of the nature of *Gratitude* to the Man who has chosen *her* to be his helpmate.' Ellen was indeed grateful. As she wrote to Shaw years later:

I'll never forget my first kiss . . . Mr Watts kissed me in the studio one day, but sweetly and gently, all tenderness and kindness . . . and I was in heaven for I knew I was to live with those pictures. 'Always' I thought, and to sit to [sic] that gentle Mr W. and clean his brushes, and play my idiotic piano to him, and sit with him there in wonderland (the studio).

Then I got ill and had to stay at Little Holland House –
and then – he kissed me – *differently* not much differently
but a little and I told no one for a fortnight, but when I was
alone with Mother one day she looked so pretty and sad and
kind. I told her – what do you think I told the poor darling? I
told her I *must* be married to him *now* because I was going
to have a baby!!!! *and she* believed me. Oh, I tell you I
thought I knew everything then, but I was nearly 16 years
old then – and I was *sure* that kiss meant giving me a baby.[12]

The wedding was small and quiet, and held at St Barnabas's
Church, Kensington, on 20 February 1864. Lady Constance, a
guest at the wedding, was reported to have said that 'the
contrast between the atrabilious bridegroom, walking slowly
and heavily up the aisle, and the radiant child bride dancing up
it on winged feet,' struck her as painful.

Ellen's own recollections of the wedding were more centred
around her clothes:

On that day I wore a brown silk gown which had been
designed by Holman Hunt, and a quilted white bonnet with
a sprig of orange-blossom, and I was wrapped in a beautiful
Indian shawl. I 'went away' in a sealskin jacket with coral
buttons, and a little sealskin cap. I cried a great deal, and
Mr Watts said, 'Don't cry. It makes your nose swell'.[13]

The reprimand was teacher to pupil rather than loving
husband to wife. And biographers are split over whether or not
the marriage was consummated. There is no proof either way,
though Wilfrid Blunt, a biographer of Watts and one-time
curator of the Watts Gallery, considers that Watts was
repressed and shy of sex throughout the whole of his life.
Marguerite Steen, a biographer of the Terry family, draws a
melancholy (and unsubstantiated) picture of the wedding night:

The ill-matched pair went back to Little Holland House. On
her marriage night Nelly was discovered, crying bitterly, on
the staircase outside the nuptial chamber. Her initiation, at
the hands of a fumbling and neurotic lover, was a sad one.[14]

The second Mrs Watts – whom he married in 1886 at the
age of sixty nine – told a woman friend of hers, according to
her son, that 'he couldn't do very much, but he liked to fumble
about.' He would surely have been more ardent, and more

G.F. Watts, photographed by Julia Margaret Cameron, in 1864, the year of his marriage to Ellen.

capable, at the age of forty seven, with a young bride to whom he was, above all, physically attracted.

There was no formal honeymoon. Instead, shortly after the marriage, Ellen and Watts, chaperoned inevitably by the Prinseps, went to the Isle of Wight to stay a few weeks with Mrs Prinsep's sister, Julia Cameron, and her husband. Ellen, relieved of her duty of spending hours posing for Watts, spent hours instead posing for Julia Cameron – each photograph requiring her to sit without moving for about half an hour. For posterity's sake it was worth it. One of Julia Cameron's photographs of Ellen at that time is perhaps one of the loveliest ever taken, showing her dreamily and sensuously leaning against a wall, half child, half woman.

Ellen was the first to admit that she had not yet left childhood behind. She became friendly with Tennyson who was a frequent guest, and would go for walks with him over the fields, finding herself quite at ease with him because of his simplicity. She admitted she fitted in more easily with the younger children. The ideal Victorian girl was dutiful, ladylike, modest and cooperative. Girls who behaved in an unfeminine way, exhibiting, in the words of the *Girls' Own Paper* 'a deplorable degree of roughness,' were dubbed 'a hoyden.' The Little Holland House menage looked on her antics disapprovingly.

'At Freshwater,' [the Camerons' house], Ellen was to say,

> I was still so young that I preferred playing Indians and Knights of the Round Table with Tennyson's sons, Hallam and Lionel, and the young Camerons, to sitting indoors noticing what the poet did and said. . . . But he and all the others seemed to me very old. There were my young knights waiting for me; and jumping gates, climbing trees, and running paper-chases are pleasant when one is young.[15]

A neighbour, Ella Hepworth Dixon, recalled her brother telling the story of Watts calling at the house to present his youthful bride during the burial of a pet bird. Ellen at once joined in the funeral rites and he remembered her kissing the dead bird as they carried it, on a grassy bier, to the tiny grave. Watts was not one of the mourners. Ellen found him 'old for his age . . . nervous about his health and always teetering about in galoshes.'

In 1923, Virginia Woolf wrote a play about Freshwater, which was staged in 1935, with Duncan Grant taking the part of Watts. The audience laughed so much, it had to be taken off.[16]

On returning to Holland House, Ellen faced immediate difficulties as Sarah Prinsep, the senior woman in the household, carried out the duties which were normally the responsibility of the wife – deciding on menus, instructing the servants, overseeing the linen cupboard and so on. Yet Ellen was Mrs Watts, and expected to act accordingly, instead of remaining as the petted child model. The abrupt transition was initially too difficult. 'I sat shrinking and timid, in a corner – the girl-wife of a famous painter.'

It was only in Watts's studio, where she posed for him for hours that Ellen could find any real contentment. It was early in the marriage that Watts painted the famous picture 'Choosing,' which shows her in her wedding dress, trying to decide between the attractions of a camellia and violets. On one occasion, when she was posing in very heavy armour, the session went on so long that she fainted. Watts jumped, and left a smear of red on the painting – which he allegedly kept there, to remind him in future to be more considerate of his sitter.

In his study of the impact of Ellen Terry on Watts's art,[17] David Loshak points out that Watts's portraits of her are charged with romantic sentiment, rather similar to that found in some Pre-Raphaelite paintings, and that several of his works during this period 'have about them an air of enchantment' missing in earlier and later works. Watts in fact destroyed many of his portraits of Ellen after the marriage broke up.

Loshak interprets one of Watts's paintings at that time, called *Knight and Maiden*, as a clear revelation of their relationship. 'The hero is unmistakably Watts himself,' he says.

No less certain is the identification of the frail young girl who delicately embraces him as Ellen Terry, the inclination of her head the very embodiment of yielding tenderness. The middle-aged knight leans on his lance and gently looks down at her, protectively, with a kind of sad satisfaction; satisfied perhaps at being able to shield her from what he conceived to be the dangers and temptations of her previous life, yet sad precisely because age and long habits of abstinence obliged him to be protector rather than lover. It is a picture full of compassion, a story of two unhappy people who find consolation by ministering to one another's infirmities.

Although Ellen was happy enough closeted with Watts in his studio, she missed the freedom of her previous life and would sometimes explode out of the cloistered atmosphere of Little Holland House and dance around the lawn. Relations between her and Sarah Prinsep deteriorated. Ellen did not fit neatly into her required role of docile child-bride: instead, she was wayward, mercurial and impetuous. Mrs Prinsep tried to correct her in quite the wrong way. According to Roddy Stanhope, Mrs Prinsep

> never ceased to treat Ellen as a naughty child who must be
> scolded and made obedient, and a high-spirited,
> unconventional girl naturally resented this treatment, while
> Watts, absorbed in his art, was little aware of the mischief
> which was preparing.[18]

The notes to Ellen's memoirs, compiled by her daughter Edy Craig and her daughter's companion, Christopher St John, say that while married to Watts, Ellen was subjected to a humiliating surveillance, with strict injunctions not to speak when distinguished guests were present. An example of such treatment was when the household, in Esher for a summer break, went to lunch with the Spencer-Stanhopes. A niece of one of the guests described it.

> Ellen Terry, as a bride, was brought over to luncheon with
> my aunt. My aunt described her as strikingly lovely, with
> brilliant eyes and very beautiful hair, but quite a schoolgirl
> and a decided tomboy. After luncheon, while my uncle and
> Watts paced to and fro in the garden talking, my aunt
> remained with Mrs Prinsep and Ellen in the drawing-room.
> Suddenly the latter, with an air of supreme boredom, leant
> back over the arm of the chair in which she was seated, and,
> shaking her head to and fro, loosened the pins from her hair
> which tumbled about her shoulders like a cloak of shining
> gold. My aunt could only gaze in delight at the beauty of the
> girl as she sat there swaying her head gently from side to side
> while the mass of shimmering hair shrouded her and swept
> the floor. But Mrs Prinsep was horrified. 'Ellen! Ellen!' she

cried, 'put up your hair instantly!' And Ellen, flashing a wrathful glance at her tormentor, grasped the waving mass of gold, coiled it carelessly upon her head, and, stabbing it with pins, sat there looking lovelier than ever, a petulant, scolded child.[19]

By the end of the year, the marriage was regarded by the 'court of married women' around Watts, and Watts himself, as being in serious trouble. Lady Lothian replied to a letter from Watts, that the first year of marriage is sometimes a trying one and with such a young bride, 'the good and the steadiness may predominate some day and that comfort may grow out of it again.'[20] Ellen herself seemed unaware of storm clouds.

She was to write.

I wondered at the new life, and worshipped it because of its beauty. When it suddenly came to an end, I was thunderstruck; and refused at first to consent to the separation, which was arranged for me in much the same way as my marriage had been.

The whole thing was managed by those kind friends whose chief business in life seems to be the care of others. I don't blame them. There are things for which no one is to blame. 'There do exist such things as honest misunderstandings,' as Charles Reade was always impressing on me at a later time. There were no vulgar accusations on either side, and the words I read in the deed of separation – 'incompatibility of temper' – a mere legal phrase – *more* than covered the ground. Truer still would have been 'incompatibility of *occupation*' and the interference of well-meaning friends.

'The marriage was not a happy one,' they will probably say after my death, but for me it was in many ways very happy indeed.[21]

Nevertheless, at the time, the breakup left Ellen 'miserable, indignant, unable to understand that there could be any justice in what had happened.' She knew that Mrs Prinsep constantly found fault with her behaviour, but she was happy enough posing for her Signor, romping in the garden, wandering through rooms full of artistic objects and dreaming of having a home of their own where she could entertain and play her part as the wife of a great painter.

The divorce petition, although not drawn up until 13 March 1877, thirteen years later, reads rather like a schoolmaster's report on a pupil who has failed to live up to her promise:

That although considerably older than his intended wife he admired her very much & hoped to influence, guide & cultivate a very artistic & peculiar nature & to remove an impulsive young girl from the dangers & temptations of the stage. . .

That the conditions of his life were perfectly well known & entirely acquiesced in by the Respondent before his marriage & it was understood that nothing was to be changed.

That very soon after his marriage he found how great an error he had made. Linked to a most *restless & impetuous* nature accustomed from the very earliest childhood to the stage & forming her ideas of life from the exaggerated romance of sensational plays, from whose acquired habits a quiet life was intolerable & even impossible, demands were made upon him he could not meet without giving up all the professional aims his life had been devoted to.

That he did not impute any immorality at that time but there was an insane excitability, indulging in the wildest suspicions, accusations & denunciations driving him to the very verge of desperation & separation became absolutely necessary unless he gave up his professional pursuits which was out of the question as he had no independent means.

It's been suggested that the use of the word 'insane' was deliberate – backed up by Watts' painting, now in the British Museum, called 'The Madness of Ophelia,' which undoubtedly shows Ellen's face expressing mental strain. The petition's charge of 'wildest suspicions, accusations & denunciations' implies she was paranoid, neurotic and even deranged. Watts was ultimately ashamed of the way he had treated her and many years later wrote to ask her forgiveness: 'What success I may have will be very incomplete and unsatisfactory if you cannot do what I have long been hesitating to ask.'

Versions differ as to the cause of the final split between Ellen and Watts – some are worthy of the lead in today's gossip columns. *Munsey's* magazine, later on, gave its readers a thrill with its dramatic account of Ellen's exit from Little Holland House:

Watts was giving a dinner party to certain staid friends. The wife was late and finally appeared, but not to sit at table. Throwing aside, for a second, the cloak she wore, she displayed to the horrified guests a highly pronounced stage costume. Then with a merry laugh, she turned and fled from the house.[22]

Another equally ludicrous contemporary version had Ellen rushing naked out of her bedroom and dancing on the dinner table before an astonished and confused audience of bishops. All that was missing was the merry laugh.

Ellen herself never gave any specific reason for the breakup. But Lady Duff Gordon in her book, aptly named, *Discretions and Indiscretions*, claimed that one night Ellen took her into her confidence and revealed 'the tragedy of her life.' Unfortunately, the account is based on romantic invention rather than truth. Ellen's memoirs show her memory to be perfectly sound: she could never have made all the factual inaccuracies Lady Duff Gordon attributed to her:

As you know I married George Frederick Watts when I was little more than a child, and he was old enough to be my grandfather. I was really tremendously innocent, just a gay little thing, without a serious thought in my head. I was fond of him, with a sort of daughterly affection, and I used to sit patiently for him for hours on end, sometimes in a dreadfully uncomfortable position with a heavy helmet on my head. You see I was a very kind little girl, and that kindness was my undoing.

We had a great friend, William Godwin. He had been friendly with the family for years and both my husband and I were on terms of the most informal intimacy with him. We used to run in and out of his house whenever we wanted. I often visited him alone and nobody thought anything of it. Then one evening I went to see him and found him very ill in bed, with terrible sickness and pain. I was so distressed for him that I never even thought of the conventions or the construction that might be placed on my actions. I spent the whole night with him, and only returned home the next morning, when he was well on the road to recovery.

To my dismay my husband was waiting there for me with my parents in solemn conclave. They accused me of infidelity

Ellen at the age of nineteen, shortly after the break-up of her marriage with the painter, G.F. Watts.

and seemed utterly horrified at what I had done in all innocence. I tried to explain that what they had imagined to be a night of love was spent in helping a sick man to and from the bathroom and heating poultices for him, but they would not believe me. They cast me out as a fallen woman and my husband refused even to see me again.

I implored the family to take my part, but they would not listen to my explanations and I had nowhere to go. In despair I turned to my supposed partner in adultery and begged him to help me to clear myself, but he either could not, or perhaps did not want to succeed with them. At any rate he was my only refuge and I went back to his house. It was some years before I grew to love him, but in the end I gave my heart to him.[23]

Ellen did not go back, as this account has it, to Godwin's house. Instead, she returned to live with her parents for three years before she finally eloped with him. Godwin was also based in Bristol during her marriage to Watts and though he visited London, he did not move to a house in Baker Street until October 1865 (his wife died in May 1865), so Ellen and Watts could not have run in and out of his house in 1864. Watts's circle of friends is also well documented and there is no reference to Godwin.

But there was some contact between Ellen and Godwin before her separation from Watts on 26 January 1865, as Godwin wrote a light-hearted note to 'the fair Mistress Watts,' in medieval script, saying

I would have you know that your request is right pleasant and delectable . . . I have strictly ordered my servitor to despatch the kettleholder with all diligence & may the saints have you in their custody. Given at Bristol the xv day of jan'y in the year of our Lord MDCCCLXV [1865].[24]

The divorce petition, which stated that Watts 'did not impute any immorality at that time' gives no hint of any extra-marital involvement – innocent or otherwise – though one provision in the immediate Deed of Separation was that Ellen would get the sum of £300 annually 'so long as she shall lead a chaste life.' The amount was to drop to £200 if she returned to the theatre.

Ellen herself wrote an undated letter to her friend, Mary Ann

Hall, swearing her to secrecy and expressing her feelings:

> I bear no malice – but I feel no love toward Mr Watts – He is
> to me *now*, as if he did not *exist*! . . . reports meet me on
> every side . . . of what Mr Watts has said of me – all most
> *cowardly* – and *most untrue*!! There is no shadow of doubt
> (for it has been *proved* to me) that *he* and not Mrs Prinsep
> only has said these things!! (I cd have forgiven the spite, and
> vexation of an *angry*, and *not* good woman) but not the
> *untruths* of one whose constant care was to make everyone
> *think me* untruthful and one to whom I *was devoted* heart
> and soul – and for one I tried to make fond of me by every
> power I cd think of, and for whom I wd *not* hve left (if all
> the *world* had wished it) had *he* not *desired* it also –
> although I thought at the time it would be my death. . .
>   I cd *tell* you in very plain words and to understand me
> when I tell you that he (Mr W.) has *not* said I was *not*
> everything that was good to him, in fact he has not brought
> any charge against me *at all* that says I was not true to him in
> every way and that I didn't do my best to please him, but he
> simply says he *cd not live with me*![25] (Ellen's writing style
> was always full of abbreviations and exclamations.)

Mortified at the abrupt end of the marriage, Ellen went back
to live with her parents. She admitted later that had she been
able to look into the future, she would have been less rebellious
– though pondering over whether she *had* actually been all that
rebellious, decided she had shown as much rebellion as a sheep.
Nevertheless, she missed intensely the elegance and grace of
Little Holland House. 'I hated going back to live at home,' she
wrote in her memoirs.

> Mother furnished a room for me, and I thought the furniture
> hideous. Poor mother!
>   For years Beethoven always reminded me of mending
> stockings, because I used to struggle with the large holes in
> my brothers' stockings upstairs in that ugly room, while
> downstairs Kate played the 'Moonlight Sonata.' I caught up
> the stitches in time to the notes! This was the period when,
> though everyone was kind, I hated my life, hated everyone
> and everything in the world more than at any time before or
> since.

It was a bleak enough time. She was bored being at home and hated losing her status as a married woman – especially as her husband had been a man of distinction. Once more she was just an elder daughter, looking after the younger ones. She didn't particularly want to act again: she hadn't been over-happy with the standard of her acting at the time of her marriage, and had left the theatre, as she thought, for ever, without a single pang of regret. Charles Dodgson (Lewis Carroll), who admired her as an actress, visited the family at this time to do some photographic studies. He was to note in his diary, 'I can imagine no more delightful occupation than brushing Ellen Terry's hair.'[26]

In contrast to Ellen, Kate was the leading lady at the Lyceum, under the actor managership of Charles Albert Fechter. Ever since 1862, when she had stepped in as understudy to the leading lady in the comedy *Friends and Foes*, Kate had been the theatrical toast of London, praised for her beauty, talent and dramatic power. Kate was to remain London's favourite actress until her last appearance as Juliet at the Adelphi in 1867, the year she left the stage to marry Arthur Lewis, a wealthy silk merchant. Ellen was pleased at Kate's success, but it only underlined what she saw as the failure of her own personal and professional life.

To get away from boredom and memories, in the spring of 1866 Ellen went on her first visit to Paris. She did not travel alone, but she refers only to 'the friend who took me every-where in Paris.' The joy of the visit was being able to surround herself once again with what she loved: good design; the fine arts; the theatre – she saw Sarah Bernhardt act; and the artistic set. She loved the way the women lay back in their carriages, 'like lovely half moons,' and at the Madeleine at Easter time, in true theatrical style, she fainted from ecstasy when the Host was raised.

After she returned home, she claimed that she was practically *driven* back to the stage by those who meant to be kind – her father and mother, Tom Taylor and others, who 'looked ahead and saw clearly it was for my good. It *was* a good thing, but at the time I hated it.' She was realistic enough, however, to see that it was Hobson's Choice between that and dwindling away at home. On 20 June 1866, she played the part of Helen in *The Hunchback*, in a benefit for Kate, at the Olympic Theatre. She

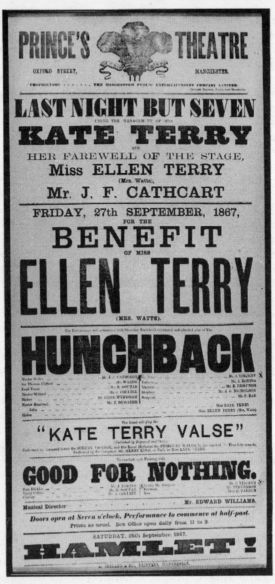

A typical playbill of the time. Ellen was angry the proprietors insisted her married name was included.

got good reviews for this, but was still depressed and cared nothing for her success. She felt wretchedly ill, and was also angry that they insisted on putting her married name on the bills. Nevertheless, in the spring of 1867 she resumed full time acting as Marion Vernon in *A Sister's Penance*, with further performances in *The Hunchback* in September. It was the final acceptance that she would never return to Little Holland House.

Ellen only saw Watts once more, when years later they met in the street in Brighton. Unsurprisingly, all he said was that she had grown. In 1892, when a mutual friend wrote to say he was going to visit Watts, she replied, 'The dews of Heaven fall thick in blessings on him.' Forgetting her anger at him, she added that she wished she could have made his sun shine, 'but I was so ignorant and so young and he was so impatient.'[27] She hoped he did not hate her.

The relationship continued in this vein, Watts as the forgiving father, Ellen the repentant daughter. After her success at the Lyceum, Watts wrote to her, saying he had watched her success eagerly, prophesied she would take a noble place in history, and asking her to shake hands with him in spirit. Little Nelly Watts was long forgotten. Ellen replied and for the next two or three years he continued to write to her 'gently and kindly.' To her evident surprise, 'this great man could not rid himself of the pain of feeling that he "had spoiled my life".' She reassured him and Watts told her he was grateful he wouldn't have to carry out of the world the sense that any malediction would follow him now that she no longer thought unkindly of him.

Ellen thought his feelings were generous and that he was taking 'a chivalrous assumption of blame for what was, I think, a natural, almost inevitable, catastrophe.' Ellen had always looked up to Watts. Her own opinion of herself was not high and if the Signor had discarded her, then the fault must be hers and not his. She kept a cutting of the announcement of their marriage in a reliquary and wrote revealing and affectionate comments in her copy of G.K. Chesterton's 1904 biography of Watts.[28] When, for instance, Chesterton comments on Watts' flowing and voluminous dark hair, saying he could have been mistaken for a hair dresser's advertisement or a minor poet, Ellen wrote next to this, 'but he was just a *boy* then.' When

Chesterton said that Watts' famous skull cap made him look like a Venetian senator, Ellen added, 'He wore it because the slightest draught gave him excruciating pain in his head.' And of the refusal to allow Watts to decorate Euston, she wrote 'Dull as it is now, it wd have been glorified by Watts.' She heavily underlined comments about Watts being precise and courtly, and there being nothing Bohemian about him; and scatters words like 'Superb' and 'Most Wonderfully Beautiful' over descriptions of his work. But against the remark that 'Now and again Watts has failed . . . for I believe that often he has scarcely known what he is doing,' she has scrawled, 'Very interesting.'

On the cover at the end of the book are the initials GFW EAW, under the last verse of a poem by Mrs Prinsep's husband, Thoby, written at the time when there were early, bright hopes of the marriage:

> Then let us unto Nelly Watts
> A shout of triumph raise
> Who cometh home at seventeen
> A bride of seven days.

CHAPTER 3

EDWARD GODWIN

Once Ellen had returned to the theatre in March 1867, she had little chance to brood. She was too busy, playing a total of eleven parts during the rest of that year.

Two plays were by Tom Taylor; and one by Charles Reade at the newly opened Queen's Theatre in Long Acre; but none of the plays fired the public's interest and many lasted just a few weeks. She and Kate also played at a charity matinee, strengthening an amateur cast which included George du Maurier, Mark Lemon, editor of *Punch*, John Tenniel, the illustrator, F.C. Burnand, a future editor of *Punch*, and Horace Mayhew, the writer. Arthur Lewis was also in the cast and on 18 October he and Kate married.

On Boxing Day Ellen teamed up for the first time with Henry Irving in *Katherine and Petruchio*, a mutilation of *The Taming of the Shrew*. There was no sound of angels singing: it was an inauspicious beginning. *The Times* critic said that, according to Miss E. Terry's interpretation, the passion in the earlier scenes belonged more to the spoilt child than to the confirmed vixen; and went on to criticise Petruchio for behaving, when he brought home his bride, more like a brigand chief with a female captive than an honest gentleman engaged in a task of moral reform.

Ellen agreed neither of them had acted well and dismissed as moonshine the well known story of Irving being so struck with her talent that he promised that should he ever have a theatre of his own, he'd engage her. In her memoirs she wrote: 'As a matter of fact, I'm sure he never thought of me at all at that time. I was just then acting very badly, and feeling ill, caring scarcely at all for my work or a theatre, or anybody belonging to the theatre.' Irving thought her a hoyden and she remembered him being incredibly conceited, even though he kindly gave up his place to her in the regular Friday night queue for salaries.

After *Katherine and Petruchio* was withdrawn in January 1868, Ellen was praised for her 'charming archness and vivacity' in the next two-part play, *The Household Fairy*. But it was not enough to rekindle her interest in acting and she now, in any case, had a different life in mind. On the night of Saturday 10 October, after the performance finished, she met Godwin by arrangement on Castle Street and disappeared with him to set up house in Hertfordshire – delightedly swapping the part of household fairy on stage for that of one in real life.

No one knew where she had gone. Whatever the truth about Ellen's innocent night with Godwin at some unspecified place, she kept her future meetings with him secret. As Godwin was now a widower, living in London, there was no problem about seeing each other and it would have been natural enough. Ellen was frustrated and disappointed with her life and the dullness and boredom she saw ahead of her, and must have been delighted to see Godwin, of whose stylish house in Bristol she was to say 'for the first time I began to appreciate beauty, to observe, to feel the splendour of things, to aspire.' Godwin had taught her the difference between good and bad taste and had opened up her responsive mind to a shining new world. He had acted as teacher and all her life she needed someone to look up to. She had found this in Watts, and had been impressed by his skills, his culture, his knowledge of art, but had lost it again.

Godwin shared with the pre-Raphaelites their love of beauty, loathing of the vulgar, and their wish to improve the public taste. A brilliant, highly cultivated man, with a wide knowledge of the arts, he also impressed Ellen with his passion for Shakespeare – much of whose blank verse he knew by heart – and his interest in costume and love of music. Through him she could meet those who moved in the literary and artistic, rather than the theatrical, world. To Ellen, he was her passport back through the looking glass.

By now, Godwin was a much respected and sought after architect – indeed, Oscar Wilde called him 'one of the most artistic spirits of the century in England.' Born and brought up in Bristol, it was his design of a church in County Donegal in

Edward Godwin, the greatest love of Ellen's life, with whom she eloped in 1868.

Ireland, where his brother worked, that first brought him to the public's notice – emphasising as it did his strongly-held contention that proportion made building art.[1] He was twenty three at the time, an ambitious man with a fervent interest in all types of design.

It was in 1861, at twenty seven, however, that he became nationally known, when he won the competition to design Northampton's new town hall. His artistic contemporaries were impressed by the result and he was approached to design a number of local projects. It allowed him to move with his wife Sarah, whose health was deteriorating, to a more fashionable address in Bristol. It was at this point that fourteen-year-old Ellen, acting at the Theatre Royal, first joined a play reading at his house and was delighted with its style.

She was equally admiring of its owners: 'Its master and mistress made me think,' she said, the highest compliment which she could pay. Its engaging master was already a favourite with women and it was hardly surprising that the youthful Ellen was flattered by his interest.

When they eloped, Godwin, at thirty five, was fourteen years older than Ellen; a dogmatic, ambitious man, but an entertaining talker and a far more picturesque and attractive character than the rather arid Watts. Though his manner could be austere, he was distinguished and sophisticated. Physically, he was lightly built, bearded, with brown eyes and drooping eyelids which gave him a hooded look. He had a pale, ascetic face and was regarded as romantically good looking. Ellen had been flattered by Watts's proposal and had thought her admiration for him was love. With Edward, it was different. For him, she felt both admiration and love and was prepared to jettison her reputation and accept the social disgrace attached to any woman who broke the moral code of the day and lived with a man without being married to him. The idealised view of womanhood held by the Victorians put a strong stress on purity.

What about Godwin's feelings? If Ellen did spend her innocent night with him, he certainly made no public attempt to explain or exonerate her. This may have been deliberate: a ploy to put her in such a position that she would have to return to him. Ellen, with her long red gold hair, youth, charm, and infectious high spirits, could well have turned his head. Both of them were careless of conventions, but Godwin was an older sophisticated man, only too aware of the social attitudes of the time, and eloping with Ellen shows a lack of responsibility, or genuine love for her. He must have known that her reputation would suffer more permanent damage than his.

Impulsive as always, Ellen went off with Godwin without saying a word to anyone as to whom she was with or where she was going. She must have realised that had she told her parents, they would have stopped her. Being in the theatre, their lifestyle differed from others, but not their outlook. Were Ellen's action publicly known, she would have brought shame and embarrassment down not only on them, but also on her sister Kate, now happily married and whose first child, also called Kate (who was to be the mother of Sir John Gielgud) was born in the July of that year.

There was no reason for Ellen's disappearance to be linked with Godwin, though she had never attempted to disguise her friendship with him. And it was unlikely anyone would query Godwin's whereabouts, as his architectural work required him to spend a lot of time out of town.

Although Godwin was now a widower, Ellen was only separated, not divorced, from Watts when she left for Hertfordshire. Watts has been criticised for not divorcing Ellen, to allow her to marry Godwin; but he does not seem to have acted vindictively as he was later apparently quite happy to divorce her in order that she could marry Charles Wardell.

There were undoubted difficulties facing Watts if he had taken proceedings at the time of Ellen's elopement. For one thing, divorce in those days was very expensive and Watts had very little money then, still relying heavily on the Prinseps for finance. There was also the problem of what grounds to cite. Later on he needed only to point to Ellen's two children to prove adultery; but in 1868, he could have been faced with trying to prove the marriage was not consummated – either for wilful refusal to consummate, or incapacity on either side. In each case, this would mean giving detailed evidence in open court of all attempts, rebuttals and failures and this would have caused an unthinkable and embarrassing scandal.

Ellen never seems to have approached Watts for a divorce, and possibly she and Godwin were simply not worried about marriage – though given the moral climate, this showed decided courage and a detached attitude towards other people's opinions ('They are saying – what are they saying? Let them be saying!' she said). She may also have thought that her flight from London and subsequent disappearance was so successful that she could merely live as Mrs Godwin the rest of her life without bothering about the necessary paper work.

She was quite right in thinking she had disappeared effectively, but seems to have been surprisingly uncaring about her family's reaction. Shortly after she vanished, a body of a young woman, fair, slight and tall like Ellen, was dragged out of the Thames. Her father identified the corpse as Ellen: she had, after all, been obviously unhappy about her marriage breakup and apathetic about acting. Her two younger sisters, Floss and Marion, then at boarding school, were put into mourning. Then Sarah went to see the body and though it resembled Ellen, she remembered her daughter was born with a birthmark – which to her relief couldn't be found. Down in the country, Ellen heard the news and, shocked, rushed back to London to her distracted parents to reassure them that she was still alive.

Delighted though her parents were to find her alive, they reacted with the horror of any middle-class Victorian parent to the news that Ellen was living with Godwin. It caused an inevitable breach between Ellen and her family, painful to both sides. Only after Ellen remarried some years later, did a reconciliation take place. In a letter Ellen wrote at that time to an old friend, she said: 'Thank God Mother is alive and I can atone to her for the pain I unintentionally caused her.'[2]

Another shock to Ben and Sarah was that Ellen had left the stage – the rock upon which the whole family was based. It was a serious disappointment; they had had high hopes that Ellen would follow Kate in her stage career. For the first time, no young Terry was on the stage. Benjamin, the oldest boy, a handsome ne'er do well, was in Australia; George was uninterested in acting; Floss and Marion were at school; Charles was only eleven and Tom and Fred hardly out of their high chairs.

But Ellen had no regrets for the stage. She had given it up perfectly happily when she married Watts and though she admired ambitious people, she said she also detested them and had 'the simplest faith that absolute devotion to another human being means the greatest *happiness*. That happiness for a time was now mine.' She may not have been married, but she was saturated in the ideals of Victorian wives: perfect happiness came from sewing and cleaning for a man and bearing his children.

The early years with Godwin in a cottage called 'The Red House' on the edge of Gustard Wood Common, a mile from Wheathampstead, were some of the happiest in her life. It was a secluded, idyllic retreat, with bay windows in the downstairs rooms and a kitchen and bake house at the back. The walls were painted pale yellow, the woodwork white; and Godwin had designed the slender, black furniture.

Ellen loved her unconventional life there and put all her energies into it. 'I experienced exquisite delight from the mere fact of being in the country,' she said, romanticising the whole scene as she joyfully played the part of the country maid. Godwin bought her a bulldog to act as guard dog when he was away on a project, and then a small monkey and a parrot.

Fortunately, she was no town miss, unused to hard work: for years she had helped her mother as the family, knee deep in young children, moved around the country from one squalid theatrical lodging to another. She therefore thought nothing of getting up at six in the morning to light the fire, prepare breakfast, feed quite a number of ducks and fowls, plus the goat, then driving Godwin to the station in the pony and trap if he was going up to London. She studied cookery books instead of parts ('I had a wonderful hand for pastry'), and developed 'a perfect mania for washing.' She would walk across the common daily to get the evening milk. To everyone around she was merely 'Nelly.'

But though she was energetic enough, she was both inexperienced and a day dreamer – a disastrous combination for house management. Previously, either her mother or Mrs Prinsep's cook had done the baking: Ellen, with the best will in the world, burnt her meals – if, that is, she returned to cook at all from wandering round the hedgerows, collecting flowers or berries; or playing with the animals. She forgot mundane matters like maintaining housekeeping accounts, putting oil in the lamps or getting water from the pump. She was untidy and spent the little money they had extravagantly. Godwin gave her about £2 a week for housekeeping – which was more than all the money Ellen's mother often received from Ben in a week – but as he was only paid by the job and had no regular salary, he was often short of money. He was also not bothered by how much or how little he had in the bank, so they were often in debt.

Though this kind of domestic chaos must have contributed later on to Godwin's growing absences from home, at the time he was still charmed by his golden goddess. In the evenings, the two of them, with their mutual delight in Shakespeare's plays, would read excerpts, discuss the play and write down their views on its presentation; or they would plan their new house Godwin was to build them in Harpenden. Godwin would sketch designs for the furniture there, when he wasn't sketching Ellen; and Ellen would plan the garden.

In order to be with Ellen as much as possible, Godwin did as much work as he could in the cottage. Two of his assignments were designing two large houses in Ireland and when he visited one of these, Dromore Castle, to see how it was coming on, Ellen went along with him, absorbed in what he had to tell her about Celtic art.

When he worked at home, she contentedly read to him while he drew. She spent many of her evenings making perfect tracings of Edward's elaborate architectural drawings, for which she could get paid a guinea, or transcribing his notes for him. When the architect William Burges – one of the few friends aware of the romance – came to stay, while Godwin was designing Cardiff Castle's tower and interior, he found Ellen happily making tracings of all the room decorations. She often worked by the light of a paraffin lamp and attributed her lifelong poor eyesight to the strain.

The serpent in the garden of Eden was to be Godwin's work. Although he managed to be at home a great deal more than most professional men, the calls on his time were increasing. He was now a Fellow of the Royal Institute of British Architects and, as a member of their council, a Fellow of the Society of Antiquarians, in the Architectural Association, attended meetings of the Archaeological Association, often held down at Weymouth, and was on a number of committees.

Ellen began to spend more and more time alone at the cottage. Without telephones, there was no way Godwin could tell her that he was going to be late, or had missed the train, or had decided not to come back that night at all. Years later, her friend, Graham Robertson, recalled some of her memories of these times:

> One dismal evening, she told me, everything had looked unusually black. She had been alone for many days, funds were very low, she was ill and anxious. She had harnessed the little rough pony and driven to meet the last train, hoping that someone, half expected, would come by it and put an end to the fears and the loneliness.
>
> But the last train played her false as it had often done before, and she drove back through the dark lanes wearied in body and brain . . . her lamp had gone out and the night was pitch dark. In a lonely lane a man's rough voice suddenly called out some obviously useless question. She answered shortly, heard the rough voice mutter, 'My God, it's a gal!' and the next minute a man had sprung into the cart beside her – she felt his hot, whisky-laden breath on her cheek.[3]

Ellen disposed of the intruder by bringing the whip handle down on his head; but the other incidents like that – including spending the night in a wood rather than squelch through a thick circle of frogs, removed her romanticised idea of the countryside and left her depressed.

Godwin was away when Ellen gave birth to her first child in 1869. Writing to Bernard Shaw in later years, Ellen recalled that

> I forgot my pangs whilst reading *The Watching of the Falcon* on a certain bitter-sweet night in December when Edy, my first child was born. They were playing in the church, 'Rest in the Lord.' I heard them as I passed through the village alone – feeling frightfully ill and afraid.[4]

Dr Rumball, a local man, delivered the child, a daughter, who was called Edith after Eadgyth, the daughter of Godwin, Earl of the West Saxons, whom Godwin, archaeologist as well as architect, believed could be an ancestor. Nicknamed Boo – Edy's attempt at pronouncing her name – Mrs Rumball was to stay with Ellen for thirty years.

Ellen's second child, Teddy, was born on 16 January 1872. Godwin was absent again and Ellen stayed the night with the midwife. She was delighted at having a son and, because he was so light in weight, called him 'The Feather of England.' He was blithely and untruthfully registered by his father as being the son of 'Eleanor Alice Godwin, formerly Watkins.'

Godwin was now overseeing the building of their Harpenden dream house which had become a necessity, as their original cottage was no longer big enough for them. The new house at Fallows Green, Harpenden, was three stories high, with a high pitched roof and vast studio. Godwin had bought an organ for the studio and covered the floors of the house with Chinese matting. It was nearly finished, and he was writing happy but frantic notes to Ellen on the progress. One, undated, read:

> I have been obliged to have Japan paper curtains for the dining room, the mule cloth wouldn't do, but I've got my own design – lucky, eh? . . . The house will be ready for habitation tomorrow night & I think you'll like the 2nd floor, our bedroom dressing room & Lady's Snuggery – the latter I shall leave pretty much for you to dress & do what you like with. I have prepared both bedroom floors the whole height of wall as it saved money — & time under the circumstances. The chimneys have been swept grates cleaned floor scrubbed & Monday morning stone stairs will be scrubbed down after the furniture is in place. . . .
>
> I am not up to fetching you although I should *so* like it, but the wet weather & the going about on my legs upstairs & down have told on me & poor Ted won't be a merry & fit companion for the party from Waterloo, so don't think me selfish if I ask you on your arrival to keep the chicks & Boo away from me at meals & give yourself as a martyr altogether to me for a day or two. . . .
>
> We shall not I fear have the curtains ready, but there are blinds & shutters & as it is summer I spose you won't mind more than I do – I have tried hard to push on so as to get one sitting room and one bedroom finished and comfy for us, but the weather & other things have conspired against us & I may not be able to do it, so don't grumble more than you can help – you see I live in mortal fear of you, don't I.[5]

Neither lived in mortal fear of the other: though they were both strong willed. But both because she loved him, and because wives of that era, strong willed or not, were also dutiful, Ellen accepted the growing number of Godwin's absences and the near poverty in which they were living. All

Fallows Green, Harpenden. The house Godwin designed for Ellen and his family, now demolished. Painted by Johnston Forbes-Robertson.

Godwin's money had gone into the house, its decorations and the specially designed furniture – he left it to Ellen to tell the tradesmen there was none left.

Despite their poverty, Ellen now being as thin as a whipping post, in the summer of 1874 Godwin took her and Edy – Teddy being left in Boo's charge – with him to Normandy, where he wanted to study the Bayeux Tapestry as part of his obsession with the origins of the Godwin family. They wandered delightedly around cathedrals, and Edy, hearing choirboys for the first time, solemnly told Ellen she'd heard the angels. It was their last holiday together, the last really happy time.

CHAPTER 4

EDY AND TEDDY: 'GROWING UP IN STYLE'

The chief comforts in Ellen's life were Edy and Teddy. 'When my two children were born,' she said, 'I thought of the stage less than ever. They absorbed all my time, all my interest, all my love.'

They were to be brought up in rather an exceptional way. Godwin had very strong ideas about the effects of environment on children, believing that their minds could be corrupted by discordant colours, unsightly objects, unattractive shapes. He designed Ellen's and Edy's clothes, in simple, unrestricted Japanese and Grecian styles.

Ellen recalled in her memoirs that the children

> were allowed no rubbishy picture books, but from the first Japanese prints and fans lined their nursery walls, and Walter Crane was their classic. If injudicious friends gave the wrong sort of present, it was promptly burned! A mechanical mouse in which Edy, my little daughter, showed keen interest and delight, was taken away as being 'realistic and common.' Only wooden toys were allowed. This severe training proved so effective that when a wax doll dressed in a violent pink silk dress was given to three year old Edy, she said it was 'vulgar'!

When telling Bernard Shaw the story years later, Ellen remembered Edy then smashing the doll to pulp. Her dislike of wax dolls continued, extending to a loathing of Madame Tussaud's exhibition:

> She would look like a murderess, the servants told me, if ever she was left alone in the room with a doll, and most people I'm certain used to think: 'That child will come to a bad

end.' Until she was about 12 she lacked sweetness and softness indeed.[1]

Even when only a few years old, Edy was a stalwart, determined small figure. Her nursemaid, confusingly called Bo because she was the niece of Mrs 'Boo' Rumball, described her as 'a piece.' Edy alone, it seemed, was impervious to Teddy's baby charm, considering him, when only a few years old herself, a great coward. Ellen recalled how 'she used to hit him on the head with a wooden spoon for crying, and exhort him, when he said, "Master Teddy afraid of the dark," to be a *woman*!'[2]

Doting mother though she was, Ellen realised that Edy was an uncompromising child. When she took her to her first theatre – Sanger's Circus – and the clown staggered around pretending to fall from the tightrope – Edy shouted at her mother, 'Take me away! Take me away! You ought never to have brought me here.' Ellen, subdued, said: 'No wonder she was considered a dour child! I immediately and humbly obeyed.'[3] Teddy wasn't much better. Once, seeing a train departing as he arrived at the station, he shouted 'Stop the train! I'm Ellen Terry's little boy!'

With Edward away so much, Ellen became totally absorbed in her children. The country girl had turned into the young mother, and Ellen wrapped up in her new part, overwhelmed her children with love and attention. 'I was born loving my mama – she was so spoiling,' wrote Teddy later.[4]

It was Teddy, however, with his straw-coloured hair and angelic smile who was later to be the downfall of half the women in Europe, who got the main spoiling. Ellen loved both her children, but differed in her attitude towards them. This, according to Teddy, was because

> my mother had the idea that women were much too soft and gentle, and men rather too hard and rough. So she set out to keep me soft and gentle and to see that my sister Edy was hard as nails.[5]

Certainly Edy quickly developed into an independent and decisive little girl. 'My little sister was just about two years older than I,' said Teddy,

> and she was not an obstinate child – she had a will. I had no

Teddy, Ellen's son, aged about twelve, who wrote of his boarding school in Kent at the time that it was 'rare jolly'.

will – I was merely an obstinate child. Our mother could note the difference immediately . . . one thing she would not do – she would never attempt to get the better of the girl.[6]

Teddy himself rarely attempted that, either. 'My sister wished from the first to brace me up,' he said, and Edy's actions bore this out. When the first snow came, Edy banged two handfuls of it on young Teddy's cheeks, saying, *'There'* – though he was honest enough to acknowledge that it was not because she was jealous of his arrival, merely generous with her snow.

Both children grew up interested in Ellen's and Godwin's preoccupations. When, a few years later, Ellen returned to the stage, she had no worries about leaving them to their own devices during rehearsals and performances, confident that they knew how to amuse themselves. She wrote in her memoirs

> I have often thanked heaven, that with all their faults, my boy and girl have never been lazy, and never felt dull. At this time Teddy always had a pencil in his hand, when he wasn't looking for his biscuit – he was a greedy little thing! – and Edy was hammering clothes on to her dolls with tin-tacks! Teddy said poetry beautifully, and when he and his sister were still tiny mites, they used to go through scene after scene of *As You Like It*, for their own amusement, not for an audience.

Ellen kept all Edy's and Ted's drawings from school: careful paintings of flowers, illustrations of classics and nursery rhymes, and marked with the time they took to do them. On the back of one done by Teddy, Godwin wrote to Ellen, 'I'm quite proud of this! No I don't mean that – but – it isn't bad, is it?' A painting by Edy of an old thatched house was signed 'Edith Terry' and, in a child's writing 'Dedicated to dear Mumy' [sic].

Edy, like her mother, was often dressed in a tiny kimono as Godwin disliked the corsets and bustles of Victorian fashion. The actor Johnston Forbes-Robertson described her as being 'a lively little girl, black-haired, with great inquiring eyes.'[7] She was also decided in her views, even when so young, and was as forthright then as when she was adult. Edward Craig, Ellen Terry's grandson, recalls his grandmother telling the story of

Edy at the age of fifteen.

the evening when she was entertaining some friends, only to see Edy appear in the doorway in her nightdress, complaining of 'having a pain in my belly.' 'Surely you mean "tummy," ' said Ellen. 'No,' said Edy vehemently. 'That's my chest,' she said, pointing to it, 'that's my tummy,' (pointing lower down), 'and' (pointing yet lower), 'that's my belly. And *that's* where the pain is.'

Conscious of the gaps in her own education, Ellen was anxious for her children to be taught quickly and well, and later, when they moved to London, but while they were both quite small, they went to a school run by a Mrs Cole, whose ideas were very progressive. She was a supporter of the new women's movement and believed that girls should be as well educated as boys. By accepting boys as well as girls, she was one of the pioneers of co-education and was highly regarded. Schoolfellows of Edy and Teddy included three of the Sickert children and one of Sir Edwin Arnold's.

The children usually spent their weekends at Rose Cottage in Hampton Court, which Ellen, once she was earning money through acting again, bought and painted. There they would run wild through the gardens, show visitors the sights, chat away to them about their mother, and take them to see the new trees. They had helped the gardeners to plant these in the wild garden, and christened them after their mother's theatrical parts – one was called Portia, for instance, another Iolanthe. They also solemnly gave performances of their favourite plays to a local audience of veterans from the Crimean War.

Ellen tried to act as both mother and father to them. And although Teddy was to say that 'the blessed lady, my mother, no more knew how to bring up a boy than she knew how to swim,' Edy sharply counter-attacked, saying she doubted if any father could have done more with a boy 'whose character was indeterminate in his abnormally prolonged chrysalis days.'

For most of their early lives Edy and Teddy got on very well; but as this remark by Edy illustrates, their relationship in later years was often to sour.

CHAPTER 5

BACK TO THE STAGE

At Harpenden, Ellen's entranced delight with her children's development was interrupted by money worries, which worsened after the holiday in France during the summer of 1874. The house had to be mortgaged and the tradesmen were so belligerent that there was now a bailiff in the house. 'Oh, blissful quiet days! How soon they came to an end!' she wrote in her memoirs. 'Already the shadow of financial trouble fell across my peace. Yet still I never thought of returning to the stage.'

The fates must have heard, as it was only by an extraordinary chance that Ellen did so. In the autumn of 1874, when Edy was four and Teddy two, the wheel of the pony cart which Ellen was driving along a narrow lane, came off. She was standing there, wondering how to fix it, when a whole crowd of horsemen in pink came leaping over the hedge into the lane. Years later, she remembered exactly what happened.

> One of them stopped and asked if he could do anything. Then he looked hard at me and exclaimed: 'Good God! It's Nelly!' The man was Charles Reade.
>
> 'Where have you been all these years?' he said.
>
> 'I have been having a very happy time,' I answered.
>
> 'Well, you've had it long enough. Come back to the stage!'
>
> 'No, never!'
>
> 'You're a fool! You ought to come back.'
>
> Suddenly I remembered the bailiff in the house a few miles away, and I said laughingly: 'Well, perhaps, I would think of it if some one would give me forty pounds a week!'
>
> 'Done!' said Charles Read. 'I'll give you that, and more, if you'll come and play Philippa Chester in *The Wandering Heir*.'[1]

Reade's play was based on the Tichbourne Case, which was arousing intense interest in England. He had taken it on a provincial run, with Mrs John Wood as the heroine, Philippa, but she had left because of another engagement. Reade, wanting to stage the play in London, was looking round for a strong replacement when he chanced on Ellen. He was a man of capricious ideas (he buried his mistress, who suffered from rheumatism, in a brick vault so she wouldn't feel the cold), and regarded his own plays as marginally this side of genius.

He felt intuitively that Ellen would be successful in the part of Philippa. Nicknaming her his 'artful toad,' he wrote a candid description of her in his notebook after taking her on:

> Ellen Terry is an enigma. Her eyes are pale, her nose rather long, her mouth nothing particular. Complexion a delicate brick dust, her hair rather like tow. Yet somehow she is beautiful. Her expression kills any pretty face you see beside her. Her figure is lean and long, her hand masculine in size and form. Yet she is a pattern of fawn-like grace. Whether in movement or repose, grace pervades the hussy. In character impulsive, intelligent, weak, hysterical – in short all that is abominable and charming in woman.[2]

His further comments about her were:

> Soft and yielding on the surface, egotistical below . . . always wanting something 'dreadful bad' today, which she does not want tomorrow, especially if you are weak enough to give it her, or get it her . . . hard as a nail in money matters, but velvet on the surface. A creature born to please and to deceive.[3]

He toned down these comments at a later date, adding a note that she had greatly improved since then and that her hardness was melting away.

Ellen, who had known Reade for years, regarded him as a quasi-father, even writing him the occasional letter in childhood beginning 'Dear Papa.' Her fondness for him continued: 'Dear, lovable, aggravating, childlike, crafty, gentle, obstinate, and entirely delightful and interesting Charles Reade,' she was to say, while he called her 'Eleanora Delicia,' to rhyme with Ellen Alicia – which Ellen seemed to think was her correct name, though she was registered as Ellen Alice.

Some forty years later, Ellen was to say that from the time she took the part of Philippa Chester, she never lost the zest for her work. Her son Teddy believed that despite 'Nelly's' protested wish to stay domestically down in Harpenden, 'her genius – E.T. – would not let her.' He knew how attracted she was to country life, the trees and flowers, the old castles and cottages, but argued that the Terry family always put work before anything else, and were fatally attracted to the theatre. 'It could be relied upon at any moment to act on any of us, and bring us to task as pins fly to the magnet.'[4]

Yet despite his firm belief that a part of Ellen willingly responded to the call back to the stage, Teddy always disliked Charles Reade. This was mostly because Reade had no time for his father, Godwin. But he also thought that, in engaging Ellen, Reade was thinking entirely of himself, and his need for good actresses to launch his propaganda plays. He was particularly angry that Reade lured Ellen back to the stage with the promise of £40 a week in salary, without being able to guarantee that she would continue to earn this amount. It depended entirely on how long his play ran for. He was not the manager of a theatre, but a tenant. Ellen and Godwin, already broke, would have the worry of setting up house in London without any real financial security.

Ellen, however, was unperturbed. She was delighted at the thought of a salary high enough to redeem the furniture in their Harpenden house, and clear the rest of their debts. Godwin seemed equally pleased: indeed, apart from the financial madness of refusing to allow Ellen to return to the stage when there were bailiffs in the house, he was conscious of how often he had been leaving Ellen alone. Edy, who was now nearly of school age, would also be able to get better tuition in London than in the country.

Godwin soon found a house for them all in London, at 20 Taviton Street – an area not too far from Kings Cross. This made it easy for them to journey down to their Harpenden house, which they could now afford to keep on. During the play's rehearsals and because of Ellen's anxiety for the children's health in London's peasouper fogs, Edy and Teddy remained in Harpenden with their nursemaid. Mrs Rumball came up to London to act as chaperone and general helper to Ellen, and Godwin set about decorating the place in his own style, based on the new aesthetic movement, which *Punch* was quick to ridicule as 'too utterly utter.'

When Johnston Forbes-Robertson, who was also to be in *The Wandering Heir*, visited Ellen in her Taviton Street drawing room, he described the floor as being covered with straw-coloured matting, with a dado of the same material. The walls were white, the hangings were of cretonne, with a Japanese pattern in a delicate grey-blue. The cushions on the wicker chairs matched the hangings, and in the centre of the room was a full-sized cast of the Venus de Milo. A small pedestal under this held a censer from which ribbons of blue smoke rose. 'The whole effect,' said Forbes-Robertson, 'was what art students of my time would have called "awfully jolly".'[5] Ellen herself added to the jolliness by floating around in a blue kimono.

The Wandering Heir opened on 28 February 1874 at the Queen's Theatre in Long Acre – the very theatre that Ellen had left so precipitately six years previously to go off with Godwin. The heroine in the play was advertised in advance as being an 'eminent actress' returning 'after a long period of retirement.' There was great enthusiasm when the 'dark lady' turned out to be Ellen and she got excellent reviews, the *Daily Telegraph* critic praising the 'undiminished brightness and buoyancy of her style.' But the play itself was less well received, even Godwin, writing in *The British Architect* (though without declaring his interest), saying that it would be almost wearying to sit it out, even if every actor in it were equal to Miss Terry.

Ellen thought it a delightful engagement. 'I felt an enthusiasm for my work which had been wholly absent when I had returned to the stage the first time,' she said and recalled how Charles Reade watched the play from his private box each night and sent her notes between each act, telling her what she had done well and what badly in the preceding act. One such note began,

> I prefer you for my Philippa to any other actress, and shall do so still, even if you will not, or cannot, throw more vigour into the lines that need it . . . you have limp lines, limp business, and in Act III, limp exits instead of ardent exits.[6]

Ellen, always anxious to learn more, cheerfully took his advice, and her swift rush off the stage became a trademark.

Ellen (top) in 1875 and Edy (below) in 1888: both influenced by Godwin's love of the Japanese style.

Reade continued to send her dozens of acting hints, suggesting she vary the pace of her speeches, her languor of diction. He even sent her £10 to go to the seaside and study her lines in peace. But despite her spirited performance, the play only lasted just over a month. Reade was unbothered: he had total belief in his own plays and after the run ended, took his company over Westminster Bridge to give a series of performances at Astley's. The disadvantage for audiences there was the strong smell of horses, as Astley's was only used as a rough kind of playhouse when Sanger's circus, its normal show, was on its annual tour. Also the gas and water had been cut off the day before the first night, because the previous tenant hadn't paid the bill.

Undaunted, Reade opened on 18 April with an old standby of his, *It's Never too Late to Mend*, with Ellen as his leading lady. Although her acting received a 'special commendation' from *The Daily News*, the play lasted barely three weeks. Undeterred, Reade decided to take his company on a tour around the provinces. Unfortunately for Ellen, her touring fee was only £25 a week.

It happened just when Ellen and Godwin needed extra money. For a year or so Godwin had been involved in a legal action over alleged poorly slated roofs at Glenbegh Towers, one of the houses he had designed in Ireland. Although the dispute was resolved about the time Ellen opened at Astley's, Godwin and his erstwhile partner had to pay legal costs at a time when Godwin had little work on hand, apart from acting as consultant over the building of Plymouth Town Hall. He spent much of his time, while Ellen was away, with friends like James McNeil Whistler at the Arts club; and in writing articles.

He was asked by Emily Faithful, editor of *Women and Work* and an early advocate of women's emancipation, for an article on women's prospects as architects. Godwin enthusiastically supported the idea, considering women had 'that equipoise which is indispensable for the creation of beauty.' His views clashed with those of other male members of the profession, who regarded his ideas as being preposterous. Possibly to irritate them, Edward took as a pupil Beatrice Philip – a daughter of John Birnie Philip, who sculpted the figure of Sir Gilbert Scott on the podium of the Albert Memorial – whom he was later to marry.

Godwin was also working hard on a series of articles for a book on *The Architecture and Costume of Shakespeare's Plays*. But this added merely to his reputation, rather than the family's finances, which were back in the same shaky state as they had been in Harpenden.

This time Ellen could not come to the rescue: she had just ended an arduous tour with Reade, which had not done well, and had no further engagement in sight. The bailiffs arrived again, and took most of the furniture away. The children were kept out of it all in Harpenden. Godwin, succumbing to an attack of Victorian vapours at the sight of the creditors, disappeared to the Isle of Wight to stay with a friend. The stronger-minded Ellen was left at Taviton Street, under orders from him to open the mail and 'detain' any unpleasant letters. Charles Reade and Tom Taylor, among other friends, urged her to leave Edward, believing he could only push her further into debt and despair.

Despairing she was. She wrote in her memoirs:

> At this time I was very miserable. I was worried to death by domestic troubles and financial difficulties. The house in which I first lived in London, after I left Hertfordshire, had been stripped of some of its most beautiful treasures by the brokers. Pressure was being put on me by well-meaning friends to leave this house and make a great change in my life. Everything was at its darkest.

And then, for the second time, Ellen was reprieved. This time, her rescuer appeared in the shape of Mrs Bancroft who was joint actor-manager, with her husband, Squire Bancroft, of the Prince of Wales' Theatre.

Clad in elegant Parisian black, Mrs Bancroft knocked at the door of the Taviton Road house and walked into the drawing room from which the furniture had been almost completely stripped. All that was left was the Japanese matting and the colossal cast of Venus de Milo.

Ellen recalled her uttering a restrained 'Dear Me!' as she caught sight of Venus, and theatrically shielded her eyes. It was hardly surprising. As Ellen said:

> The room, the statue, and I myself must all have seemed very strange to her. I wore a dress of some deep yellow woollen

material which my little daughter used to call the 'frog dress' because it was speckled with brown like a frog's skin. It was cut like a Viollet-le-Duc tabard, and had not a trace of the fashion of the time. Mrs Bancroft however, did not look at me less kindly because I wore aesthetic clothes and was painfully thin.[7]

Her reason for coming changed Ellen's mood from despair to delight. The Bancrofts had decided to put on *The Merchant of Venice* at the Prince of Wales' Theatre, but as Mrs Bancroft had to rest for health reasons, she and her husband wondered if Ellen would be interested in playing Portia, at a salary of £20 a week. This was regarded as a high wage in those days, even though it was only half the salary paid – for a short time – by Reade.

Ellen accepted the offer joyfully and incoherently. With her love of Shakespeare she already knew every word of the part, and every detail of the Venetian background of the play. She was even more delighted to learn that Godwin – whose articles on the design of Shakespeare's plays were highly regarded – would be asked to take charge of the scenery and costumes. With one bound, it seemed, the family was free of its financial misery and Ellen and Godwin could work together on their mutual passion, Shakespeare.

It was the Bancrofts' first venture in Shakespeare. When Mrs Bancroft – then Marie Wilton, a young actress – had first gone into management in 1865, at the age of twenty six, she had done so because she wanted to play comedy and had found very few theatres would stage comedies. She rented a small theatre, called Queen's, and took the comedy writer, H.J. Byron, into partnership with her. When he retired two years later, his place was taken by Sidney 'Squire' Bancroft, whom Marie Wilton married. Together, they quietly revolutionised the theatre. Instead of the melodrama and spectacle that London audiences were used to, and on which Ellen Terry had been reared, they concentrated on light comedies, mainly written by Tom Robertson, which confounded critics by being immensely successful.[8]

Other changes brought about by the Bancrofts were equally startling for the times. They put the orchestra below the stage; and introduced modern scenic effects with the use of genuine objects on stage – like furniture, china, rugs and even door knobs. So impressed was the audience by these realistic effects that the Robertson comedies were known as 'cup-and-saucer' drama. Robertson himself, who acted as dramatist-director, was held to have invented stage management and his notes to actors ('No tragedy, no tears, no pocket-handkerchief') also helped damp down the long-accepted declamatory and melo-dramatic school of acting.

Squire Bancroft, as a young actor, had also always disliked the custom whereby everyone, from cleaner to principal actor, had to queue up weekly outside the treasury for their salary; and he introduced the idea of wages being taken direct to the dressing-rooms. He also believed firmly that actors should be paid enough to live on, without having to depend on benefit performances, and started the idea of increasing their salaries, when profits allowed.

But the major change the Bancrofts effected was the way they made the theatre respectable: an entertainment fit for the middle and upper classes. When Marie Wilton, as she then was, had first bought the Queen's Theatre in ungenteel Tottenham Street, it was known as 'The Dust Hole.' She re-christened it The Prince of Wales', carpeted the auditorium, painted the stalls blue and white and turned it into London's most fashionable little theatre. Its middle-class audiences, who dined late, expected to see two or more short burlesque pieces, but found these had been cut to a single, longer play. Matinees were another innovation.

It was the Bancrofts' enthusiasm for realism in stage design that made them make Godwin archaeological adviser to *The Merchant of Venice*. He began work immediately, sending the scene painter to Venice to get the authentic feel and colour. Deciding the play was set in 1590, he made detailed notes on scenery and costume:

> Portia's stockings would be silk or the finest thread worked
> with clocks and even seams. Her shoes, of slipper form,
> would be of morocco or of velvet, embroidered with gold,
> cork being used for the soles.

The dress he designed for Ellen as Portia was like almond blossom.

The play opened at the Prince of Wales' on 17 April 1875

and flopped. Three weeks later it closed. The main reason for this was Charles Coghlan's hesitating performance as Shylock; another, ironically, was the authenticity of Godwin's set, which disconcerted the audience by looking more like an old Italian picture than a theatre. Squire Bancroft liked it, but thought it a bit before its time. Some of the more eminent among the audience, like the poet Edwin Arnold and painter and sculptor Sir Frederick Leighton, regarded it as the renaissance of theatrical art and offered to keep the play going by subscription.

There was one undeniable success: Ellen as Portia. When the curtain rose and showed her in a china blue and white brocade dress, with one crimson rose at her breast, there was rapturous applause. The critics praised her in the most extravagant terms: 'Very perfect acting, in the style of art which cannot be taught,' said the *Daily Telegraph*. Oscar Wilde, enthralled by Ellen, sent her a sonnet.

Ellen considered she played Portia more stiffly and slowly than in later years, because the costume seemed to demand this. But she felt transformed as an actress:

> Never until I appeared as Portia at the Prince of Wales's had I experienced that awe-struck feeling which comes, I suppose, to no actress more than once in a lifetime – the feeling of the conqueror. In homely parlance, I knew that I had 'got them' at the moment when I spoke the speech beginning, 'You see me, Lord Bassanio, where I stand.' 'What can this be?' I thought. '*Quite* this thing has never come to me before! *This is different!* It has never been quite the same before'.[9]

Ellen was elated by her new-found enthusiasm for acting, the critical acclaim, and the letters of admiration from the public. 'Everyone seemed to be in love with me!' she said. But although the Bancrofts, too, were delighted with their leading lady, they had no particularly exciting play to offer next. Robertson, their comedy writer, had died in 1871 and they finally cast Ellen as Clara Douglas in Lord Lytton's old-fashioned comedy, *Money*.

She rather enjoyed the part of the well-balanced Clara, though Tom Taylor, in the tradition of Ellen's older male friends, wrote to admonish her about her acting:

But you were nervous and uncomfortable in many parts for want of sufficient rehearsal. These passages you will, no doubt, improve in nightly. I would only urge on you the great importance of studying to be quiet and composed, and not fidgeting. There was especially a trick of constantly twiddling with and looking at your fingers which you should, above all, be on your guard against . . . I think, too, you showed too evident feeling in the earlier scene with Evelyn. A blind man must have read what you felt – your sentiment should be more masked.[10]

While Ellen was with the Bancrofts, Charles Calvert, manager of the Prince's Theatre in Manchester, offered her the parts of Juliet and Rosalind. The offer finally fell through, but not before Godwin had planned her wardrobe. He wrote to tell her that he was designing her a square mantle of fluffy transparent eastern stuff about six feet six inches square, 'worn *anyhow*, but your how especially.' And in another, dated 24 July, from the Verulam Club in St James Street, illustrated with an intricate drawing of Juliet's scent bottle, he wrote:

Darling – one word – you took away all memory, thought, archaeology & the rest today.
   Of course you can have *silk* for Juliet – pale red – pale blue – violet & a *kind* of vermillion were used mostly in 1300-10. Swell dresses like her ball dress may be *embroidered all over* (blue & white embroidery) . . . you might also get a silver box made with open work . . . but then you might be happier if *you* were Juliet from top to toe. I can't trust myself to write two words apart from what you call 'business.' You will *believe* this & credit me with *something* human.[11]

Why the letter from the club? And why did he want to be credited with being human? The answer was simple. Despite the lover-like beginning to the letter, despite his evident desire to continue to design her stage costume – Edward had left her.

As so often in Ellen's private life, there can only be speculation as to what caused the break-up. It was likely that the relationship had been frayed by poverty. Ellen was under constant pressure from friends to extricate herself from her precarious financial existence with Godwin. They also pointed out that living openly with Godwin could harm her and her children more in London than in secluded Hertfordshire.

The fact that Godwin was to marry his pupil, Beatrice Philip, on 4 January the following year suggests another reason: that Ellen suspected his affections had been transferred elsewhere. Beatrice was a lively, handsome brunette, who had a tendency to hero worship – although Godwin may have slipped off his pedestal when, immediately after their wedding, he dropped her off at his house-cum-office and went off to dine at his club. Such casual treatment implies, however, that Godwin was not sufficiently infatuated with Beatrice to leave Ellen and his children for her. It's more likely that Beatrice was around *after* he had left Ellen, when he was lonely, and that he made a snap decision to marry her. He had, after all, made a similar, sudden decision to elope with Ellen.

He and Ellen might possibly have fallen out over Ellen's new absorption with the stage and her career. But this is unlikely: Godwin had shown by his writings, and by taking on a woman pupil, that he was unlike the reactionary men of the age. He respected women who were active in the arts, and was always to admire Ellen's acting. He continued to design her dresses and was evidently proud of her career.

Ellen's daughter Edy, in her notes to her mother's memoirs, writes that an old friend of Godwin told her that he had left Taviton Street 'in a fit of pique.' It could have been over anything. Ellen was, after all, no obedient Victorian mistress, demure in a love nest: she was highly strung and impetuous, Godwin might have had his latest carefully designed dress for her chucked at his head. Ellen's son, on the other hand, said of his parents' separation, 'Then, by mutual disagreement, they parted. Sad: but there was no unkindness, no dissension – they were neither of them desertable people.'[12]

Certainly the letter Ellen wrote in 1890, four years after Godwin's death, to a friend of Harpenden days, gives the impression that she, too, hardly knew how the break had come about:

> The times, of which you were part, were my best times, my happiest times. I can never think of him but at his best, and when he died, he thought only so of me. I could never suffer again I think as I have suffered, but I joy in the remembrance

of him. He loved me, and I loved him, and that, I suppose, is the reason we so cruelly hurt each other. He went away and shut the door after him. It seems like that to me, but *he knows*.[13]

After Godwin left, Ellen and her household moved to 221 Camden Road, which had an attractive large garden. It was from there (according to a letter written by Ellen that came into the hands of her grandson, Edward Craig), that Edward took part in a curious attempt to 'snatch' Edy. Faced with a threat to one of her beloved children, it was one of the few recorded times that Ellen stopped professing love for Godwin and showed her claws. A letter, headed '221 Camden Road Villas, N.W. Saturday night,' and addressed to a Mr Wilson, reads:

> In all gentleness and kindness of feeling, I must beg you not to act as mediator between Mr Godwin and myself. Our separation was a thing agreed upon by *both* of us many weeks before it actually took place. The first steps were taken by *him* and I certainly am much astonished to hear that he professes any strong feeling in the matter. Part of our compact was that we should always maintain a kindly, friendly relation to one another – He has since Tuesday last made this an IMPOSSIBILITY. He tried by unfair means to get my little girl from me (I *had offered* to let him have the boy) and I now distinctly refuse to hold any communication whatever with him.
>
> I do feel sorry that he is ill – Glad that he has some good friends – may he CONTINUE to appreciate them through his lifetime. I thank you for many kindnesses you have shown me and my children but I thank you still more for the fact that you are Mr Godwin's friend now.
>
> Your letter arrived AFTER your departure last evening.
>
> If Mr Godwin's friends knew his temperament as I do and the effects of change of scene upon him, they would advise his leaving London and *staying with friends*, for a time at least. He should not go alone as he is apt to brood and imagine all kinds of ills which do not exist. You say in your letter '*I really fear for his reason*' – When I knew him in his home life 13 years ago I had the same idea, and at that time he had an *utterly sorrowless life* – a devoted help-mate –

success – friends – *everything*. He never was happy – he never will be. If you choose to show him this letter I will find no objection. At the risk of being called utterly heartless I again say I will hold no further communication with Mr Godwin, and I also say that this hard behaviour on my part has been brought about entirely by his own rash conduct since the last time we were together in Taviton Street.[14]

She never forgot the incident. Her son Teddy remembered her asking him, when he was six, if he would like to see a picture of the devil. Teddy expected to see a hideous picture of a fiend with long teeth, claws and a tail and instead was shown a portrait of his father.

Ellen was to marry twice more and have a long involvement with Henry Irving; but though she tended to romanticise her days at Harpenden with Godwin, she was evidently deeply in love with him. Among her books at her house in Smallhythe, Kent, is a copy of *The Nutbrown Maid*. Ellen wrote inside it 'This own wee book from EWG' and altered the verse inside to read:

> Though it be sung of old and young
> That I shall be to blame
> Theirs be the charge that speaks so large
> In hurting of my name . . .
> For in my mind of all mankind
> I love but you alone.

Her friend, the artist and writer Graham Robertson, was to write in 1931 that Ellen often told him her litany of really beloved names, which started 'Edward – and Edward.' Even though Robertson thought few would agree, he himself believed that Ellen 'loved (in the true sense of the word) one man only – and for ever.'[15]

From the time Edward left Ellen, until he married on 4 January 1876 (now aged forty two), he divided his time between his office and his club, and wrote weekly for *The Architect*. On return from his European honeymoon, he supervised the building of the new Bedford Park Estate in west London for 'middle class people of superior taste,' as *Building News* put it. He was still involved with the theatre and in 1876 designed some stage settings and costume in a production of *Henry V* at the Queen's Theatre. Ellen, gradually recovering her spirits, had returned to the stage herself in the November of 1875, some two months before Edward's marriage. The Bancrofts were staging a revised version of Charles Reade's and Tom Taylor's play *Masks and Faces* and Ellen, in the part of Mabel Vane, which one critic said scarcely extended beyond looking tasteful in the artistic dresses provided, was nevertheless cheered ecstatically by the audience.

This embarrassed Ellen, who wrote in her memoirs that it was the fault of her following that

> it got about that I had hired a claque to clap me! Now it seems funny, but at the time I was deeply hurt at the insinuation and it cast a shadow over what would otherwise have been a very happy time.

Her daughter, Edy, however, watching her mother act for the first time, was short on compliments: 'You *did* look long and thin in your grey dress,' was her verdict. 'When you fainted I thought you was going to fall into the orchestra – you was so *long*.'

Ellen said that had she listened to Edy, she would have left the stage in despair. But in the public's eyes, she had replaced her sister Kate as the idol of the London stage. Aware of this, the Bancrofts commissioned the playwright H.J. Byron to write a play with a leading part in it for Ellen, but he bungled it, producing a bad play, called *Wrinkles*, without an acceptable part for her. On the first night, adding to the general gloom, there was the sound of sawing wood during the last interval. Asked what it was, the depressed author replied: 'I don't know, but I hope they're cutting out the last act.'[16]

In the May of the following year, 1876, Ellen appeared for the last time under the Bancrofts, in yet another revival of Robertson's comedy, *Ours*. It was notable mainly because she accidentally stabbed Mrs Bancroft in the arm during a bayonet charge on stage and admirers of Mrs Bancroft, who had been angered at their favourite getting a less enthusiastic reception than Ellen, claimed it was no accident. Ellen, in fact, got on very well with Mrs Bancroft and had a lot to thank her for: she had learned the more intimate style needed for playing modern plays in a tiny theatre; and at last had a stable income.

Although Ellen had been earning well while at the Prince of Wales', she now received an even better offer from John Hare, who operated in friendly rivalry with the Bancrofts at the Court Theatre – a suburban little bandbox in Sloane Square which had been a dissenting chapel. She accepted Hare's offer and was now in a position to leave the lodgings in Camden Road and move to a more permanent home at 33 Longridge Road, in south west London. In addition she found a small cottage at Hampton Court – the first of many small cottages she fell for – where she and the children could rest and play during the summer months.

Ellen's first part at the Court Theatre, in November 1876, was that of Kate Hungerford in *Brothers*, an original comedy by Charles Coghlan. It did not 'draw the town' and was promptly replaced by another comedy, *New Men and Old Acres*, by Tom Taylor and A.W. Dubourg. Ellen was worried about one scene in which she had to play the piano and talk at the same time: she practised it incessantly at home, only to hear Edy say scathingly: '*That's* not right.'

But by joining the Court, Ellen's life took another turn. One of the actors in the cast was Charles Kelly, about whom Ellen had written to Mrs Bancroft to say, 'Have you ever seen *Mr Kelly* act? . . . He can show *gradation* of feeling – and has the *tenderest voice I've ever heard* . . .' In a little over a year, Ellen was to marry him.

CHAPTER 6

MARRIAGE TO KELLY: 'THE MANLY BULLDOG'

Charles Kelly was one of the trio that John Hare was banking on to bring success to the Court – the other two being Ellen Terry and Charles Coghlan, a friend of Hare's who was both playwright and actor. Kelly's reputation as an actor was growing. Clement Scott, the drama critic, said of him that he had 'that extraordinary power of "grip" that so few Anglo-Saxon actors possess.'[1]

Nevertheless, Charles Kelly (whose real surname was Wardell) came to the stage by chance: his ambition was to be a soldier, not an actor. He came from an educated background – his father, the vicar of Winlaton in Northumberland, was a friend of Sir Walter Scott – and was commissioned in a crack cavalry regiment, the sixty-sixth. He fought in the Crimean war but, after being wounded in action, retired from the army.

Describing Kelly as an actor, Ellen said that:

> Charlie, physically a manly bulldog sort of man, possessed as an actor great tenderness and humour. Owing to his lack of training, he had to be very carefully suited with a part, but given one that was in his line, he could do as well as many actors twenty years ahead of him in experience.[2]

The parts Kelly played best were one dimensional: he could easily be bluff and soldier-like, but had difficulty in extending his range beyond that.

Ellen had acted with him before. When she had returned to the stage as Philippa in *The Wandering Heir*, she and Kelly had both appeared in an 'after-piece' by Charles Reade, called *Rachael the Reaper*. The script called for farm animals and Charles Reade, with his passion for realism, decided to use real pigs, sheep, goats and a dog. Although Charles Kelly, with his robust, hearty, appearance, looked just like a farmer, this was too much for him.

Ellen never forgot the sight of Charles Reade arriving at the theatre with his entourage of animals, which promptly escaped and ran off in all directions. 'That's a relief, at any rate,' she heard Charles Kelly say, as he watched the flight of the pigs. 'I shan't have those damned pigs to spoil my acting as well as the damned dog and the damned goat!' Her amusement increased on the first night, when 'the real dog bit Kelly's real ankles, and in real anger he kicked the real animal by a real mistake into the orchestra's real drum!'[3]

At the time of *Rachael the Reaper*, Ellen was still living with Godwin in London. When she met Kelly again, at the Court, in 1876, Godwin was married to Beatrice Philip. This might have turned her own thoughts towards matrimony. But what made marriage possible was that Watts filed for a divorce, which was granted in the autumn of 1877, citing Godwin as the guilty party. Commenting on the divorce, Edy said she had no idea why it was so delayed and assumed that the need for it only arose after her mother and Godwin had separated.

The implication here is that Ellen had never approached Watts for a divorce while living with Godwin; but might have done so when she and Charles Kelly wanted to marry. Marrying Kelly had undoubted advantages for Ellen. Having two illegitimate children was totally unacceptable in those days: even Lewis Carroll, devoted though he was to her wouldn't introduce a young girl to her without the permission of the girl's mother. Although Ellen cared little about such censure herself, she adored her children and feared their lack of a surname would cause them to be ostracised.

Marriage would also heal the breach with her parents caused by her liaison with Godwin and allow her sister Kate to receive her at her impressive home, Moray Lodge on Campden Hill. Kate's husband Arthur Lewis, owner of a fashionable haberdashery shop in Conduit Street, was also an amateur painter and singer and he and Kate entertained constantly, holding concerts and large parties.

Edy, while agreeing that one of the reasons for Ellen's remarriage was to regularise matters for her and her brother, admitted 'it is conceivable that she was strongly attracted by Charles Wardell. All through her life the man of brains

Ellen, photographed around the time of her marriage to the actor Charles
Wardell, known as Charles Kelly, 1877.

competed for her affections with the man of brawn.'[4] Bernard
Shaw believed she was attracted to men of brains to
compensate for her own poor education, but could not resist
stupid men who were devoted to her, because 'their distress at
being repulsed by her was more than she could bear.'

Ted could never understand why she selected Kelly:

> on what terms did they marry? Certainly not love –
> admiration? . . . Of course E.T. admitted that she would
> always try *to please everyone* – and here I suppose she was
> trying to find a father for Edy and Ted – AND a sort of hefty
> protector for herself – and a practical daily assistant – and
> then, when H.I. wished her to sack Charlie K., she doubtless
> did so to please H.I.[5]

Ellen married Kelly during the run of *Olivia* in the spring of
1878, and he moved in with the family at Longridge Road. Edy
and Teddy were now Edy and Teddy Wardell and Ellen had
visiting cards printed, with the respectable name of
Mrs E. Wardell.

Kelly got on reasonably well with the children. Teddy, who
was about four when his mother married Kelly, remembered
him as being 'something large and heavy footed, a kind of
stranger who, I thought, growled and clumped his way along
the passages, whereas Mother had seemed to sing or whisper
her way, and had flitted in and out.'[6]

He also recalled his mother objecting to Kelly 'flourishing his
hunting-crop at us in the Lord of the Manor style, when we
made a beastly noise in the morning,' but said that his step-
father was 'really as kind a bear as it were possible to find.
Once he devoted over an hour to trying to teach me the way to
read the clock.'[7]

Olivia was written by W.G. Wills, but based on Oliver
Goldsmith's *The Vicar of Wakefield*, and John Hare's decision
to stage it saved the fortunes of the Court. The story was set in
the seventeenth century: at the time there was a seventeenth
century craze going on. George du Maurier had started the
fashion with his *Punch* drawings and as a result people had
gone mad about blue china, Chippendale chairs, Sheraton
sideboards, old spinets and brass fire-irons.

Ellen played the female lead, but Kelly was furious at not
being offered the leading part of the vicar, as he considered

himself the company's leading man. Clement Scott, the drama critic, said of Kelly that he was 'a man of excellent talent, of firm determination, and who could argue and argue well on any given subject.'[8] This time, however, he lost the argument; and then refused to act any other part. 'Alas!' said Ellen Terry. 'Many actors are just as blind to their true interests.'

She herself sent a letter to W.G. Wills, saying she was delighted with the play and her part. Judging by the way Wills wrote his plays, it was surprising any of them got as far as being produced: he used to lie in bed, jotting sentences down at random on his wristbands, the backs of old envelopes and in untidy copy books. He would chuck the pages out of bed and then summon his servant to pick them up and collect them together, in any kind of order.

But *Olivia* was a resounding success, both for Ellen and for William Terriss, who played young Squire Thornhill. The critics were ecstatic. Clement Scott, praising her for her dramatic pathos, wrote that 'When Olivia struck Squire Thornhill in her distraction and impotent rage, an audible shudder went through the audience.'[9] Another critic, Dutton Cook, wrote that the modern theatre had rarely seen such emotion and tragic passion.

Edy and Teddy had walk-on parts for the first time. According to Ellen, Teddy had such red cheeks that the other rouged cheeks on stage looked quite pale in comparison; while Edy delighted Ellen by giving her a bunch of flowers she'd picked the day before in the country.

The audiences were as appreciative as the critics. Ellen became the idolised heroine and fashionable London went *Olivia* mad; the milliners' windows were jammed full of Olivia caps, which were as sought after as the Langtry bonnet; photographs of Ellen Terry were everywhere; and hundreds of newborn girls were christened Olivia.

Neighbours of Ellen in Longridge Road counted themselves especially lucky. One young man living opposite, D.S. MacColl, had watched her from the day she and the children had moved in. Having caught 'the flicker of an elbow in the bay-window of the dining room,' he found 'even so little of the owner was fascinating.' When he saw her 'dazzling shape,' he was overcome and called his sisters to share in his rapture.[10] They had no idea, at that stage, who the vision was and called her

'The Greek Lady' because she still dressed in the flowing garments Godwin had liked. Only later, when they knew who Ellen was, and that she was appearing at the Court Theatre, did they make a point of watching her leave every day. It was an excellent performance. Ellen was playing at being herself.

'Each morning, when the Greek Lady went off to rehearsal,' her young male admirer noted,

> there was a scene as pretty as anything she played upon the stage. She appeared upon the steps like April morning, lifting wide eloquent lips, hooded eyes and breathless face to the light. She raised and kissed two little tots . . . greeted the next door neighbours, family of a Rabbinical scholar, who had promptly become slaves of her apparition, and stood ready on the pavement. Her cushions were brought out, placed and patted in the open carriage; herself installed; the air became tender and gay with wavings and blown kisses; the wheels revolved, and greyness descended once more on Longridge Road.[11]

The success of *Olivia* changed Ellen's career. A friend of Ellen's, a Lady Pollock, knew that Henry Irving had just become sole lessee of the Lyceum Theatre and was looking for a leading lady. She told Irving that Ellen would be ideal for him; that apart from being the current star of London, and thus able to bring her personal following to the Lyceum, she had experience of Shakespeare under the Bancrofts. With total trust in this reference, and without even going to see Ellen act the part of Olivia, Irving wrote to Ellen on 20 July from 15a Grafton Street – where he lived throughout his management of the Lyceum – to say that he would like to meet her.

He intended to ask her to play Ophelia to his Hamlet. Ellen could never recall their precise conversation, but she noticed the change in him since they had played together in *Katherine and Petruchio* in 1867; then she had thought him sensitive to ridicule and deeply unhappy at being unable to express himself through his art. She said

> In ten years, he had found himself, and so lost himself – lost, I mean, much of that stiff, ugly, self-consciousness which had encased him as the shell encases the lobster. His forehead had become more massive, and the very outline of his features

MR. CHARLES KELLY.

A SOUND ACTOR

Charles Kelly, the actor (whose real surname was Wardell), whom Ellen married two years after separating from Godwin.

had altered. He was a man of the world, whose strenuous fighting now was to be done as a general.[12]

Ellen had greatly admired Irving's successful *Hamlet* at the Lyceum in 1874 and, two years later, his Philip I, which she thought a perfect study of quiet malignity and cruelty. Irving suggested that Ellen go to Birmingham, where he was currently playing Hamlet. She did so and thought he was even more wonderful than before: 'The Birmingham night he knew I was there. He played – I say it without vanity – for me ... that night I saw what I shall always consider the *perfection* of acting.'[13]

Although Irving told a friend he had engaged Ellen for the Lyceum, Ellen had been unable to interpret his friendly smiles and embarrassed grunts, and was forced to write to him in August, asking his theatrical intentions. Once they were made clear, it was agreed that Ellen would start after the Lyceum's summer break had ended at a salary of forty guineas a week. With two children to support and a husband who earned comparatively little, Ellen finally had long-term financial security.

Meanwhile, in the summer of 1878, before she joined the Lyceum, Ellen and Kelly toured the provinces in a couple of comedies. Ellen said she had never had to work harder in her life, but they enjoyed it all, nevertheless. Charles Reade wrote to Ellen, after seeing them in *Dora* at Liverpool, congratulating them both on a masterly performance: 'Be assured nobody can appreciate your value and Mr Kelly's as I do. It is well played all round.'[14] The tour was so successful that the two of them repeated it for the next two summers, until 1880.

But there were already difficulties between the couple. Ellen was finding it hard to run a home for her children with a man who drank as much as Kelly, a habit which was to kill him. And Kelly, who had hitherto regarded himself as Ellen's leading man, felt Irving had supplanted him in that role – something a man of so jealous a temper could not accept. In talking of his domination, Ellen was to say 'one cannot live with a steamroller.'

When she wrote to Bernard Shaw some fifteen years later, declining the part of the jealous, ill-tempered Julia in *The Philanderer*, she said:

Ellen aged thirty two, drawn in pencil by Violet, Duchess of Rutland, in 1879, and purchased by the Watts Gallery.

I could play it from the life, if I played it. For three years I lived with a *male* Julia. He was my husband, Mr Wardell ('Charles Kelly') and I'm alive! But I should have died had I lived one more month with him. I gave him three-quarters of all the money I made weekly, and prayed him to go.[15]

Ellen was fortunate in not having to give up her house, too. The year she and Kelly judicially separated, 1881, the Married Women's Property Act was passed. Until then, all property belonging to a woman automatically became her husband's at marriage – a neat reversal of the marriage service, which had the husband promising to endow all *his* worldly goods.

Commenting in later years on why Ellen's marriages always ended so lamentably, her son said he supposed she was impossible as a wife:

Her husbands were not to blame – it was she who was not a marriageable person – because she was too passionately the servant of the stage . . . I don't see how you can rock the cradle, rule the world, *and* play Ophelia perfectly, all in the day's work.[16]

Ted's views of women, however, was that their real role was in the home.

The MacColl neighbours, still watching the family, approved of the separation, having always thought that Kelly, a 'manly bulldog sort of man' was not really worthy of their 'Phantom of Delight'. 'We resented the conjunction for her as a false concord.' About a year after Kelly had left Longridge Road, they were to see a new figure visiting Ellen, 'spare, and grim-jaunty in close-fitting short jacket, and tilted wide-a-wake; Henry Irving.'[17]

CHAPTER 7

IRVING AND ELLEN: 'TILL DEATH DO US PART'

In 1878, when Ellen joined Henry Irving at the Lyceum, she was thirty one and he was forty. He had been acting at the Lyceum for seven years, but it had been his melodramatic and haunting performance there as Matthias in *The Bells*, in 1871, that dazzled London audiences and made him the greatest drawing power in the theatre.

Irving always had a taste for melodrama. It was he who had persuaded the American manager of the Lyceum, Hezekiah Bateman, to put on *The Bells* – adapted from a French play. In it, Matthias murders a man travelling in a jingling sleigh and when, later, his conscience invokes the sound of imaginary sleigh bells, he collapses and dies. Irving looked so livid with fear in the part, audiences were terrified.

When Bateman died in 1874, his wife took over as manager, as well as remaining leading lady. Four years later, in 1878, Irving asked her permission to engage his own leading lady. Mrs Bateman agreed reluctantly and transferred the Lyceum's lease to him. For the next twenty or so years, the quality of the productions at the Lyceum Theatre, off the Strand in London, were unequalled.

Unlike Ellen, Irving, whose real name was John Henry Brodribb, did not come from a theatrical family. He was the son of Samuel Brodribb, a travelling salesman, and Mary Behenna, a devout Cornish woman. He was born in Keinton Mandeville in Somerset, but when he was four his parents moved to Bristol to try and find work and he was sent to an aunt in Cornwall. A lonely, reserved, child, he spent much of his time reading the bible and Shakespeare. Once he let his emotions show through, when he came across an endearing little lamb and threw his arms round its neck and kissed it. It bit him.

He retreated from people through play-acting and even as a child wanted to be an actor. As he stammered this seemed unlikely, but a headmaster of a new school took him in elocution lessons and practically cured him. On leaving school at thirteen, he became a clerk by day and did amateur acting at night, despite his religious mother's conviction that hell fire was now waiting for him.

Left £100 by an uncle, John Brodribb spent it on stage properties – actors then having to provide their own wigs and other accessories – and got a job in a stock company in Sunderland. His mother promptly severed all connection. At eighteen, he took the stage name of John Henry Irving, then dropped the John. He spent ten hard years in the provinces in various stock companies, sometimes unemployed for weeks. It was a life of near starvation which only a dedicated actor would choose.

He also had to try to overcome his physical limitations; a dragging leg, which made his walk unusual; and a high, thin voice, which lacked the depth of tone needed to convey passion. In trying to overcome this, he prolonged his vowel sounds in a most peculiar and irritating manner. Instead of saying, for instance, 'To trammel up the consequence,' he would say, 'Tram-mele up-p the cunsequence.'

In the autumn of 1871, he joined the Lyceum, where his immediate success with *The Bells*, revealed, said Max Beerbohm, 'an incomparable power for eeriness.'

It was on the first night of *The Bells* that Irving left his wife. He had married Florence O'Callaghan two years before in July 1869, and it proved a disaster. Irving, with his perfectionism and obsession about work, was not easy to live with, but even before their marriage Florence worried Irving by her 'unsurmountably cold' manner. She remained unloving and though becoming pregnant shortly after the marriage, was jealous over the actor friends her husband kept bringing home to supper. Irving left her to live in some cheap lodgings. The birth of a son briefly reconciled them and led to Florence becoming pregnant again.

However, Florence remained disapproving when Irving was lionised at the supper party to celebrate the first night of *The Bells*. Driving home from the party in a brougham he said to her, 'Well, my dear, we too shall soon have our carriage and

Henry Irving as Matthias in *The Bells*, in 1871, the part that made him the greatest drawing power in London.

pair.' Florence's reply, ungenerous and cutting, was: 'Are you going on making a fool of yourself like this all your life?'[1] Irving banged on the side to stop the driver, got down and walked away. He never lived with, or spoke to Florence again.

After *The Bells*, Irving's next success at the Lyceum was his unconventional playing of *Hamlet* as a gentleman scholar instead of the usual over-dramatic, funeral-plumed prince. His version of *Macbeth* as a craven, and *Othello* as a Venetian general, were equally unconventional. His reputation as an actor grew and seven years after joining the Lyceum, he had earned enough money to take over the lease, engage Ellen Terry, and begin the start of their twenty four year partnership.

Before opening with *Hamlet*, Irving spent £4,000 on transforming the Lyceum. The faded auditorium was repainted in sage green and turquoise blue; the ornaments and figures cleaned and burnished; the seats in the stalls and dress circle made more comfortable; and the plain benches in the pit and gallery given backs. There was new scenery and a new drop curtain.

By making the Lyceum an inviting theatre, concentrating on Shakespeare, and creating glittering and elaborate productions, Irving attracted an intellectual, middle and upper class audience who expected, and got, a higher standard of acting at the Lyceum than elsewhere. The working class who, in the early and mid part of the nineteenth century had formed the bulk of the audiences, turned increasingly to music halls and the playhouses, which still staged a mixture of farce and burlesque, and where the acting style was declamatory.

Irving was a perfectionist about acting. He would often study a play for months before he put it on. At the first rehearsal of *Hamlet* he read everyone's part except for Ellen's. She remembered that

> The power that he put into each part was extraordinary. He threw himself so thoroughly into it that his skin contracted and his eyes shone. His lips grew whiter and whiter, and his skin more and more drawn as time went on, until he looked livid but still beautiful. He then constantly re-rehearsed the first scene on the battlements, in order to get from the actors the intensity required to 'start the play a living thing.'[2]

His actors learned to watch his arrival on stage for rehearsals carefully. If he wore a silk hat, it meant he had a social engagement and the day would be peaceful; if he wore a broad brimmed soft felt hat – which they were to christen his 'storm hat,' they knew they had better watch out.

Ellen worked hard on her own part of Ophelia and visited local asylums to study inmates' behaviour. It confirmed her belief that an actor must imagine first and observe afterwards. She hadn't the advantage of one actress, a Mrs Mountford, whose favourite part was Ophelia, and who subsequently went mad herself. In a lucid interval, she discovered *Hamlet* was being played at her old theatre. Giving her attendants the slip, she concealed herself in the theatre and, waiting until the mad scene, shouldered her way past the real Ophelia and, in front of the amazed audience, played the scene perfectly.

A further worry for Ellen was her costume. She had decided to wear a transparent black dress for the mad scene, but Irving gently commented that surely Ophelia wore white? Ellen said that black was more interesting, and the subject was dropped. Irving used diplomacy, rather than threats, when he meant to have his own way and sent Walter Lacy, his Shakespearean adviser to her to say that she surely could not have been serious about wearing black. She asked why not. 'My God, madam, there must be only one black figure in this play and that's Hamlet.'

Ellen wasn't sure whether Irving was right or not, but she didn't argue. The incident, she said, showed her that 'he had a finer sense of what was right for the *scene*.'

Irving was increasingly to rely on Ellen's judgment and, after this, he always consulted her about the costumes. She proved very useful to him, having developed a good sense of colour and design after years of living with Godwin and discussing with him how Shakespeare's plays should be presented. Although her son, Ted, believed she had only 'a woman's taste' for beautiful things, and no creative skill as a stage producer, her help over artistic decisions strengthened Irving's reliance on her judgment.

Ellen's other concern during *Hamlet* was that Irving rehearsed everyone except her. She was in awe of Irving, despite being his leading lady, but finally approached him about this and told him she was very nervous about her first appearance with him. Couldn't they rehearse their scenes?

Top: Ellen as Ophelia in 1878, the start of her partnership with Irving at the Lyceum. Below, as Juliet, 1882.

Irving dismissed her fears, with: 'We shall be all right, but we're not going to run the risk of being bottled up by a gas man or a fiddler.'[3]

The play opened on 30 December 1878, with Ellen feeling nervous and irritable about her lack of rehearsal. The audience roared a welcome when she first appeared; but after the fourth act, when her part in the play was over, she flung herself into the arms of a friend, repeating, 'I have failed, I have failed!' She then left the theatre and frantically drove up and down the Thames Embankment half a dozen times, missing her curtain call and finally going home.

Ellen was to remain unhappy, still considering she had not rehearsed enough. But though one critic said damningly that she played the mad scene 'with a realism which was happily kept in check by fine taste,' most praised her performance with extravagant adjectives: 'Picturesque, tender, and womanly throughout'; 'Infinite pathos'; 'Wonderful charm.' ('Blow that word charm!' Ellen often said after reading the critics. 'There is something more in my acting than charm.')

Irving's Hamlet was also praised – Tennyson saying he had lifted the part to heaven. But his voice and self-conscious gait was criticised. Hurt, he asked Ellen later on if she thought this was justified, and whether he really said 'Gud' for 'God.' She said straight out that it was true, he did pronounce his vowels in an odd way and did drag his leg. Irving admitted that as a young actor he had been jeered and hooted at because of his thin legs, so now he padded them. Ellen at once told him to take the padding off; what did he want with fat, prize-fighter legs?

Irving, finding that Ellen helped him rather than laughed at him, made her one of his few confidantes. It was an important off-stage role. Despite holding supper parties in the Beefsteak Room at the Lyceum for up to three hundred and fifty at a time, Irving, a reserved man, had only a small circle of real friends and Ellen said that he never wholly trusted these or discussed his intimate thoughts with them.

Ellen was dispassionate enough to see that her importance to Irving was a curious mixture of professional and personal. Her son remembers her saying,

Yes, yes – were I to be run over by a steamroller tomorrow,

Henry would be deeply grieved: would say quietly, 'What a pity!' and would add, after two moments' reflection: 'Who is there – er – to go on for her tonight?'[4]

They both saw as much of each other outside as inside the theatre. Her son, in his memoirs, recalled his mother's usual weekend routine at the time:

Saturday was always a half-holiday, spent in promising her advisers that she would be good next week – and on Sunday she generally drove away to [her cottage at] Hampton Court with Irving, waving her lily white hand.[5]

The mid-Victorian age was a censorious time but throughout her life Ellen sunnily disregarded conventions.

She and Irving patently cared for each other, but there is no conclusive proof that they were lovers. Yet the electricity between them as stage partners, their admiration for each other as actors, the euphoria of their success, Ellen's strange beauty and Irving's romantic disposition – all this must surely have led to a love affair. Ellen destroyed almost all her letters from Irving, but the few notes from him that survive clearly show that his early feelings for her were near infatuation. One undated fragment reads: 'Soon – Soon! I shall be near you on Sunday. God bless you my only thought. Your own till Death.'[6] Another reads: 'My fairest – sweetest, loveliest Ophelia. Only this. *Your* Hamlet.'[7] A third, says: 'We must bring the summer to ourselves by being together;'[8] and a fourth ended, 'My own dear wife as long as I live.'[9]

Nevertheless, their precise relationship still provokes argument. Those who point to Ellen's undoubted love for Godwin – the crucifix, made by her son, and at her bed when she died, had 'EWG – 1886 the 6 Oct. My love (and my only lover) died. God rest his soul' on the bottom – are convinced she did not take another lover. Her son for years vehemently maintained they were not lovers, though admitting that his mother said the loveliest things about Irving every day for years. Edy, in private, said that they were.

Different biographers have taken different sides – as they have over whether Ellen had a sexual relationship with Watts, and with Kelly, and the precise circumstances of her marriage break-up with Watts. Margaret Webster, whose parents were members of the Lyceum company, said they would both have been amazed at the idea that there had never been more between Ellen and Irving than good comradeship and professional association, and that her mother never had the slightest doubt that they were lovers.[10]

Laurence Irving, in his biography of his grandfather, says Irving adored Ellen, who was to him, 'the Queen of every woman,' and once told Ellen that the proof of his love for her was that he was not jealous of the public's devotion to her. However, Laurence Irving felt that fundamentally Irving looked on Ellen as a gifted, irresponsible daughter; while she saw him as a son of genius, who needed protection from his rasher actions.

Ellen herself covers her tracks neatly by telling different people opposing stories. Marguerite Steen, biographer of the Terry family, says Ellen and Irving's love affair began after the first night of *Hamlet*, when Irving followed her home after she had left the theatre so abruptly, thinking she had failed as Ophelia. When she asked Ellen directly if she had been Irving's mistress, Ellen told her,

> Of course I was. We were terribly in love for a while. Then, later on, when it didn't matter so much to me, he wanted us to go on, and so I did, because I was very, very fond of him and he said he needed me.'[11]

Lady Duff Gordon, on the other hand, says in her memoirs that she often saw Irving drifting in and out of Ellen's house at all hours, and that although Ellen understood him perfectly and knew how to manage him, it struck her that their association was one of closest friendship rather than of love. Ellen, she said, told her the same herself: 'People always say that Henry is my lover, of course. He isn't. As a matter of fact he never sees further than my head. He does not even know I have a body.'[12]

Nevertheless, there was open speculation about the relationship. The novelist Violet Hunt wrote of a supper party Irving attended at which he alluded to the scandal about Ellen and himself, very rife at the time, and said that if he were free, he would marry her the next day. This was confirmed by Laurence Irving, who said his grandfather

believed, no doubt sincerely, that he loved her, and was

prepared to sacrifice his jealously guarded independence for her sake. There was a time when he had hoped she might marry him – indeed he pressed her to do so.[13]

Perhaps in hope, Irving bought the lease of 'The Grange' in Brook Green, west London, and spent a lot of money refurbishing it and replanting the garden on the same lines as Ellen's much loved garden in Harpenden. He never moved in permanently. When he bought it, he and Ellen were acting in *Romeo and Juliet* and Ellen was to say that, at the time, Irving 'felt like Romeo.'

For Irving, banned by his wife from even seeing his children, the thought of a happy marriage, surrounded by Ellen's warmth and charm, must have been tempting. Yet paradoxically, the two would really have caused a scandal if they had decided to marry. A divorce action would have meant him admitting to being the guilty party and, given his wife's open hatred of him (she called Ellen 'the wench' and brought Irving's two young sons up to loathe him), the case would have attracted enormous publicity and ruined Irving's career. On the other hand, if they did not marry and Ellen became pregnant, her career would be ruined.

Over the years, they managed to avoid serious scandal, helped perhaps by there being no gossip columnists to contend with. Although Ellen and Irving were in newspapers and magazines, and although first nights at the Lyceum stopped the London traffic, actors and actresses were still not accepted in the best social circles in Victorian times. To be on the stage at all cast doubt on your morals. As late as 1844, a reviewer in the *Theatrical Journal* wrote of the theatres as 'great public brothels.'

Despite their attachment, Ellen, the extrovert, would often bewilder Irving, the introvert. A melancholy man himself, he was taken aback when he was passing the foot of the stairs which led to her dressing room one day, and caught her sliding down the bannisters. 'He smiled at me, but didn't seem able to get over it,' said Ellen. Sir Frank Benson was equally shaken when he claimed he saw her catching hold of scenery being hoisted to the flies and hanging on until she was several feet above the stage. When the horrified carpenters realised they were hauling up one of the mainstays of the Lyceum and hastily lowered her, she did an impromptu Irish jig to show how much better she felt for her aerial flight.[14]

Irving was also puzzled by her quick changes of mood, from happy gossiping in the actors' green room, to tragic tears on stage a few minutes later, as he needed time to think himself into his part. He also found it hard to accept her 'unprofessional' behaviour: her uncontrollable laughter on stage if anything amused her; the way she could forget her lines or alter dialogue; her constant late arrival for rehearsals, which forced stage hands to call her for her cue some five minutes before necessary.

They did share the same sense of humour, however. One night, as they left their dressing rooms to go home, they came across a small girl sitting forlornly waiting for her mother. Irving asked what part she was playing. 'Please, sir, first I'm a water-carrier, then I'm a little page, and then I'm a virgin.' Ellen and Irving collapsed in tears of laughter.[15]

Irving had nothing of the impulsive in him. Describing him, Max Beerbohm said:

> He was always courteous and gracious, and everybody was fascinated by him; but I think there were few who did not also fear him. Always in the company of his friends and acquaintances – doubtless, not in that of his most intimate friends – there was an air of sardonic reserve behind his cordiality. He seemed always to be watching, and watching from a slight altitude.[16]

Asked what she remembered about her early years at the Lyceum, Ellen said Irving so loomed across them, that all events and feelings were reduced to insignificance. All she could recall was work. What with acting and rehearsing, she was rarely out of the threatre.

The early production of a play was always the same: at the first rehearsal, Irving, having studied the play, would read all the parts, making notes about the position of the characters and the order of the crowds and processions. He then handed out the handwritten parts. The next day, actors compared their parts on stage and checked their cues. This was followed by a stand-up rehearsal in which one set was done straight through, under Irving's personal supervision. Until the result satisfied him, it was done again and again – taking all day, if necessary.

He regarded timing as essential. Nothing was left to chance. There was no break for lunch, actors grabbing a sandwich if and when they could.

Ellen admitted 'it was a long time before we had much talk with each other,' and he was as unyielding to her as everyone else in the case. On one occasion, a year or so after she joined the Lyceum, she had a long and intense argument with him about the precise line in a play at which the curtain should come down. She used every argument, artistic and otherwise, and implored him to change his decision, but he was adamant. 'After holding out for a week,' she said, 'I gave in. "It's my duty to obey your orders and do it, but I do it under protest".'[17]

Apart from occasional disagreements, she was happy enough to obey Irving's commands, because she knew he was anxious for her success – though she was also realistic enough to know that this was not just for her own sake, but for the perfection he sought throughout the entire production.

No woman who was personally ambitious would have stayed twenty four years with an autocratic manager like Irving, losing, for instance, the chance to play Rosalind in *As You Like It* because there wasn't a suitable part in it for him. But Ellen lacked such ambition. She was to say she was more woman than artist – though in the next breath, she showed the conflict within her by saying, 'I love to work.' She admired Irving and was proud to work under him. In the same way, she had looked up to both Watts and Godwin: had been equally proud to do long hours of modelling for the one and innumerable architectural tracings for the other.

Bernard Shaw railed at her for the way she allowed Irving to dominate her, unable to understand that she was happy to defer to him. She once told Clement Scott, the critic,

> My aim is usefulness to my lovely art and to Henry Irving. This is not a very high ambition, is it? But long ago I gave up dreaming, and I think I see things as they are – especially see myself as I am, alas!, both off and on the stage, and I only aspire to help a little.[18]

She was quick to defend Irving over what her father crossly called her 'second fiddle' parts, claiming that in some plays she had better – or at least equal – acting opportunities. And in her memoirs, she said: 'I have sometimes wondered what I should have accomplished without Henry Irving. I might have had "bigger" parts, but it doesn't follow that they would have been better ones.' The painter Graham Robertson, agreed with her. In a letter he wrote in 1931, he said,

> As to her [Ellen's] career being sacrificed to him [Irving] –
> does anyone in their senses suppose that she would have
> gained her unique position without him? She has little
> ambition – no 'push' – little business capacity. She loved to
> serve and would always have served *somebody*.[19]

After *Hamlet* ended, Irving decided to alternate Shakespeare with popular melodrama. In one of these dramas, *Eugene Aram*, Ellen had little to do, but Irving, fascinated by melancholy and the horrors, much enjoyed his own role which allowed him to spend much of his time wrapped in a black cloak in the graveyard.

When the Lyceum closed for the summer break that year, Ellen and Kelly took a small company on tour. Although Edy was to accompany her mother on a similar tour the following year, being then aged ten, this year she and Teddy were left behind. Ellen missed them and one night, while playing the part of a dying woman who is shown a locket with a picture of her child in it, she opened the property locket to find Kelly had inserted two coloured photographs of Edy and Teddy. She promptly burst into tears and often wondered whether the audience spotted the difference between her real and assumed tears.

The Lyceum re-opened on 1 November 1879 with a sumptuously staged *The Merchant of Venice*. Although Ellen had played the part four years before under the Bancroft management, she re-studied Portia in great detail and tried out five or six different ways of playing the part. When she later gave her lectures on Shakespeare's heroines, at a time when the suffragettes were questioning male superiority, she admitted it must jar them to hear Portia say to Bassiano that her spirit 'Commits itself to yours to be directed, As from her lord, her governor, her king.'[20]

She then argued the case for Portia, saying that though modern women, wanting to see their sex less servile, had told her this speech was a serious obstacle to their admiration of

Ellen as Portia, in *The Merchant of Venice*, in the Lyceum Theatre production of 1879.

Portia, she thought the significance of her actual words should not be exaggerated:

> In spite of her gracious surrender, she retains her independence of thought and action. The first thing she does after her marriage is to lay her own plans for saving Antonio's life without so much as a 'with your leave or by your leave' to her lord and master.

Ellen also believed that the trap set for Shylock

> was just such an inspiration as a woman might have when she is at her wits' end, and willing to try anything. She [Portia] screws her courage to the sticking point and plays her last card for all that it's worth.

When Ellen had played Portia previously, she had done so with restraint, to contrast with the robust Shylock of Charles Coghlan; this time, Irving gave a thoughtful, non-traditional rendering of Shylock and Ellen in turn made Portia more tempestuous. Critics were mainly favourable, admiring her 'bubbling and infectious high spirits.' She got more letters from the public than for any of her other performances and Oscar Wilde sent another admiring sonnet.

But she did attract some hostile criticism. *Blackwoods* magazine gave a whole list of her shortcomings: that she turned Portia 'to favour and to prettiness'; that her characterisation lacked dignity, depth and subtlety; and that she had a 'coming-on disposition' towards her lover. Ellen was particularly affected by the last comment, saying that for years it made her self-conscious and uncomfortable as 'any suggestion of *indelicacy* in my treatment of a part always blighted me.'[21]

Six years later, she was blighted again. While playing Margaret in *Faust*, Lewis Carroll brought a little girl to see her. When the script required Margaret to start undressing, the child, a true Victorian, averted her eyes and said, 'Where is it going to stop?' Carroll suggested to Ellen that as her undressing had such a disagreeable effect on his companion, she should alter this. Ellen was furious and told him she thought he only knew *nice* children. But although she didn't take the criticism meekly, she still felt ashamed and shy whenever she played the part.[22]

The Merchant of Venice had a record run of seven months,

ending on 31 July 1880. Ellen then left for another summer tour with Kelly, playing Beatrice in *Much Ado About Nothing* – a performance, she said, she never bettered. It was to be their last tour together before they separated.

She returned to the Lyceum in time for rehearsals of *The Cup*, a trite play by Tennyson based on a story by Plutarch – redeemed only by Godwin's costumes for Ellen. When Tennyson first read the play aloud at Irving's house, the audience included Ellen and Edy. Tennyson read in a low monotone, jumping to a high pitched voice for the women's voices and Edy's laughter even infected the solemn Irving. When the listeners discussed whether two of the characters' surnames were too similar, Edy announced in a loud clear voice that she hadn't known one from the other all the time. Irving was delighted at her forthrightness, but Ellen had a sudden onset of feeling the Victorian mother, and was ashamed of her.

Irving got on very well with both Edy and Teddy, even allowing them to go backstage, a rare concession. Teddy recalled going with his mother under the stage when a ghost went up, to see how the trick was done. He in turn liked Irving, who 'proved as kind as a father.'

It was a role that Teddy wanted him to play, saying 'Every other boy I knew had his mother *and* father. Not having mine – not hearing of mine – this grave sensation of *something being wrong* grew into a fixed sort of small terror with me.'[23]

After *The Cup*, the next production at the Lyceum, in May 1881, was *Othello*. In this the parts of the Moor and Iago were played alternatively by Irving and the American actor, Edwin Booth. When it was Irving's turn to play Iago, he was so moved by Ellen's attempts, as Desdemona, to accept comfort from him, that when she raised her eyes to his at the line, 'Oh, good Iago, what shall I do to win my lord again?' she would find his eyes were full of tears.

Ellen loved playing Desdemona – though found it hard to act her weakness and passiveness – and thought the opening scene with Desdemona and her father was one of the finest in any play she knew. It was Edy, however, who pointed out how many times Shakespeare draws fathers and daughters (for example, Desdemona, Cordelia, Rosalind, Miranda, Hermione, Ophelia, Hero), and how seldom *mothers*. Ellen thought it a singular fact. It helped make her reassess Shakespeare with a more feminist eye — apparent in her later lectures on Shakespeare's women. She explored the idea further, noting that while there are plenty of examples of mothers of sons (Constance, Volumnia, Gertrude), the few mothers of daughters were poor examples, like Juliet's mother and Mrs Page.

Othello was followed on 8 March 1882 by *Romeo and Juliet*, the most elaborate of all the Lyceum productions: very sumptuous and Italian. But although the play ran for six months, it was a critical failure for both the leading actors. Irving at forty four was considered too old for the part. His wife, Florence, who always claimed her 'rightful' place in a box on first nights, wrote spitefully in her diary, 'First night of *Romeo and Juliet* at Lyceum — jolly failure — Irving awfully funny.'[24]

The *Saturday Review* said of Ellen that she was very charming, but not Juliet, 'and when really tragic passion is wanted for the part, it is not forthcoming.' Irving disagreed. After the dress rehearsal, he wrote to her saying 'Beautiful as Portia was, Juliet leaves her far, far behind. Never anybody acted more exquisitely the part.'[25]

Ellen herself regarded her Juliet as a failure. For one thing, she felt she did not look right. Edy, sharp critic as ever, told her, 'Mother, you oughtn't to have a fringe.' Ellen also wished that instead of studying how different actresses had played the part and reading the opinions of philosophers and critics, 'I had gone to Verona and just *imagined*.' In her lectures on Shakespeare's women, she said of Juliet, 'She is no school-girl, no debutante; she has no coquetry. She is something more than a girl in love . . . she is a *poet* in love.'

At supper on stage after the hundredth performance of the play, Ellen met Sarah Bernhardt for the first time, whom she admired both as an actress and for the way she had shown herself to be the equal of any man as a manager. Sarah praised Ellen's performance as Juliet, particularly her 'real tears.' The two actresses differed in their style of acting, Sarah striking Ellen as being, on stage, 'more a symbol, an ideal, an epitome, than a *woman*.' Hollow-eyed, thin and looking, Ellen thought, as transparent as an azalea, Sarah astonished her by openly making up her lips in front of Irving — unheard of behaviour.

The acclaim Ellen received for the next production, *Much*

Ellen as Beatrice in *Much Ado about Nothing* at the Lyceum in 1880, a performance that drew full houses.

Ado About Nothing, on 11 October, wiped out all memory of any poor reviews as Juliet. 'It is only in comedy that people seem to know what I am driving at!' she said.

After studying the part, she was sure that Beatrice was ruled by both the mind and the heart.

> Then I was struck by her pride – pride without an ounce of vanity. Vanity makes women feeble – Pride makes them strong. . . . Beatrice has been brought up and educated by men (there is no mention of her mother except to say that she cried when B. was born!) and her uncles take pleasure in hearing her talk, for all their reproofs to her for her incisive tongue. Notice how chivalrous Beatrice is. How generous! At the happiest moment in her life, when Benedick has just told her of his love, her cousin's wrongs burn more in her than her own passion. What a lesson she teaches to those women who seem to think that because the world has treated them well, there is no need for them to interest themselves in efforts to help those who are not so happy or so fortunate![26]

Much Ado About Nothing ran to full houses, but was withdrawn early in June 1883 so that the cast could prepare for their first tour of America. It was to take meticulous planning. Apart from organising a hundred-strong company, the scenery for each play had to be packed up – including 1,100 wigs with three wigmakers to maintain them.

But in late August, just before going to America, Irving and Ellen sandwiched in a six-week provincial tour. Ted went along with them and, while in Scotland, in a typical casual fashion, Ellen bestowed a new surname on her children – who until then had taken Kelly's real surname of Wardell.

It arose by chance. Irving, Ellen, Teddy and Bram Stoker (Irving's secretary and touring manager) went off in a boat from Greenock around the famous rock, Ailsa Craig. 'What a good stage name!' said Ellen. 'A pity you can't have it, Ted. I shall give it to Edy.'[27] And, indeed, Edy was christened Ailsa Edith and her first stage appearances were under the name of Ailsa Craig. Only when she found another actress had the same name did she drop Ailsa in favour of Edith, though retaining the surname Craig.

Teddy too adopted Craig as a surname, and when he was christened at sixteen the names he was given were Edward, after his father; Henry, after his godfather Irving; and Gordon after his godmother, Lady Gordon. He registered this name by deed poll when he reached twenty one, and decided from then on that the name he would use, both on and off stage, would be Gordon Craig. Ellen was always to call him Ted.

After the tour, Ellen arranged for Edy to become a boarder at Mrs Cole's school, which had now grown in both size and reputation and moved to larger premises. Since January of that year, Teddy had been boarding at Southfield Park, a boys-only school, in Tunbridge Wells, Kent. In his memoirs, he recalls disliking it to begin with, writing home: 'I feel so unhappy, Mother.' Ellen was to scribble across it: '1883 − 1st week at school − *poor kid*.' But shortly after he was writing about their fine larks and by March he was to pronounce the school '*Rare Jolly*.'[28]

As the American tour was to take six months, plans had to be made for the children to stay with Ellen's friends during the school holidays. Teddy was later to recall, rather vaguely, that

Edy and I may now have been at Dixton Manor House where Mrs and the Misses Malleson lived. It was a delightful time: I recall this − Dixton Manor House and Edy and I there − on the roof, eating biscuits and fruit and chocolates . . . Edy was thirteen, I was eleven. I was never happier than when with Edy.[29]

For six weeks before leaving, if anyone mentioned the word America, Ellen burst into floods of tears. 'I was leaving my children, my bullfinch, my parrot . . . to face the unknown dangers of the Atlantic and of a strange, barbarous land.'[30] Her emotion was shared by the audiences at the Lyceum, who flung bouquets and laurel leaves on the stage at the farewell performance, and became almost hysterical with cheers and tears.

The tributes, toasts and dinners continued for weeks. It was an extraordinary show of national mourning at the loss of the public's two idols to America for six months. There were drawings of a weeping Britannia; and special cards were sold, with emotional couplets and an illustration of a sailing ship.

On 11 October, tearfully waved off by a mass of friends and

well-wishers, including Mrs Lily Langtry and Oscar Wilde, Ellen and Irving set sail from Liverpool for New York in the *Britannic*.

CHAPTER 8

AMERICA: 'A VOYAGE OF ENCHANTMENT'

For Ellen, the journey to America was 'a voyage of enchantment,' even though the ship was laden with pig iron, and rolled and rolled. When the *Britannic* arrived in New York, on 21 October, it was greeted by river steamers; one of which had thirty Italian musicians on board, who played *God Save the Queen*, then *Rule Britannia*.

Also on board were reporters – and American reporters were reputed to be the toughest in the world. Irving dealt with them in what Ellen called 'his best Jingle manner ... full of refinement, bonhomie, elegance and geniality.' He gave a fine solo performance, ending, 'I have brought my company and my scenery – and Miss Ellen Terry, one of the most perfect and charming actresses that ever graced the English stage.'[1]

Asked if she had a message for her English friends, Ellen was urged by Irving to 'Say something pleasant! Merry and bright!' Instead, the very thought of England made her burst into tears. She was described the next day as a 'woman of extreme nervous sensibility,' but the *Tribune*'s reporter, at least, was impressed:

As she stepped with a pretty little shudder over the swaying plank upon the yacht she showed herself possessed of a marked individuality. Her dress consisted of a dark greenish-brown cloth wrap lined inside with a peculiar shade of red; the inner dress, girt at the waist with a red, loosely folded sash, seemed a reminiscence of some 18th century portrait, while the delicate complexion caught a rosy reflection from the loose flame coloured red scarf tied in a bow at the neck. The face itself is a peculiar one. Though not by ordinary canons beautiful, it is nevertheless one to be remembered, and seems to have been modelled on that of some pre-Raphaelite saint, an effect heightened by the aureole of soft golden hair escaping from under the plain brown straw and velvet hat.

Ellen had expected New York to be ugly and noisy. She had a vague idea 'that American women wore red flannel shirts and carried bowie knives,' and that she might be sandbagged in the street. She was depressed by 'the muddy sidewalk and the cavernous holes in the cobble-paved streets' and on arriving at the Hotel Dam – Irving was staying at the Brevoort House Hotel – she cried for two hours. But she was cheered as her room became ever more full of roses from admirers.

On 29 October, at the Star Theatre, the company opened with *The Bells*. There was torrential rain on the first night and the first act, constantly interrupted by latecomers, went badly. Irving, in his dressing room, slated the Yankees for being 'icebergs, blocks, stone ... I might as well play to a churchyard!' But at the end he received tumultuous applause. Afterwards, Irving and Gilbert Coleridge, the son of the Lord Chief Justice, escorted Ellen to her hotel. Ellen, jubilant, broke into a dance and the three of them did a *pas de trois* all the way back.

The next stop was Philadelphia, then Boston, Baltimore, Brooklyn, Chicago, Cincinnati, St Louis, Detroit and Toronto. The company travelled everywhere in a private train which had eight coaches – with the scenery and costumes packed in two sixty-foot box cars and a huge open railway car. It was an impressive sight.

Unless there were blizzards, the theatres were packed out, and in Philadelphia, after *Hamlet*, Ellen was serenaded by eighty six musicians. Wherever she went, she was a personal success, in her dashingly cut top coats, feathered hats and billowing scarves. Her own impressions of America were mixed. She considered the women dressed too grandly in the street and too dowdily in the theatre; she also thought them naive, but admired their vivacity, energy and culture.

She liked the way everyone always looked so happy, compared to the 'hopeless' expressions of the English; she hated the steam heat of the theatres, which affected her voice; thought tram cars no substitute for hansom cabs; and was impressed by the cool, dry wit of American stage comedians. America's bitter weather in no way put her off: during one particularly bad train journey in driving snow, she passed the time by reading, singing and eating grapes.

Financially, as well as professionally, the tour had been a success: the final profit, after costs, was £11,700. Irving saw that tours like this would allow him to experiment with the plays he put on at home without financial risk.

In his farewell speech in New York, he thanked his audience, and all America, for showing 'that no jealous love of your own most admirable actors had prevented you from recognising the earnest purpose of an English company.' To ecstatic shouts, he promised the company would return in the autumn 'for a parting embrace.'

Ellen and Irving returned to England in May 1884 and opened the sixth season at the Lyceum with a revival of *Much Ado About Nothing*. They were greeted rapturously, though Irving warned the audience that the season would be short as the company was returning to America in four months. *Much Ado*, he said, would be followed by *Twelfth Night*.

Irving genuinely wanted to put on a play by a contemporary writer, but there was a dearth of playwrights, worsened by the deaths of both Charles Reade and H.J. Byron while the company was abroad. It was a perennial problem: in his four years of managing the Lyceum, Irving had spent over £3,000 in advances to playwrights who had failed to come up with any good material.

The audience, however, was well pleased with the thought of *Twelfth Night*. Irving had commissioned a very decorative set and the play opened on a sultry July night to a packed house. But to Irving's dismay, boos and hisses greeted his first night speech. He sharply rebuked the audience, asking how a company that was 'sober, clean and word-perfect,' could fail to please. One critic attributed the uproar to foul first-nighters; others criticised Irving for making Malvolio too tragic a figure.

Ellen, at least, was a success, the critic Clement Scott saying her Viola was 'tender, human, graceful, consistently pictur-esque, and with humour as light as featherdown.' She herself thought the production

dull, lumpy and heavy. Henry's Malvolio was fine and

Ellen as Viola in *Twelfth Night* at the Lyceum, 1884. Owing to a poisoned finger, she sometimes played sitting down.

dignified, but not good for the play. I was handicapped as Viola by physical pain. On the first night I had a bad thumb – I thought it was a whitlow – and had to carry my arm in a sling. It grew worse every night and I felt so sick and faint from pain that I played most of my scenes sitting in a chair.[2]

Bram Stoker's brother, a doctor, happened to go behind the scenes, took one look at the thumb and lanced it. He was just in time. Ellen had blood poisoning, and without the lancing could have lost her arm. Her sister, Marion, had to take over her part: Fred, their brother, was already playing Sebastian.

Ellen was so ill that Irving had straw laid down outside her house to blanket the noise of passing horses and carriages. This provoked a sour comment, in a speech at the Social Science Congress, about 'actresses who feign illness and have straw laid down before their houses, while behind the drawn blinds they are having riotous supper-parties, dancing the can-can and drinking champagne.'

During the summer break, Ellen decided to rent a cottage in Winchelsea, Sussex, for herself and the children, next door to Alice Comyns Carr, who helped design Ellen's stage dresses. It was a busman's holiday as she became happily involved in the local amateur theatricals. Edy helped her, and Alice Comyns Carr, in her reminiscences, said that she could still remember the incongruous sight of Ellen, fresh from her Shakespearean triumphs, 'going through ancient amateur gags in the bare and comfortless stone hall at Winchelsea, with the rows of smelly oil lamps for footlights.'[3]

Ellen's off-stage behaviour was equally incongruous. Alice recalled with amusement that

One of Nell's favourite pastimes was going out in the early morning and dancing on the lawn in front of the house with bare feet, and clad only in the flimsiest of long white night-dresses.

When my husband suggested that the prim old lady next door but one might disapprove of such unconventional behaviour, Nell only laughed gaily as she replied, 'Who's to see me, Joe, at five o'clock in the morning? There are only the labourers going to work, and I don't mind amusing them. It's so good for the poor dears.'

Irving was a frequent guest and the following year, when Ellen rented the Comyns Carr's own cottage – which she was to buy in 1896 – the next-door neighbours, the Smiths, remonstrated with Joe Comyns Carr for having let his cottage to people whose manners were such that Mr Smith could not walk at ease in his own garden. Alice Comyns Carr commented:

> They were not in the least appeased when Joe pointed out that Mr Smith could scarcely be molested by the view of Miss Terry unless he climbed into his pear-tree. Henry Irving did not go to such length in *déshabillé*, but we often caught glimpses of him in rather queer get-ups as he sat taking his ease in Nell's garden.[4]

Blanche Patch, Bernard Shaw's secretary for thirty years, also remembered the Winchelsea summers well as her father was Rector there. In her autobiography, she said she often watched Ellen rehearsing with Irving in the meadow beyond the Rectory garden. As there were no cars in those days, a visit to London was a rare event, so few local people had heard of Irving's fame. He was simply known as a constant visitor of Ellen Terry's.

Blanche Patch recalled

> His presence in her house did not lessen the doubts of those ladies who held fast to Victorian taboos about whether a London actress was the sort of person who should be 'called on.' Evidently they overcame their scruples, for she was soon very popular with everyone, and I remember she attended a bazaar which we held in the Rectory garden, subscribing to raffles and visiting every stall.[5]

Ellen was consistently generous like that, one winter writing to say that every child who needed boots or shoes was to have a new pair.

'Nellen Terry,' as the Comyns Carr children christened her, was a great favourite with all the local children and the pony trap which she always drove – she hated trains – was invariably full of children and dogs. Two of these dogs were fox terriers: Charlie and Fussy. Ellen had given Fussy to Irving and they became inseparable. She once came across the two of them sitting in opposite armchairs, 'mutually adoring each other.'

Ellen with her two fox terriers, Drummie and Fussie. She was to give Fussie (right) to Irving, and they became inseparable companions.

After the summer break, the Lyceum company prepared to return to America. Financially, the tour was essential as, for the first time, the latest season at the Lyceum had shown a slight loss. The company opened in Quebec on 30 September in a theatre that was a cross between a chapel and a very small concert room – having first got rid of some members from the previous troupe still on the stage: two hens.

Christmas was spent in Pittsburg, and Ellen was given a silver tea-service by the gentlemen of the company. Irving's secretary, L.F. Austin, wrote home to his wife, saying,

> ET's face I shall never forget. The surprise, the pleasure, and the choking emotion made her such a picture as she never has looked on the stage. Then she stood up, with great tears rolling down her cheeks – while Henry tried to conceal his behind his glasses – and said a few broken words more eloquent than any speech.[6]

What made Ellen's Christmas, however, was the arrival of Teddy, her son – even if the longed-for Christmas pudding he had brought out with him reeked of camphor, having been packed in with Ellen's furs. Ellen knew she couldn't manage both children, so she had cabled some friends, who were about to leave for New York, to 'bring one of the children' – thereby, Solomon-like avoiding favouritism.

Teddy was given a sledge and whenever the company's train stopped, would romp around with Ellen who, Austin said, 'was just like a schoolgirl, every bit as young in feeling as her boy.' The high spot of the tour for her was Chicago. Not only did she play Ophelia to a highly sympathetic audience, but Teddy also made a successful stage appearance there and, as she said, 'Was it not a Chicago man who wrote of my boy, tending the roses in the stage garden in *Eugene Aram*, that he was "a most beautiful lad".'

Ellen loved having Teddy with her, but she missed Edy and wrote frequently to her. One of her letters, dated 17 March from New York, reassured Edy that all Ellen's friends in America 'are ready to love you for yourself alone' and then went on to give her some advice on drawing:

> I don't like your dog's head as well as a little sketch you once did of Fussie and Charlie, but the flower was very pretty. I

Ellen playing Olivia, a favourite part, with Irving as the Vicar of Wakefield, in *Olivia* at the Lyceum, 1885.

think it's a very *difficult* way to learn drawing – *by letter* – still Mrs Malleson is sure to do her best for you and I am very grateful to her for being so ingenious . . . meanwhile observe all *angles* in natural objects and *proportion*, note too the *unequal balance* in flower-life and shell – all will be of use to you should you one day for instance play Lady Macbeth! I'll explain 'because why' when we meet, my little noodlemus – Please study *Jessica* (M of V) next (what a comedown) and get done with the only, to my mind, *Cat* in Shakspere. It is a very effective *part* tho' *played properly* and 'looked' as you could look it. Poor Ted has a little cruel pain in his little stom-ack and I must go and make a fuss of him and rub it!! Your own Mummy.[7]

On 17 April 1885, while the company was still sailing back from America, Charles Kelly died. Ellen, generous as always, paid his debts and for years supported the sisters of his first wife. Ellen hardly had time to mourn Kelly. A few days after returning from America, on 2 May, the seventh Lyceum season opened with a revival of *Hamlet*. Since first staged seven years previously, production costs had doubled. Irving failed to see the financial writing on the wall. He cut down on advertising, but otherwise failed to reduce expenses. He followed *Hamlet* with another lavish revival: this time of *Olivia*, Ellen's earlier triumph. But the over-elaborate set, the large Lyceum stage, and the slower pace at which Irving took this essentially slight play, made it ponderous going.

Ellen loved doing the play again and had none of her usual first night nerves. It was 'about the only comfortable first night at the Lyceum' she had ever had. Irving was less happy with the part of Olivia's father, the Vicar. Ellen remembered him being far too melodramatic at rehearsals:

One day when he was stamping his foot in the manner of Matthias in *The Bells*, my little Edy, who was a terrible child *and* a wonderful critic, said: 'Don't go on like that, Henry. Why don't you talk as you do to me and Teddy? At home you *are* the Vicar.' The child's frankness did not offend Henry, because it was illuminating. . . . When the first night came he gave a simple, lovable performance.[8]

Teddy remembered *Olivia* because he was allowed backstage

and would leave the theatre each night with his mother. Her cab would be waiting, with sticks laid across the seats, so that she could immediately lie down.

Olivia ran successfully until the end of July. The same month, Godwin pulled off a theatrical coup. He had been made 'The Director General of Entertainments' of the Pastoral Players, a group Lady Archibald Campbell and her friends had recently formed to give plays in the open air. At that time, actor-managers totally controlled a performance, and commissioned plays to suit their requirements. Godwin asserted the importance of the *producer* in the presentation of the play. He was in charge of costume design and stage settings, often selected the actors, told them how to move on the stage and controlled the pace of the production.

His personal life was less successful. He had parted from his wife, Beatrice, the year before and she and Whistler, the painter, formed an open attachment. His health was getting much worse, not helped by constant overworking. Apart from his theatrical productions, he was also designing The White House in Chelsea, for Whistler, writing articles, exhibiting his elegant furniture, designing wallpaper, drawing plates for the Costume Society and completing architectural commissions. His social world overlapped that of Ellen, as they had so many mutual friends. One Christmas, for instance, Liberty's closed its doors to the public and allowed a select few to choose presents. Besides Godwin, there was Ellen, Lily Langtry, Dante Gabriel Rossetti and Whistler.

With *Olivia* over, Irving planned to produce W.G. Wills's version of *Faust*, with Ellen as Margaret. To get the set right, he invited Ellen, Edy, Ted, Alice and Joe Comyns Carr to go on an excursion to Nuremberg. Delighted by the nearby medieval town of Rothenburg, he wired his scenic artist, Hawes Craven, to leave London and join him. Alice, as Ellen's dress designer, poured over old German books and the tightly kilted full skirt Ellen was to wear as Margaret became the season's fashion.

Alice, in her reminiscences, recalled Irving and Ellen going on light-hearted shopping expeditions, which she joined in to act as interpreter as neither of them spoke German. Later, during the rehearsals for *Faust*, Alice was taken aback to find Irving's other side.

Gone was the debonair, cheery holiday companion, and in

his place was a ruthless autocrat, who brooked no
interference from anyone, and was more than a little rough
in his handling of everyone in the theatre – except Nell.[9]

Irving undoubtedly had a habit of digging, punching and
slapping people both on and off the stage. The actor H. Chance
Newton recalled that when George Alexander was acting at the
Lyceum, Ellen stopped him in the corridor to ask him how he
was, adding that he looked most unwell. 'No wonder,' he
replied. 'Not only have I come here when I ought to be in bed,
but the "Chief" has been banging me about till I'm sore all
over, and can scarcely crawl.' Ellen told him he should bang
Irving back. '*I* did so when he unconsciously banged at me once
or twice. He never tried it on *me* any more!'[10]

The *Faust* production was full of authentic stage effects.
Ellen made valiant efforts to learn how to spin before she
played Margaret, disliking the 'property' spinning wheel; while
Irving, as Mephistopheles, arrived in a cloud of steam, courtesy
of a steam engine. The swords were connected to primitive
electric mains and flashed with genuine electric sparks:
unfortunately for Irving's duelling opponent, his glove was
punctured and he got an electric shock. Altogether, four
hundred ropes had to be used to shift the scenery – each one
being given its own name to avoid confusion.

Faust opened on 19 December. Three days before, Irving sent
Ellen this letter:

No rehearsal this morning for you, my darling.

Tonight at seven dress. . .

It was quite amusing last night – the absolute fog of some
of 'em.

It will be all right – of course – but it is a stern business.

Yes a Good drive today – perhaps you will drive down.

But do not wear yourself out – & you shall not tonight
either if I can persuade [you] to take it quietly.

What a worry you are, you see.

With all my love my dearest dearest.[11]

Purists shook their heads at *Faust* and considered it more of
a pantomime. W.G. Wills had adapted the original, but then
Irving in turn adapted Wills – using scissors, paste pot and a

pile of American and English versions of the play. Still, the
public loved it, Gladstone wrote to congratulate Irving, and it
was a huge financial success.

Ellen herself said she liked playing Margaret better than any
other part, except for Shakespeare. Her rehearsal notes, as
usual, were copious and echoed her personality. At the point
where Faust kisses Margaret, for instance, she wrote: 'Startled!
a little ashamed – happy.' The word 'Happy' is scrawled in
large letters five more times down the margin. In the final act,
Margaret, in a prison cell and condemned to die the next day,
sings in a harsh voice about her family. In the margin of her
rehearsal copy, alongside Faust's remark, 'Alas! her mind is
shaken,' Ellen has written, 'Rather!'[12]

At that time, Irene Vanbrugh, before she became a well-
known actress, lived across the road from Ellen and recalled
that:

> Life was never dull when there was a chance of catching sight
> of her driving in her comfortable landau and of being greeted
> with a wave of her hand. Then there was the added thrill of
> being offered her box at the Lyceum. I often contrived to
> push myself in on this with the result that I saw Faust about
> twenty times.[13]

She remembered one of the many occasions that Ellen started
to laugh on stage. She was playing a pathetic scene, speaking of
her baby, and instead of saying, 'Sometimes a crying fit would
seize it and I would gently lift the tiny babe,' she said,
'Sometimes a frying kit would seize it' ... and became too
hysterical to continue. 'Red-letter evenings' for her were when
Ellen 'would let me drive down with her and sit in the little
stool in the prompt corner, keeping well out of sight of Irving
who rather discouraged these visits.'

Violet Vanbrugh, Irene's older sister and another aspiring
actress then, also remembers Ellen smuggling her into a
rehearsal of Faust. (One can only sympathise with Irving for
trying to curb this habit of Ellen's.) In her autobiography, Dare
to be Wise, Violet recalls how kind Ellen was to would-be
actresses – though Ellen herself said she had discouraged more
stage aspirants than she had encouraged, 'so great is my horror
of girls taking to the stage as a profession when they don't
realise what they are about.[14] Certainly would-be actors and

actresses had a hard time of it then: there were no theatre schools and the stage was dominated by the big theatre families. Nepotism was expected and accepted.

J.L. Toole, the comedian, gave Violet Vanbrugh her first part – in a burlesque of *Faust*, called *Faust-and-Loose*, which mercilessly parodied Irving and Ellen. In later years she was to say, 'I simply adored Miss Terry, as I do still.' Lynn Fontanne was another actress who stayed with Ellen and was given small jobs to help her out – like reading to Ellen in the afternoon – until she got a footing in the theatre.

Ellen attracted a bevy of such young women and she was worshipped by them to the point of idolatry: the first actress to have fans. Before she even met her, Marguerite Steen remembered her own mother being hurt, because Marguerite gave Ellen Terry the adoration she withheld from her mother, and admitted that the hours she spent away from her mother's flat were spent patrolling Ellen Terry's doorstep.[15]

Lady Duff Gordon, who met Ellen for the first time during a colonial reception on the Lyceum's stage during *Faust*, says she too immediately fell for Ellen's extraordinary charm and was delighted to be invited to call at Ellen's house in Longridge Road:

> I found her sitting in the midst of a group of girls who were sewing. She was wearing a flowing robe of blue velvet and her fair hair was bound round her head like a coronet. . . . Although I went to the house many times I rarely saw Ellen Terry without her little circle of girls. I think that any one of them would gladly have laid down their lives for her sake. I never knew any woman who possessed in such a degree the art of inspiring affection in her own sex. She was not a young woman then, but she was the friend and confidante of dozens of girls, who adored her and loved to serve her in all sorts of little ways. They would do her shopping for her, arrange the flowers, dress her to go to the theatre, mend her clothes, and write her letters for her.[16]

Ted, Ellen's son, was bemused by all these women. His theory was that Ellen confused reality with theatrical dreams and thought of them all as Shakespearean heroines.

Lady Duff Gordon, by now a constant visitor at Longridge Road, was warned by Ellen of the social consequences of visiting an actress who had broken society's rules. But she was excited by the theatre people she met both at Longridge Road and in the house Ellen shortly rented in Barkston Gardens:

> Henry Irving used to drift in and out at all hours, looking very eccentric sometimes. She understood him perfectly and always knew how to manage him. Once or twice I saw him in a towering rage, working himself up to fever heat over something that had happened at the theatre, but she could calm him in a moment.[17]

In her eyes, Ellen created happiness just by sitting there. Sometimes, according to Lady Duff Gordon, Ellen would read over one of her new plays to them, sometimes they just gossiped and sewed pieces of stuff, which Ellen fished out of her large and very untidy workbag.

Ellen's hopeless untidyness gave them all enough to do, as she could never find anything without a long hunt. Every few weeks, her entourage turned out and tidied the drawers and cupboards, but in a day or two they would be as bad as ever.

As Lady Duff Gordon recalled

> She was absolutely indifferent to dress, and thought very little of her personal appearance. Her hair was often tumbling down and she would push it impatiently back from her face when she was interested in something. I could never persuade her to let me make her a dress, although I used to drape pieces of material on her. It would have been impossible to picture her in fashionable clothes, they would not have suited her personality.[18]

This casualness was in interesting contrast to her theatre clothes, over which Ellen was immensely particular.

As Margaret in *Faust* she wore a yellow dress, with her golden hair in braids to her waist. There were postcards of her on sale throughout England. She was thirty eight at the time and managed to convince the audience that she was a pure, innocent girl in her teens. Her rehearsal notes show how she established this: when Faust first accosts Margaret and offers to escort her home, she wrote in the margin,

> Taken Aback – a little frightened – look straight in his eyes – be simple – not as if she were *used* to being spoken to –

surprised, thinks he's making fun of her.[19]

Faust seemed set to run for ever. On Valentine's Day 1886, Irving sent Ellen and Edy bouquets of flowers, writing a verse which pleased Ellen by alluding to Edy's part:

> White and red roses,
> Sweet and fresh posies,
> One bunch for Edy, *Angel* of mine –
> One bunch for Nell, my dear Valentine[20]

While *Faust* played to full houses, Godwin produced Euripedes' *Helena in Troas*, with a cast that included Beerbohm Tree and Oscar Wilde's wife, Constance. Oscar wrote in *Dramatic Review* that Godwin had 'given us the most perfect exhibition of a Greek dramatic performance that has as yet been seen in this country.'

In May that year, Teddy was sent to a public school, Bradfield College. He stayed there only a year and achieved little. He explained this by saying,

> It was all right in a way – but one wasn't exactly trained
> there – except for the cricket and football and the occasional
> military drill, it was dull and meaningless. Latin,
> mathematics, history – this for a dull boy as I was, was
> money thrown away.[21]

The following year, he was sent to Heidelberg College to learn German, and was duly expelled from there.

The Lyceum company took its usual break at the end of July, and a newspaper report, dated 1 August, announced:

> Mr Henry Irving and Miss Ellen Terry left Waterloo in a
> saloon carriage at 10.15 am yesterday for Southampton. . . .
> Mr Irving informed a representative of the Press that he
> proposes on reaching America to go yachting with a friend
> on the East Coast and he expected to be back in England in
> five weeks' time.

Ellen usually took Edy and Teddy with her when she went on any form of holiday with Irving, making it a family affair rather than a private liaison. This time, there was no mention of the children.

CHAPTER 9

LADY MACBETH: 'A WOMANLY WOMAN'

Faust restarted at the Lyceum on 11 September 1886; but despite the summer break, Ellen was still tired, unwell and unusually depressed. Her letters to her friend, Bertha Bramley, revolve around her health: 'My vocal cords are *that* red!' said one. 'I'm obliged to act in spite of the torture. . . . My Edy goes back to school Saturday and I can't bear to think of it.'[1] Another letter was headed: 'Private (or they'll say I'm lunatic)' and went on

> in truth I've been brave in the long-while-ago, through heavy sorrow and trial, and now that there's nothing to bear with, now that the Sun does shine for me, I am in the tight merciless grip of *Melancholy* for the first time in a very long life.[2]

Unknown to her, Godwin had become ill again. None of his friends took it too seriously, as he often suffered from ill health and usually recovered after a few days. But he got worse rather than better and a letter he wrote to his friend and theatrical colleague, Louise Jopling, at the end of August ended: 'The next move I make is to St Peter's Hospital, where I have bespoken a ward all to myself; then the next ward may be 6 x 4 x 2. I feel completely done with life.'[3] He was fifty two.

Beatrice Godwin was summoned home from Paris and Whistler visited him daily. He was operated on but never recovered from the anaesthetic and on 6 October, just before midnight, he died. Whistler, Beatrice and Lady Archibald Campbell were with him. At dawn, Whistler went around to Louise Jopling, who was also a friend of Ellen's and asked her to break the news to Ellen before she read the morning papers.

Ellen received the news with the great cry: 'There was no one like him!'

The conventions of Victorian society prevented Ellen from paying a public tribute to Godwin's memory. All she could do was keep various mementoes; two newspaper obituaries pasted on pink paper on a card which said 'Mrs E.W. Godwin'; another obituary, which she lent to a friend, marked '*Very* precious. Please read & return, ET.' Found among her papers after her own death was a sonnet addressed to him – possibly written by Oscar Wilde – which ended

> They tell me he had faults, I know of one/Dying too soon, he left his best undone.

Godwin was an eminent architect; a pioneer in the reform of domestic furniture and decoration; and had an influence on stage scenery and costumes. But like his son and daughter after him, he got less recognition in England than he deserved. His obituary in *The Architect* was ungenerous:

> Like all men, he was not without his weaknesses. Edward Godwin assumed an air of superiority at times, but he found many who willingly recognised his right to it. We have often thought that his removal to London did not help him as an artist. He found there too many distractions. If he had remained in Bristol he must have been more successful as an architect.

There was general praise for his influence, but it was muted. Beatrice Godwin was shortly to marry Whistler and Godwin was all too soon remembered mainly for having been the first husband of Whistler's wife. Not even a gravestone marked his grave, as he objected to them.

Ellen was now unwell herself, owing to the shock of Godwin's death and the strain of playing Margaret too long, and was forced to leave the Lyceum for a time to rest. On 23 December, she was to write to Bertha:

> Dear – I'm here – at home 'doing' nothing (trying to rest). I'm not acting the last month because I've been ill for three months! But I'm better now and commence work again on the 3rd.
>
> I *couldn't* write in answer to your last letter – Edward

Godwin died *just* then and I have been *finished* by that – I shall seem well soon I think but I didn't know how terribly it would alter me. I went on at my work for a time but broke down at last and sent for Edith [now 16 years old] to be with me – selfish and wrong but I *couldn't* help it – I think I shd have lost my wits from misery. I'm all right now – *Edith did that*. She and Ted are with me now. . . . Yes! Ted my boy has altered lately – looks rather shy now sometimes and is much quieter – Edith the same *rum* queer old Frump!⁴

Ellen had a curious, dual attitude towards Edy. Teddy jealously recalled that when Edy was a young child, her mother thought her 'wonderful' and that 'she had but to frown and say "Won't" for the greatest actress of the age to cry "marvellous!" and "hush!" to everyone, and repeat, "isn't she really marvellous!" ' As she grew up, Ellen turned to her for emotional support, which Edy unstintingly gave. But in her comments about Edy to other people, Ellen could be quite heartless. She complained about Ted, too, as he grew older, about his career, his inconstancies, or continual cadging, but she openly adored him as her letters to him, invariably addressed to 'My dearest Ted,' showed:

'I sent Edy a pound for a Xmas box – I sent *you two* with my same old love which never alters to more (cos' it couldn't) nor to less (I don't think it *could*).' She was constantly concerned, too, about his health. 'Don't rub your skin off with Elliman's embrocation,' she wrote, 'keep *your feet dry* – and don't lie in the grass – nearly always cause of rheumatism is damp feet – *don't take sugar* – nor pastry – keep flannel next yr skin *bottom of back, dry feet*, or it will affect you in various painful ways.'⁵

Ted claimed to have a special relationship with his mother, and in his book about Ellen, he said that unlike him, Edy never really knew their mother, 'for she always persisted in looking down on what she held to be little Nelly's "weaknesses".'⁶

Bernard Shaw had a theory about the different attitudes towards Ellen, held by her son and daughter. Interviewed by the *Observer* after he had published his correspondence with Ellen, and was bitterly attacked in a book by Gordon Craig (Teddy) for besmirching the image of his mother, he said

Edy was unsympathetic to her mother in her early years

because she was developing her powers of resistance to this domestic tornado. Edy finally got the upper hand, and so lost her fear of her mother, and with it her hatred of her – the word is a hard one; but children do really hate their parents in their struggles for independence.

Craig flew away from the nest the moment his wings were fully fledged; and he saw very little of his mother afterwards. And he was perfectly right. He had to save his soul alive. Make no mistake about it: Ellen Terry, with all her charm and essential amiability, was an impetuous, overwhelming, absorbing personality.

What makes this book of his so tragically moving . . . is his desperate denial of the big woman he ran away from and his assertion of the 'little mother' he loved. He still resents the great Ellen Terry, the woman who would have swallowed him up if he had stayed within her magnetic field.

Edy, who did stay within her magnetic field, found herself at times less swallowed up by Ellen, than just treated as just one of her coterie. In a magazine column called *Sylvia's Journal*, for instance, the writer, who had gone to one of Ellen's tea parties made up of the usual collection of young girls, recorded that

Her own daughter is of the party, but it would be hard to single her out, so little does her mother do so by anything more than a rather happier laugh than usual at the quaint fun and a rather more sensitive appreciation of her smallest fancy. But the girls might all be her daughters, so sympathetic is she to all.

However, only the best would do for Ellen's children. When Edy – at the age of seventeen – was confirmed shortly after Ellen returned to *Faust*, it was no minor ceremony, but held in Exeter Cathedral. Ellen's diary entry reads:

Edith confirmed today (January 11, 1887) by the Bishop of Exeter (Dr Bickersteth). A private single ceremony by the Bishop for Edith. Strange! Over thirty years ago Father and Mother (with Kate and me) *walked* (necessity!) from Bristol to Exeter, and now today my child is given half-an-hour's private talk with the Bishop before her confirmation.[7]

Ellen was now forty and at the height of her popularity.

Wherever she went in Britain, she was immediately recognised and was often mobbed. Alice Comyns Carr recalls her rushing in to the theatre just a few minutes before the curtain was due to go up,

> humming a tune in the way she had when she thought she might be to blame. 'That you, Henry?', she remarked demurely as Irving, watch in hand, came in . . . 'I've been down to the Minories [an unsalubrious area, near Aldgate, in the East End] to see a fellow who sent me a begging letter this morning. I just wanted to make sure that it was genuine.' 'The Minories!' grunted Henry. 'A nice place for you at night. I suppose you didn't think of what would happen to the play if you had been attacked by some roughs down there?' But Nell only laughed. 'Why every man Jack in the crowd knew me or had heard tell. I let down the window of the four wheeler and shook hands with them all. It's because there were so many that I'm so late.'[8]

Faust was to run until the spring. In June, Ellen appeared in a single performance of *The Amber Heart* – a 'poetical fancy' by Alfred Calmour, which her acting redeemed from total banality. Irving – who was not appearing in it – was able to watch Ellen from the front of the house and wrote to her: 'I wish I could tell you of the dream of beauty that you realised.' He made her a present of the sole rights in the play. Despite this, a growing number of entries in Ellen's diary that year read, 'Quarrelled with Henry.'

With *The Amber Heart*, Alice Comyns Carr moved from assistant to chief designer of Ellen's dresses. Until then, the position had been filled by Patience Harris, the sister of Augustus Harris, manager of the Drury Lane Theatre, who preferred to make elaborate dresses. Ellen decided she wanted more of her dresses in the style of a crinkly dress of Alice's – achieved by using a potato steamer. Patience disapproved and Alice was appointed. After a provincial tour with *Faust* from August to October, the company took the production on a further three month tour of America. Despite hitting the worst blizzards ever recorded, the tour was a success.

Edy, who had left school that year and gone to Germany to study music and art, had wanted to go with Ellen and Ellen wrote to her saying:

And so America – the going to America is what you most desire? Well then, work away now. You must give up some of your present pleasures, and work at your German, and *speak* it. I shall not be able to gratify this wish of your heart, which is for your own pleasure, if you don't gratify the wish of my heart (which is for your own benefit) and make good use of the present time, and work.[9]

Edy made good progress as a pianist, but had to give up hopes of turning professional because of rheumatism, which had plagued her ever since childhood. While she was in Germany, Ellen sent off a barrage of letters, which were a mixture of do's and don't, fondness and critical advice:

Remember, my dear darling, not to (just from thoughtlessness) give too much trouble and anxiety to Mabel, for she is so very conscientious that you will have to guard against being selfish in regard to her, and if you only know this, and think of it, I'm in the best hopes you will remember not to forget! . . . By the way I've asked the doctors, and you must on no account drink beer, even of the *smallest* kind! Claret, or any wine of the country, but not beer. (A glass once a moon would not hurt, just to *feel* German!).

Oh you bad girl about writing that letter to the German actor! Be careful, my pet. It's all well enough with N. I know him pretty well (know too that he's a young monkey) but be careful, for I would be vexed if some fool or other thought you vulgar.

Remember you must be more reserved with a pack of folk you don't know *well* (and one changes one's first opinion of some people) than with old friends and people who know *you*. You know I used (long ago) to have to tell you to keep a little steadier in shops and places where strangers were about.[10]

It says much for Edy's sweetness of character that on re-reading these in later years she merely said: 'If I could have done all Mother advised me to do, been all she wanted me to be, I should now be a very splendid and wise woman.'

The next big production at the Lyceum was to be *Macbeth*. The announcement of this caused a minor public uproar as no one could see Ellen as the inhuman, unsympathetic Lady Macbeth, agreeing with the critic, Charles Hiatt, who asked: 'How could the graceful, gracious, tender-eyed, sweet-voiced, gentle Ellen Terry grasp such a part as this?'[11]

On stage, Ellen was everyone's ideal woman. Anyone who had marched across the stage with a placard announcing that Ellen had been an unmarried mother, had two failed marriages behind her and a questionable relationship with Irving, would have been howled down.

The parts Ellen played were very much identified with her. Indeed, her son claimed that she could play 'but one part – herself.' Was the audience watching Beatrice in *Much Ado* (lively, bubbling with laughter), Juliet in *Romeo and Juliet* (youthful charm), Portia in *The Merchant of Venice* (intensity of feeling) or were they just watching different facets of Ellen Terry? Bernard Shaw said that she never needed to perform any remarkable feat of impersonation as the spectators would have resented it: 'They did not want Ellen Terry to be Olivia Primrose; they wanted Olivia Primrose to be Ellen Terry.' However, the naturalness of Ellen's acting was achieved through back-breakingly hard work.

Ellen certainly had an extraordinary rapport with her audience. Irene Vanbrugh described it this way:

> [Her] charm enveloped every being in the audience. It is a bloom, but the bloom has to have a rare foundation to hold it; a foundation of generosity, of giving out to your audience, a quality of crystal clarity which lets your audience see into your soul and understand your feelings.[12]

Irving had considered plays other than *Macbeth*. One contender was *Anthony and Cleopatra*, though Ellen said 'I could not see myself as the serpent of old Nile.' Another was *The Tempest*, as Irving wanted to play Caliban. Ellen unselfishly told him to go ahead and not to bother about it having no part which attracted her, but Irving finally decided against it.

She was less sanguine about his decision not to stage *As You Like It*. She was now forty one and time was running out: not even her devoted public would relish a Rosalind in her late forties or fifties. But Irving put his objections to the play so convincingly that she said, 'although I was dying to play Rosalind, I believed he was right to give it up.'

Her admirers were angry, but Edy, in her notes to her mother's memoirs, points out that it was not in Irving's interest as a manager to keep Ellen in the background in his theatre. 'There is no proof that he sterilized her greatest possibilities. It is pure speculation that she would have developed into a finer actress, with less restricted opportunities than her partnership with Irving afforded.'

Once *Macbeth* was decided upon, the usual meticulous planning started. Ellen and Irving went to Scotland in the summer of 1887 to get ideas for the scenes – with Ellen noting in her diary, 'Visited the "Blasted Heath." Behold a flourishing potato-field!' Nevertheless, Irving got his inspiration and the overall sombre effect of the Highlands was such that when, in one scene, Birnam Wood was seen in brilliant sunlight, one member of the gallery called out, 'Good old England! Hurrah for Good Old England!'

Ellen had a clear idea of how to play Lady Macbeth. In her lectures on Shakespearean heroines, she was to list Lady Macbeth unexpectedly under 'Pathetic Women' rather than 'Triumphant Women,' writing in the margin of her notes, 'There is more of pity than of terror in her end.' She felt that

> Lady Macbeth is no monster . . . she is a woman in everything. . . . Her strength is all nervous force; her ambition is all for her husband. She has been the 'dearest partner' of all Macbeth's thoughts and actions; she must needs be the partner of his crime.[13]

Her margin notes add: 'I suppose I can say, "That's *just* like a woman." '

In a letter to the veteran actress, Mrs Keeley, she said:

> I have never had the passion of ambition, but watching my own mother, and some few friends of mine, all good women, I have wondered at the lengths to which ambition – generally for some son or husband – drove them, and long ago I concluded that the Thane of Cawdor's wife was a much be-blackened person. She was pretty bad, I think, but by no means abnormally bad.[14]

She made the same point in a conversation recalled by the critic, Clement Scott:

> I don't even *want* to be a 'fiend,' and I *can't* believe for a moment that Lady Macbeth did *conceive* that murder – that *one* murder. Most women break the law during their lives; few women realise the consequences of what they do to-day.[15]

During the summer of 1888, she and Irving took a break from planning Macbeth and went to Lucerne. From there, on 9 August, Ellen wrote to a friend, Marie Casella, to say it was lovely,

> but for my part I like a much *quieter* place – but Henry asked, 'Is it a lively place' and being told it *was* he settled upon it for our headquarters from which to make excursions. Ted arrived last night and is looking splendid and seems rather nice I think and improved – he and Edy are *glued* together.[16]

She ended by saying she and Henry were getting so fat they would soon only be fit for Barnum's show or Thorley's food for cattle, and drew a caricature of the two of them. A few days later she wrote again, this time from Venice, to say that she and Irving were there alone, apart from the courier, 'for H. thought it a little too much of a joke for us all to come so Miss Held is taking care of the children until we go back to Lucerne on Thursday.' Usually, Ellen and Irving kept Edy and Ted with them when they holidayed, so that to outsiders it looked like a happy family outing.

On their return to London rehearsals began, and Ellen started to worry about her interpretation of Lady Macbeth. She was calmed by a reassuring letter from Irving:

> I want to get these great multitudinous scenes over and then we can attack *our* scenes . . . your sensitiveness is so acute that you must suffer sometimes. You are not like anybody else – you see things with such lightning quickness and unerring instinct, that dull fools like myself grow irritable and impatient sometimes. I feel confused when I am thinking of one thing, and disturbed by another. That's all. But I do

feel very sorry afterwards when I don't seem to heed what I so much value.[17]

Against this, Ellen was to scribble, pathetically, the words, 'How seldom!'

It may be that Irving found it easier to express his feelings in writing. Certainly he wrote constantly and lovingly to her, his letters a mixture of tenderness, encouragement and advice. 'You will be splendid in this part,' he wrote again during *Macbeth* rehearsals.

> The first time it has been *acted* for many years. The sleeping scene will be beautiful too – the moment you are in it – *but* Lady M. should certainly have the appearance of having got out of bed, to which she is returning when she goes off. The hair to my mind should be wild and disturbed, and the whole appearance as distraught as possible, and disordered.[18]

Alice Comyns Carr made some spectacular costumes for Ellen, the most exotic being the one in which John Singer Sargent painted her. It was made from green cotton and blue tinsel, sewn all over with real green beetle wings. She also made Ellen a vivid, blood-red cloak, to wear after the murder of the king. Irving, seeing it, congratulated her on such a wonderful splash of colour and, never one to be upstaged, promptly appropriated it for himself. Alice hurriedly designed Ellen a heather-coloured velvet cloak, embroidered with Scottish lions and fake jewels.

The play opened on 17 November 1888 and queuing started before seven in the morning. The eminent audience included Sir Arthur Sullivan, who was responsible for the musical setting; Oscar Wilde and his wife, Constance; Arthur Pinero and his wife, Myra; and most of the Terry family, including Ellen's sister, Kate, who sat in state in the centre box accompanied by her four daughters all dressed in white.

The first night audience was wildly enthusiastic. The critics neither damned nor enthusiastically praised it. The staging was thought magnificent, but they regretted Irving's interpretation of Macbeth as an anxious, haggard, man, lacking in physical valour, though he was to get a letter from Joseph Chamberlain thanking him for such an intellectual treat.

There was controversy, too, over Ellen's interpretation of

Lady Macbeth as a womanly woman, whose behaviour stemmed from wifely devotion. The critic of *Truth* felt Ellen had produced 'an aesthetic Burne Jonesy, Grosvenor Gallery version of Lady Macbeth, who roars as gently as any sucking dove.' The *Daily Chronicle* praised Ellen's 'delicious tenderness and abnegation of self,' called her sleepwalking scene, 'refined,' while Burne Jones said Ellen filled his whole soul with her beauty and her poetry.

Writing to Edy, who was in Germany at the time, Ellen said:

> Yes, it is a success, and I am a success, which amazes me, for never did I think I should be let down so easily. Some people hate me in it; some, Henry among them, think it my best part, and the critics differ, and discuss it hotly, which in itself is my best success of all! Those who don't like me in it are those who don't want, and don't like to read it fresh from Shakespeare, and who hold by the 'fiend' reading of the character.
>
> Oh, dear! It is an exciting time! I wish you could see my dresses. They are superb, especially the first one: green beetles on it, and such a cloak! . . . The whole thing is Rossetti – rich stained-glass effects. I play some of it well, but, of course, I don't do what I want to do yet. Meanwhile I shall not budge an inch in the reading of it, for that I know is right. Oh, it's fun, but it's precious hard work for I by no means make her a 'gentle, lovable woman' as some of 'em say. That's all pickles. She was nothing of the sort, although she was *not* a fiend, and *did* love her husband. I have to what is vulgarly called 'sweat at it,' each night.[19]

Macbeth ran until the end of June 1889. At its close, Ellen left for Germany to join Edy, while Teddy went down to Ramsgate with Irving – writing to his mother with all the news and ending, 'My best love to the dear old *frump* [Edy] & to you.'

Both Irving and Ellen were often better at handling each other's children than their own, Ellen developing a particularly close rapport with Irving's younger son, Laurence, calling him 'My Irving boy.'

At the time of *Macbeth*, Laurence was eighteen and his elder brother Harry was nineteen. Estranged from Irving as young boys, having been brought up to hate him by their mother, they now sought him out for help with their careers. Harry wanted to act, but Irving wanted his sons to have a life of less hardship. For a time he got his way: he persuaded Harry to go to Oxford and Laurence to study modern languages in preparation for the diplomatic service.

Ellen, however, wanted her children to go on the stage and warmly appreciated Irving asking Teddy if he would like to join the Lyceum company that year. But when, in September, he cast seventeen-year-old Teddy as the young Count St Valery in *The Dead Heart*, she was not over-pleased. Whereas Irving, with his passion for melodrama, wanted to play in it, Ellen said: 'Here was I in the very noonday of life, fresh from Lady Macbeth and still young enough to play Rosalind, suddenly called upon to play a rather uninteresting *mother* in *The Dead Heart*.' For the sake of her beloved Teddy, she accepted, merely commenting, 'The crafty old Henry! All this was to put me in conceit with my part!'[20]

During the run, in the January of 1890, Ted reached eighteen, and in between rehearsals and performances, he regularly went to the irreverent but immensely lively music halls. He was particularly fascinated by Albert Chevalier as the Cockney Coster, thinking this 'British mask' ranked equal with the French pierrot. Ellen never appeared at the halls herself, but she was friendly with Marie Lloyd and would drop in and see her show.

As well as music halls, Ted visited all the galleries, taking notes of costume design in which he was becoming increasingly interested. Both he and Edy had inherited their father's talent in this area, Edy showing an early gift for improvisation. Ellen recalled her writing from school to ask for some money, in order to go to a fancy dress ball. At the time, Ellen was short of money and just sent a postal order for two shillings and sixpence, saying that if she could make a fancy dress for that, she might go to the dance. Edy squandered most of it on chocolate, then spent sixpence only on some burnt cork for her face, brass curtain rings for her ears, and made her dress – the success of the evening – from Turkish towels in her bathroom.

Improvisation was one of Edy's main skills when she started a business making theatre costumes. But that was in the future. In March that year, after returning from studying music in Berlin under Hollander, she joined the Lyceum company. A tall, thin, dark girl of twenty one, she was to play minor roles

Ellen and her son Ted (Gordon Craig), playing mother and son on stage in *The Dead Heart*, 1889.

for some ten years, though not progressing further than that, and inevitably remaining under Ellen's shadow. Bernard Shaw said of her that she was too clever for her profession.

Ellen had by now moved to Barkston Gardens, Earls Court, and Edy's return made Ted even more conscious of being the solitary man in a houseful of women.

'They were kind enough to me,' he recalled in his own memoirs, 'and not uncommonly noisy – but women all the same.' He felt oddly cocooned by the female household, consisting of Ellen and Mrs Rumball, her lifelong companion; Miss Harries; the housekeeper; Edy and three servants. Occasionally a man came in, to bring the heavy flower boxes. Otherwise it was,

> Ring at the front-door bell – another woman; ding-a-ling-a-ling – a girl this time: they trickled in all the time and out again . . . there were actors who might call at odd times and go away again. But ours was not planned as a sociable house, or a society house – it was a working house. It was E.T.'s house, and run for her, and for her alone, and this demanded quiet.[21]

Ted gives a clear picture of the household and Ellen's daily routine. She spent most of her time upstairs on the second floor, where there were two rooms: at the front, a large bedroom with one window. After the evening performance was over, she would drive back to Barkston Gardens, getting there just before midnight. She would then have a quick supper with Edy and Ted, read her letters, and go up to her bedroom. There she would reply to her correspondence – sitting up in bed, a board on her knees – read a little and try to calm down after the exertion of her performance.

She slept late in the morning, then from midday to about two p.m., she would drive out to see a friend, or get some air, or go shopping. She usually returned for lunch at two or two thirty to find, her son recalled, 'all the women talking a good deal, something to her annoyance I think; though it represented to some extent the life of the place.'[22]

He also remembered the continual cleaning that went on in that house: the brushing, scrubbing, polishing, tidying and carpet beatings out in the garden. Such 'gardens' were really standard London back yards, enclosed by soot-blackened brick walls. Nevertheless, property like this was expensive enough to rent – Ellen had to pay £250 a year for her Barkston Gardens house, plus taxes and rates. She also had all the household expenses, food bills, and salaries for her housekeeper and three servants, as well as occasional extra expenses: tutoring in Germany for both Edy and Ted, holidays abroad. Ted's salary at the Lyceum was £5 a week then, and when he went touring for the summer, he was paid £4 – half of which he remembered sending to his mother. Edy had earned little money as yet, a habit she continued.

In April, during the run of *The Dead Heart*, Queen Victoria asked Irving and Ellen and the company to act scenes from *The Bells* and *Macbeth* at Windsor. They had a successful evening, an audience with the Queen, and supper with other royal guests like the Prince of Wales. Irving was pleased: for the acting profession it was another step on the road to respectability.

The end of the Lyceum's summer season simply meant having to act elsewhere. Ellen and Irving went off to tour, giving readings from *Macbeth*, Ted went off on a different tour, then briefly joined Ellen for a holiday in Winchelsea. They made a day trip to London to see an exhibition of paintings by Burne-Jones. Ellen slipped easily into the world of painters. Edy once said of her,

> Put her in a room full of artists of the most advanced and unconventional type and she seemed completely one of them. On some other occasion, you might observe her in a room filled with aristocrats holding an utterly unconventional set of ideas and you would never know she had not always shared them completely.[23]

Irving was in Lowestoft, working on *Ravenswood*, the next production at the Lyceum, and wrote to Ellen from there saying, 'I want to get to Winchelsea, my Nell, and be by you. It *is* dull here, upon my word – but I'll walk it off and stick to my work or perish in the attempt.'

He got down in the end, and he, Ellen, Edy and the dogs explored the countryside in the pony trap. In her diary, Ellen wrote: 'Henry got the old pony along at a spanking rate – but I had to seize the reins now and again to save us from sudden death.' In Tenterden once, they found a marionette show and paid the proprietor to put on a special performance for them.

'Henry and I,' recalled Ellen, 'and Edy and Fussy [Henry's dog] sat in solemn state in the empty tent and watched the show which was most ingenious and clever.'[24] It was a pleasant, Darby and Joan existence.

Ravenswood, a boring adaptation of Scott's *Bride of Lammermoor*, opened at the Lyceum on 20 September 1890 and did little for Ellen apart from the riding dress she wore in the play setting the fashion for ladies' coats. But it offers an example of Ellen's casual attitude as against Irving's meticulousness. At one point, Ellen had to break into hysterical laughter and, coming offstage afterwards, she was greeted by an exceedingly cross Irving. 'Why did you alter the laugh?' he said. 'It put me out altogether, I was waiting for you to finish.' Ellen replied that she had laughed as usual. 'No you didn't. You always say ha-ha seventeen times – you only said it fourteen times tonight.' Ellen said later: '*I* knew nothing about those seventeen ha-ha's, it was pure luck my getting the same number every night. But now I am sure to get it wrong – I shall see Henry standing there counting!'[25]

In the same play, Ellen and her friend Graham Robertson, decided to watch a particularly effective scenic transformation from behind a stage rock. Not realising their rock, too, was going to move, they had to crawl along behind it frantically as it slipped away. Ellen devoutly thanked God that Irving had gone straight up to his room and not noticed them.

She was equally cheerful in her private life. On 11 December, she wrote to her friend, Bertha Bramley, to say that Ted had had jaundice and that there had been

> a still more fearful happening on the 9th. It was Edy's 21st birthday – and that's an expensive period – Altogether I'm a tired and very poor woman – and Edy and Ted and I are all as happy as happy can be – spite of the fog and the jaundice.[26]

The three of them spent New Year's Eve having dinner at Irving's London flat in Grafton Street, and playing games. The year to come, 1891, was not so happy. *Ravenswood* had not been a success, and Irving hastily put on a series of revivals. One of these was *Nance Oldfield*, an eighteenth century pastiche, in which Ellen was pleased to be playing opposite Ted – though neither of them knew their lines on the first night, and pinned their parts all over the furniture. It was well received, and Burne-Jones wrote to Ellen to say, 'As for your boy, he looked a lovely little gentleman . . . and you were you – YOU – and so all was well.'

The pace of the productions was exhausting and Ellen, tired out, could not fight off influenza. On 3 June, Irving wrote to her saying,

> My Nell. . . . The worst will be over now I hope – but you have had a terrible time. No one thought – nor did I dream how bad you were. Do pray be careful. . . . You gave me a lovely letter to take away with me on Monday.[27]

Ellen began to improve and Irving wrote more cheerfully on 12 June:

> You are coming back tomorrow I hope – I want to see you – & to know & feel that you are getting stronger. Let me know if you are coming & I'll be with you the moment I can.[28]

He then mapped out the Lyceum schedule until the end of July – a punishing mixture as before. It was surprising Ellen returned.

For the rest of the year, the company went on tour and from Edinburgh, in November, Ellen wrote to a friend of hers, Aimee Lowther, to say she had managed to get Irving to raise Ted's salary as 'I *must* see that he "gets on," must not I?' She was not quite so excited about Edy.

> Edy walks on in some of our plays and now and then has a line or so given her to speak, but although I *never* should be surprised if she did something great some day, either as a writer, or an actress or a musician, the fact remains at present a hard fact that she does *nothing whatever* well! Ted says, 'Ah, but remember, Mother, George Eliot wrote her first book when she was 40!!' Ted and I too, believe most firmly in the damsel, only we wish she'd hurry up![29]

On 5 January 1892, Irving staged a spectacular *Henry VIII* at the Lyceum, with himself as Wolsey, Ellen as Katherine and Ted as Cromwell. Ellen at forty four was hardly thrilled at being white-haired Queen Katherine, and though admitting the

Ellen and Edy (Edith Craig) as Queen Katherine and one of her
ladies-in-waiting, in *Henry VIII*, 1892.

production was magnificent, 'was not very interested in it, or in my part.'

Ellen's disenchantment with such parts was fuelled by her first letters this year from George Bernard Shaw, which told her bluntly that she was wasting her talent. He had earlier watched her in *Nance Oldfield* and considered she was simply playing a charade, hardly taxing the strength of the top joint of her little finger. She knew that she was not being stretched by such parts and was sufficiently intrigued by Shaw's siren voice to enter into a correspondence that lasted some thirty years.

Shaw was to say that he had trained his batteries on Ellen and the Irving management and would not rest until its end. He had not very long to wait. With *Henry VIII*, Ellen entered her last decade at the Lyceum.

CHAPTER 10

BERNARD SHAW AND ELLEN: 'A PAPER COURTSHIP'

Shaw's broadsides were aimed at a ship that was already foundering. Ellen called the last ten years of the Lyceum 'the twilight of the Gods,' saying, 'During that time the vogue of the Lyceum declined, very gradually and not always perceptibly to us, for we had ups as well as downs, and the ups created an illusion that nothing was changed.'[1]

There were various reasons for the decline. The electricity of the early partnership between Ellen and Irving had gone; and they were plagued by ill-health. They were both getting older and there were simply fewer roles open to them now in Shakespeare and the revivals they normally appeared in. There was competition now, too. When Her Majesty's Theatre opened in 1897, under Sir Herbert Beerbohm Tree, it lured in the fashionable public with glittering productions of Shakespeare's plays.

The Lyceum's finances were also in a serious state, because of running expenses and the high costs of the magnificent sets. Irving could see no way of economising. He was not a man to move with the times – even ripping out the electric light that had been fitted at the Lyceum by a summer tenant, as he felt only gas could give the subtleties of lighting he needed. Under his management, the Lyceum had always followed the grand theatrical tradition. In his view, modern dramatists' plays were all on too small a scale for the large Lyceum stage. And he loathed their concern with social problems.

The correspondence between Shaw and Ellen began in 1892, when Shaw was music critic of the newspaper, *World*. Ellen asked the editor for his opinion of a composer-singer friend of hers and he sent Shaw to cover the concert. Ellen was giving a recital there and he was much more impressed with her than with her friend. He wrote and told her so and they continued to correspond for some twenty six years.

It was a paper courtship only. Shaw was to say that he did not want to complicate their 'wholly satisfactory love affair' by meeting. And, indeed, it was years before they did meet and then it was for business reasons only.

Meeting each other could have raised the question of a more permanent relationship: both were legally free to marry, even though Ellen, who was forty five at the start of the correspondence, was nine years older than Shaw. Shaw had a great fear of commitment, preferring dalliance. Although swearing lifelong devotion to Ellen, he was also emotionally entangled with other women. Indeed, each was to marry during the correspondence.

Both knew that they could not have achieved the same unembarrassed intimacy face to face. Their delight was in writing unreservedly: they were theatrically extravagant in the way they expressed themselves ('Ellen, Ellen, Ellen, Ellen, Ellen, Ellen, Ellen, Ellen, Ellen, Eleanor, Ellenest,' wrote Shaw; 'Tear this up, quick, quick!' wrote Ellen). They could hardly wait to comment on each other's letters and say what they were thinking, feeling, or doing. They poured out confidences; argued; advised; admonished and comforted each other. Their letters were a mixture of theatrical gossip, teasing, tenderness and intimacy.

They were also love letters. And for Ellen, whose emotional and professional life was in the doldrums, it was exhilarating to get a letter from Shaw after a first night starting,

> Dearest and Everest – I could not go any nearer to you tonight (even if you had wanted me to – say that you did – oh say, say, say, say that you did) because I could not have looked at you or spoken to you otherwise than as I felt

and to join in the game with replies like,

> Darling! I haven't said that yet! And now I'll say it again. Goodbye, Darling![2]

Ellen had to perform a difficult balancing act between Shaw and Irving – particularly when Shaw later became drama critic of the *Saturday Review*, and his attacks on Irving became intense. Despite the position this put Ellen in, she managed to retain the friendship of both men.

It was fortunate that Shaw was not yet drama critic when Irving staged *King Lear* in November 1892, as even Ellen considered it one of their failures. She thought Irving marvellous, but indistinct – one critic noted on his programme that Irving had pronounced the word 'sterility' as 'stair-ril-la-ta-a.' She was fairly pleased at the way she played Cordelia, 'a wee part but a fine one.'

The year had had its sadnesses. Ellen's mother had died, though Ellen had been comforted by Irving's thoughtfulness: when she turned up at the Lyceum that night, he had filled her dressing room with daffodils, 'to make it look like sunshine.' Tennyson, too, had died and Ellen, who attended the funeral, wrote to a friend that his great coffin, moving up the centre of the Abbey wrapped in the flag, had been a harrowing scene. The new year held little promise. 'H.I. not well,' Ellen wrote in her diary in December. 'Business by no means up to the proper point. A death in the Royal Family. Depression – depression!'

To get the Lyceum back into profit, Irving decided to take the company on an American tour in the autumn. Ted's name was down for it but, to Ellen's dismay, he talked of marriage rather than America. He was to be twenty one in January, free to do as he liked and was as susceptible to women as they were to him. Irving sent Ted a gold watch for his birthday, along with a letter to say he hoped he would think better of it and come on the tour:

> Of the anxiety to [your] mother I say nothing. Such a mother as yours has no peace when you are disturbed – or your interests are at stake. This tour will be a very hard one for her, and her work, as much as she can possibly bear, and your presence would be a comfort to her I know.[3]

Ellen's spirits were not improved with the opening of Tennyson's *Becket* on 6 February 1893 – Irving's fifty fifth birthday – in which she played Rosamund. As a play, it was a great success, but Ellen's part, as one critic said, 'had been dragged in by the hair.' Ted didn't help. Playing the youngest Knight Templar, he got stage fright on the first night and fluffed his three lines. He took his acting duties lightly, too lightly for Ellen's peace of mind.

During the Lyceum's Easter break, while Ellen was relaxing at her Winchelsea cottage, she received a telegram from Ted dated 27 March to say that he had married May Gibson at a registry office. May was the daughter of a close friend of Ellen's, though Ellen had hoped Ted would marry another actress girlfriend. Her only comment, against the diary entry of the event was 'This is the 19th century!' Irving thought him a fool and Ted later agreed with him.

Ellen told Ted and May they could have her Uxbridge cottage – with her passion for cottages, she had three at the time, at Uxbridge, Hampton Court and Winchelsea. The result, by chance, switched Ted's interest from acting to the graphic arts. Returning home one evening, Ted met the painter James Pryde on the train. Pryde was staying nearby with his sister, who was married to another painter William Nicholson, and they agreed that the three of them would meet the next day.

For the next few years, the three met frequently. Ted was fascinated with the way Nicholson engraved on wood, and spent much of his time copying him. He continued to act, just to earn a living, but his interest in design grew. When in 1894 he joined a small acting company and went touring with *Hamlet*, the posters he persuaded the manager to use were done by the almost unknown Beggarstaff Brothers – Nicholson and Pryde. By now the simplicity of design, so evident in the Beggarstaff posters, was becoming increasingly popular as public reaction grew against the over-elaborate versions of the Victorian era.

In the summer, Ellen went to Canada for a holiday before the Lyceum company's American tour began in September. Edy and their friends the Lovedays went with her. Ellen had hoped her father might join them, but on 13 September she wrote in reply to his letter to say she was sorry to hear he was not coming

and that you are troubling about Tom [a younger brother of Ellen's] is quite naughty. Of course, all along our dear mother has been the practical *doer* of the family, but she was far too brave to let her thought and care for Tom (and for all of us – *you* too my dear) overwhelm her.[4]

The company was going out west for the first time and Ellen joined it in San Francisco, where the old favourites were put on and the audience stamped, cheered and howled its approval. It continued to do well throughout the country, until the company left New York for England on 17 March 1894.

While Ellen had been away, Ted had written to tell her that May was pregnant. The child, Rosemary, was born on 8 April 1894. Financially, it was not a propitious time. Ted had not acted since the previous summer, enjoying himself instead by producing an Alfred de Musset play for charity. Ellen, worried, had sent him weekly letters of advice from America, enclosing £3 a time.

On 14 April, the Lyceum re-opened with *Faust* which ran for more than five hundred performances. During the summer lay-off, Ellen went down to her Winchelsea cottage and Ted, May and the baby came to stay for a week. Being a mother-in-law instead of a mother didn't suit her at all. Writing to her friend, Bertha, she said:

> Ted, May and that sweetest babe have been with me a week and they leave me tomorrow – oh, Bertha – I can't be all sorry, for my experience is that it's bitterly disappointing being a Grandmother – and I had thought it would be so lovely (I'm a *very* patient person but my patience wd go if that Baby were here much longer without my being able to have any 'say' concerning her and I'm *more* than 'tactful' about interfering).
>
> I'm more pleased that Ted shd 'go touring' with other folks than to go touring with 'his own company' (the plan fell through because he cd not find the money for which he will rejoice some day – as I do now). . . . His wife contrives to irritate me more I think than any other person I *have ever met with* but she's Ted's wife and I'll do my best to keep from *spanking* her.[5]

The next production at the Lyceum, on 12 January 1895, was *King Arthur*, a verse play by Joe Comyns Carr, with scenic ideas by Burne-Jones. A writer in the magazine *Mainly About People* recalled seeing Ellen sprawled under a may tree on Hampstead Heath, rehearsing her part of Queen Guinevere, her hair looking like fibre on a coconut, and holding the play first in one hand and then the other, according to which hand she was gesticulating with.

The same month as *King Arthur* opened, the theatre critic of the highly-regarded *Saturday Review*, Edmund Yates, died and Shaw was asked to take his place. It gave him the weapon he wanted against Irving, a chance to carry out a public crusade against him, his style of acting, his preference for Shakespeare, his ignoring of the new dramatists like Ibsen, and his – in Shaw's eyes – often insensitive casting of Ellen Terry.

He started his attack with *King Arthur*, writing in *Saturday Review* that it was pathetic to see Miss Terry speaking

> arid sham-feminine twaddle in blank-verse, which she pumps out in little rhythmic strokes in a desperate and all too obvious effort to make music of it . . . what a theatre for a woman of genius to be attached to!

Irving could afford to brush criticism aside. On 25 May 1895 he was to receive a knighthood – the first for an actor and the accolade he needed to achieve his long fought-for aim of making the acting profession respectable. 'The dear fellow deserves any honours, all honours,' said Ellen.

CHAPTER 11

ELLEN AND EDY: 'A TUG OF WAR'

Irving's knighthood was announced on the same day, 25 May 1895, that Oscar Wilde was convicted of homosexual acts of gross indecency at the Old Bailey. Irving knew Wilde a little but Ellen had been on very friendly terms with him, having met him through Godwin and thinking him a remarkable and audacious man. Wilde, in turn, along with Burne-Jones, was one of her most devoted admirers and her son remembers her sitting with Wilde and talking about nothing, like a pair of fools. He thought Wilde 'A great-hearted being,' while Wilde, in agreement with the general opinion that Ted was 'such a beautiful boy,' once wrote and told him so. Ellen gently stopped any further correspondence. However, on the day Wilde was sentenced, a veiled lady, rumoured to be Ellen, left a bunch of violets and a message of sympathy at his house. Irving was one of the few people who sent a message of encouragement to Wilde, two years later, when he left prison.

On 18 July, Irving went to Windsor to receive his knighthood. Max Beerbohm glimpsed him in a brougham on his way to Windsor, his hat jauntily tilted and his face full of 'ruminant sly fun.'

That summer, Irving was working on a stage version of *Coriolanus*. When in August he joined Ellen and Edy in Winchelsea for a few days, he read it to them. 'As it went on and on, we thought it duller and duller,' said Ellen, 'and at the end I felt convinced it was no good as an acting play, and said so . . . the next morning he called out to me from his bedroom to mine: "I shan't do that play." Joy! Joy!'[1] He was to change his mind six years later, when it was to be Ellen's last role at the Lyceum.

At the end of the month, Irving and Ellen left for another

tour of Canada and the United States. The rest of the company travelled separately and they all met in Montreal on 12 September. Ellen commented on how odd it was that Irving should hate such reunions, involving him in 'shaking their greasy paws.' Ellen's own warmth and affection was scattered around indiscriminately. She wrote to a friend from America once to say that she had spent New Year's Eve alone, sitting among her photographs, and having 'a long think' about all her dear friends. Irving's coldness was a mystery to her. 'I think it is not quite right in him that he does not care for anybody much,' she said. 'I think he has always cared for me a little, very little, and has had passing fancies, but he really *cares* for scarcely any one.'[2]

The ten month tour ahead was the longest and most gruelling yet undertaken. In Philadelphia, Eleanora Duse, the Italian actress who tried to revive classicism on the Italian stage, was acting at another theatre and pleased Ellen and Irving immensely by congratulating them. Wherever they went, the company was given banquets, receptions and applause. Ellen could forget a letter she had had in England signed 'An American gentleman' which, she complained to a friend, 'tells me I am far too old and fat to be acting and that no one wants to see me any more on the stage and warning me not to go to America or I shall be shot!'[3]

As it happened, she almost did lose her life when crossing the Mississippi, where floods swept the tracks away. May Webster, whose husband Ben was one of the company, recalled in her autobiography that one night the train crossed a deeply flooded river and the water almost reached the engine fires.

> Edy Craig rushed to her mother's compartment to see
> whether she was all right and found her completely dressed,
> gloves neatly buttoned, tying her veil. 'Edy darling!' she said,
> 'hurry and dress yourself properly; we shall probably have to
> swim!'[4]

It was no fanciful idea. As they travelled through the south, with its magnolia trees and huge firs, they crossed other lakes on perilously low bridges and in one they saw the remains of a train that had been wrecked three weeks before. Ellen was to write: 'This rushing, tearing America, so full of hope! but oh, so rough – so rough.'

Ellen and Edy on their American tour, 1895-6.

In New Orleans they started to rehearse Laurence Irving's play *Godefroi and Yolande*, about leprosy, which Ellen had persuaded Irving to run. He did so on the condition that she took charge of it and May Webster, on the tour with her husband, Ben, was unimpressed. In a letter to her sister-in-law, she wrote: 'We're rehearsing that filthy leper play every day, takes up all our time, and it's in such a muddle owing to the erratic Nell's stage management.' At one point, when Ellen was worried about the lights, May Webster rushed to the stage manager, saying, 'For God's sake get that lime on her or she'll go mad!' Then she heard a chuckle from the darkness and Irving's voice saying drily: 'Better get it right, Loveday. Don't want her to go mad, y'know. Pity.'[5]

It gave Ellen the only chance she ever had in America to play a new part. But she put the play on to help Laurence. He had given up the idea of being a diplomat to become an actor and after joining the Lyceum company formed a close relationship with Ellen, who was more encouraging to him than was his father. Shortly after he had read the play to her, he wrote thanking her for her generous enthusiasm over it.

Edy was indispensable during Laurence's play. As it was not in the company's repertory, everything had to be done from scratch. She devised the scenery, the effects and the clothes, and did so on a very small budget. She had always been extremely inventive and managed by gathering odd bits of scenery from other plays and transforming them into something quite different. Despite her talents, Edy was still a nebulous, shadowy figure, always in the background, acting like a lady in waiting to Ellen. Whereas her mother and brother left memoirs, detailing their lives, Edy's day to day activities went unrecorded, save when the other two mentioned her. She was still testing her ideas and trying to develop her own personality behind the glare of Ellen's. Ellen thought both her children brilliant actors, but Edy, who had several walking-on parts in the current tour, was never over-enthusiastic about acting.

Unlike her brother, Edy in no way traded on the family endowment of easy charm, indeed she seemed to make a point of not being charming. But May and Ben Webster, who were staying in the same hotel as Edy and her mother, found that behind her initially brusque manner she had knowledge and judgment, humour and loyalty. 'She was talented in a determined, almost belligerent way,' said May Webster, 'passionately and possessively devoted to her mother, beset by all the problems which surround the daughter of a famous actress and a beautiful woman, especially when she herself is illegitimate.'[6]

May Webster relates an episode on the tour that showed Ellen, sympathetic enough to Irving's son Laurence, totally lacking in perception with her own daughter. Edy until then had had no boyfriends or any involvements with men, cocooned as she was inside her mother's house, with its constant women callers.

Amy Leslie, an actress, remembered Ellen once saying to her,

> Wouldn't it be a fearful thing if some dear comfortless young gentleman should coax Edy to marry Him? She would take collar buttons as seriously as twins, and the blessed man would die of fright at her consuming arguments over laundry bills and dotted veils. Really, two or three benighted youths have come to me praying to be allowed to pay attentions to Ailsa [Edy], but I have warned them of the fearful fate waiting anybody bold enough to ask her. She won't have any of them – that's the only consolation. She never really laughs heartily at anything but beaux. I have given her up, just as she has me.[7]

On this tour, however, Edy fell deeply and passionately in love with a married man, painter Joe Evans. Interestingly, he suffered from a facial disfigurement, like another man whom Edy was to love.

Ellen reacted ruthlessly, ending the romance at once and threatening to send Edy back home. Although any mother would be justifiably concerned at her daughter loving a married man, Ellen seemed unaware of and uncaring about Edy's feelings, and gave her no comfort at a time when, despite being twenty six, her first emotions had been aroused and she was bewildered and unhappy. Used to her mother receiving all the adulation, she felt she had at last been loved for herself. The abrupt cessation of the romance, with no advice or understanding, or cooling-off period allowed, could hardly have helped her feelings to heal.

This unthinking indifference was more the reaction of mistress to slave, than caring mother to her daughter and showed more than a hint of the same possessiveness that Edy felt about Ellen. This two-way possessiveness – particularly about each other's relationships with the opposite sex – coloured their lives. Men as devotees were accepted, but the possibility of one becoming a husband threatened their own dependent relationship and was always violently opposed.

In this instance, Ellen consolidated her unnecessary heartlessness towards Edy. At the time Ellen was having a mild flirtation with a handsome, rather wooden, actor in the company called Frank Cooper – in effect, a retread of Charles Kelly. According to the Websters, she would bring Cooper back to supper at the hotel after the performance and then insist that Edy – who would return with them from the theatre – stay up to act as chaperone. If Edy had not been in the play, and so was in bed, Ellen insisted she get up. Both Edy and Ellen talked to the Websters about the situation, but the Websters felt powerless to help. Edy stayed with the company, quietly doing what she was told. And the whole episode was never mentioned again.

During the tour, Ellen continued to write to Shaw. In the autumn of 1895 he had completed *The Man of Destiny*, a play about Napoleon. He then discovered that Irving had acquired the English rights of *Madame Sans-Gêne*, a comedy about Napoleon and a washerwoman by the French playwright, Victorien Sardou, and wrote to Ellen in America in exasperation to say he had heard she was playing the title role, while he had just completed 'a beautiful little one-act play for Napoleon and a strange lady – a strange lady who will be murdered by someone else whilst you are nonsensically pretending to play a washerwoman.'[8]

Laurence Irving in his biography of his grandfather, Henry Irving, queries what Shaw was up to, writing *The Man of Destiny* for a theatrical partnership that he was openly trying to disintegrate. But Ellen was anxious to encourage Shaw, warning him, 'If you give Napoleon and that Strange Lady (Lord, how attractively tingling it sounds!) to anyone but me I'll. . . . Ah, but be kind, and let me know that "lady".' Shaw sent it and Ellen, after reading it, telegraphed 'Delicious.' She tried to persuade Irving to use it, and he did indeed consider it, but she knew he found it difficult to fit a one-act play into the Lyceum bill.

Shaw also knew that Irving considered him to be a pamphleteer, rather than an author, so when the *Chicago Tribune* mentioned that Irving might be producing the play, Shaw promptly wrote to Ellen asking if 'His Immensity's' intentions were really honourable and threatening to give the Strange Lady's part to the beautiful Mrs Patrick Campbell. For months afterwards Ellen badgered Irving to do the play, while the tragi-comic negotiations between the two men fuelled their emnity.

The tour ended in New York. Irving made a farewell speech of thanks for the Americans' reception of his 'merry little band,' who, after some eight months of togetherness, were hardly on speaking terms with each other. On 16 May 1896 they sailed home and, according to May Webster, slept almost the whole way back to Liverpool.

After a week's break, there was a five week tour of the provinces. This prevented Irving from attending his son, Harry's, wedding in July 1896 to a young actress called Dorothea Baird. It was a fortunate excuse, allowing him to avoid meeting his wife whom he had not seen for twenty five years. Before he made his decision, however, his wife's family had been feverishly discussing whether he would bring 'the creature' – the hated Ellen – with him to the wedding. Harry wrote to his fiancée, saying:

I am sorry all this E.T. business is cropping up again in South Kensington. How wretched it is! I had hoped they would have spared you all unpleasantness. Whatever the whole business means my father is now at an age when the matter may surely be set at rest, and the family linen not washed to every newcomer. Heaven knows it is distressing enough to Laurence and myself to be planted in the midst of all this scandal and we have done our best to steer some sort of course between it. And why all this excitement? I don't anticipate any trouble from E.T. She is not so blind or foolish as yet.

You will have to meet her as I met her and be rather bored by her, but she will not want to come to the wedding or to our house or do anything that might be inconvenient.[9]

Despite the disparaging remark about Ellen, both Harry and

Laurence were grateful that she ultimately succeeded in reconciling them with their father.

Irving returned to London to discuss *Cymbeline*, the next production at the Lyceum, with the classical artist Laurence Alma Tadema, whom Irving had asked to design the sets. Meanwhile the negotiations – or arguments – between Irving and Shaw were in full spate, with Shaw announcing that Irving could only have *The Man of Destiny* on his terms and Irving counter-announcing *his* terms.

Spurred on by these acerbic negotiations, Ellen and Shaw were now writing to each other almost daily. This year and next, the correspondence was at its height. It was an involvement that Irving must have been hurt by and found hard to understand: how could his leading lady be on such intimate terms with his leading critic? He called Shaw 'Mr Pshaw,' and told his son Laurence that he would cheerfully pay Shaw's funeral expenses any time.

In the August of 1896, while Ellen was trying to rehearse her role of Imogen in *Cymbeline*, Shaw was sending her a jealous torrent of criticism about Irving and the play ('Shakespeare is as dead *dramatically* as a doornail'). But despite Shaw's dismissive attitude, Ellen argued, in her later lectures on Shakespeare's heroines, that Imogen was 'perhaps the most complete and lovely of all Shakespeare's heroines. . . . In every situation she shows such perfect "good sense.". . . Dignity in meeting a foul accusation, and unwavering love in spite of it, are also characteristic.' In the margin of her notes, she wrote, 'I'm *foolish fond* of her.'[10]

Shaw also sent her pages and pages of detailed advice on how to play the part. Ellen, always eager to learn, took his hectoring to be concern rather than conceit, and was genuinely pleased that many of their ideas coincided. Irving, had he known, would have been appalled at this usurping of his own professional right to direct Ellen's playing of the part – though Irving himself was mostly to blame for this as Ellen, in thanking Shaw for his advice, said:

> You must understand I am the one person at the Lyceum
> who is never advised, found fault with, or 'blackguarded'
> before the production of our plays. . . . It is *frightful* not to
> be found fault with. Henry wont, cant find time, and the rest

are silly and think me a very grand person indeed, and would not dare.[11]

Ellen's and Irving's strong relationship was essentially based on their work. But Ellen's dissatisfaction with the roles she was given, Shaw's continual attacks on Irving, which insidiously destroyed her belief in him, and the worrying state of the Lyceum's finances, weakened then finally broke the bond between them. A selection of the entries in a notebook she kept, found after her death, shows her detached assessment of Irving over these years:

1896
H.I. appears to me to be getting impatient as other actors come on. He is tired. . . .

    H.I. is much handsomer now than when I first knew him in 1867. Handsomer, but somehow more furtive-looking. Is his dominant note intellectuality? Yes, I think so. He has so much character. The best in him is his patience, his caution, his strong, practical will, and his gentle courtesy. His worst is his being incapable of caring for people, sons, friends, any one, and his lack of enthusiasm for other people's work, or indeed anything outside *his own* work. . . .

1897
Very odd. He is not improving with age. . . . He never admires the right thing. (This tells against myself since I know he has always 'admired' me! Perhaps, though, he has only 'admired' my usefulness to him!). . . .

1899
I wonder how his other friends and lovers feel to him. I have contempt and affection and admiration. What a mixture! . . .

    His illness has made him look queer. He is stouter, very grey, sly-looking, and more cautious than ever. Bother![12]

Cymbeline opened on 22 September 1896. Ellen, despite her worries about the part, charmed everyone, particularly Shaw, who damned the rest of the cast and called the play stagey trash. Ellen wrote to him, saying, 'Well, they let me down very kindly, but – you and I know it was all rubbish, and as I only care for what "you and I" think.'[13] Despite writing in her diary at the time that 'Nothing seemed right. Everything was so slow, so slow,' in her memoirs, she noted: 'I think as Imogen I gave the *only* inspired performance of these last rather sad years.'

During the run, Ellen nearly bumped into Shaw while he and Irving were discussing, yet again, *The Man of Destiny*; but she told Shaw that her resolution had deserted her at the door of Irving's office: 'Heard your voice and then skedaddled home again full tilt and, oh, I was laughing.'

Ellen's health had been poor that year: her eyes had deteriorated and she'd had a small operation on them. Making light of it in her letters to Shaw, she asked him to send her his play *Candida* to read – her verdict being that it touched her more than she could say. She wanted to read it to Edy, who 'is the clever party, but the most simple, single person I have ever met. . . . I love Edy even better than you. I think I love her better than me.'[14] But reading to Edy could be unpredictable. When, that October, Shaw read *You Never Can Tell* to Edy and a young American woman, Edy seemed so busy with her embroidery, and paid Shaw so few compliments about his play, that he complained afterwards that she behaved as if she had been married to him for twenty years.

Writing to Shaw about Edy, Ellen exclaimed:

I think you think she takes care of me! Of course she does in a way, because I care what she thinks and I love her best, but I'm not her child.

Edy *looks* a tragedy, and is about the most amusing, funniest creature living, a casual wretch. Oh she is odd. Envy was not in the mixture that made her up, nor me. (It's quite odd, and we cant help knowing it.) She says she could not live with any set of people in the world, that no one would put up with her but me. ('Put up' with her!) She'll try and go away for a whole month sometimes, and hates it, and always gets into a difficult corner. . . . She's high, she's low. She's a perfect Dear. She loathes emotional people, yet adores me. I scarcely ever dare kiss her, and I'm always dying to, but she hates it from anyone. It 'cuts both ways' I assure you, the having an impersonal person for a daughter.

Until she was about 12 she lacked sweetness and softness. But oh she's really sweetness and softness indeed. Only she's odd. She doesn't spoil me, I tell you, but let anyone try to hurt me! Murder then, if it would save me.

I've prayed she might love, but I dont pray for that now. I'll tell you some day when we've time to meet.

P.S. Edy says she'd never marry because she would not stay anywhere where she was not entirely happy. I heard she said once: 'Not a minute would I stop with Mother, but that I do just as I like.' (She thinks she does, but really she does as I like.) To my mind she never wants to be naughty in any way. One thing I desire. That she shall never be frightened at me. She's such a baby – and yet so clever.[15]

In reply, Shaw wrote that he expected Ellen had spoiled her children, and whereas she had probably succeeded handsomely with the man, had overshot the mark a little with the woman and made her cynical. Edy should be told that Ellen wasn't in the least free, had picked up her happiness in casual scraps on her way to work – while she, Edy, was quite free and had nothing to do but be happy.

In December, Ellen went to Germany and Monte Carlo for a six week holiday. Irving was putting on *Richard III*, in which there was no suitable part for her, and her doctor had also told her she must rest. Unfortunately, Irving badly ruptured the ligatures of his kneecap on the first night and without an understudy – Irving never expected to be ill – the theatre was closed. The season's losses were £10,000.

Shaw's review of *Richard III* was ambiguous at points, and Irving's friends read into it a suggestion that Irving had been drunk on stage. It was a ludicrous idea, but Irving's supporters had an almost hysterical dislike of Shaw and were quick to believe the worst of him. Shaw wrote personally to Irving to say he had not meant to imply he had been drunk. Irving replied, saying he had never read a criticism of Shaw's in his life: 'I have read lots of your droll, amusing, irrelevant and sometimes impertinent pages, but criticism containing judgment and sympathy – I have never seen by your pen.'[16]

A couple of months later, Irving, who had been holding on to Shaw's play, *The Man of Destiny*, finally rejected it. Shaw started a barrage of correspondence with Irving, and Ellen wrote to him saying, 'Oh dear oh dear, My Dear, this vexes me very much. My friends to fight! And I love both of them, and want each to win. . . . Don't quarrel with H. That would add to my unhappiness.'[17]

Shaw's *You Never Can Tell* was in production at the Haymarket, but rehearsals proved catastrophic, with actors walking out ('no laughs and no exits,' said one) and Shaw finally withdrew the play. Ellen asked Shaw to give Edy a chance in one of his plays, and though Shaw agreed she had a remarkably beautiful voice and was very capable, he said she was too sane to be a hysterical leading lady and too young for heavy parts of any value. His influence, he thought, like Ellen's, would only tell against Edy.

On 10 April, 1897, *Madame Sans-Gêne* opened at the Lyceum and was well received, even though Edy had told Ellen she was going to be very bad in her part, and Irving was far too tall to play Napoleon realistically. Shaw called Ellen an 'exceptional actress,' and Ellen wrote in her diary: 'I acted courageously, and fairly well too. Extraordinary success.' She didn't mention that she didn't know her words properly.

Audiences fell off only because in the June of that year they were flocking instead to the celebrations marking Queen Victoria's Diamond Jubilee. Troops from the colonies and representatives from all parts of the Empire joined the Jubilee procession and cheering crowds greeted the Queen as she drove to St Paul's in a landau.

Ellen meanwhile was juggling her relationships. In June, Irving had accused her of being in love with Shaw, and Ellen had written to Shaw in amusement to say that her curses of children had discovered his handwriting and Edy was being exceedingly pert to her aged mother. But the gossip in theatrical circles was now over Ellen's evident partiality for the Lyceum company actor, Frank Cooper – a flirtation which had begun during the last American tour. Cooper sent her presents, signed 'from an admirer,' in distinctive handwriting; his landlady would tell him 'a lady' in a carriage was waiting for him. Ben Webster, who shared Cooper's lodgings thought Ellen was degrading herself. Irving was furious one night when Ellen called him 'Frank' all through supper.

The flirtation may just have been Ellen's need for reassurance. She was forty eight, and fifty was looming. She knew the links with Irving were weakening, and even the pillar-box romance with Shaw was no substitute for the real thing. Yet judging by a letter she wrote to Bertha Bramley later that year, regarding the press rumour of a romance with Frank

Cooper, her flirting was not too serious:

> No – I fear I can't snap up Frank Cooper (!) and marry him,
> for he happens to have a wife – and she's nice too – so he
> can't 'cut her throat with a bar of soap' – She is a jealous
> little lady too, but *not* of me – and I'm fond of her. They
> marry me to every man I act with. . . . Mrs Hatton told me a
> few days since that she saw in a paper that my Edy was
> engaged to be married – I knew nothing about it, but as Edy
> is away I sent her congratulations!!! She thought it very
> polite of me but knew nothing about the matter!![18]

There was gossip about Irving as well; during the summer
break from the Lyceum he too had found other attractions. He
had been working in Cromer with his son Laurence on
Laurence's play, *Peter the Great*, planned for the Lyceum's next
season. They had both been asked to tea by a Mrs Eliza Aria,
who wrote gossip and fashion pieces for the weekly paper, *The
Truth*. Irving had met her at a supper party in Jubilee year and
had liked her: she was intelligent, with a dry wit. After the tea
party, he and Laurence often took her on carriage drives
around the country.[19] For Irving, it was the beginning of a
friendship that lasted for years and, in Ellen's eyes at least, was
the *coup de grâce* in their long relationship. The Terry family
biographer, Marguerite Steen, reported that when she gave
Ellen a biography of Irving by Mrs Aria, twenty four years
later, Ellen put it aside, saying, 'Thank you, my dear. . . . Henry
left me for Mrs Aria.'[20]

Irving never mentioned Mrs Aria to Ellen. It was not until
January of the following year that she wrote to Shaw to say:
'Henry is so nice to me lately that I'm convinced he has a new
"flame" (he is always nicer then, which I think is to his credit).'
One month later she asked him,

> 'But who is Mrs A.? I only know she is "a journalist" and "a
> friend" of H.I.'s. I never set eyes on her and she had no idea I
> know of her (This is fun, and would be better fun, if I knew
> something about her.) If you know her personally dont "give
> away" that I know of her existence.'

Shaw had met her once, casually, so was able to report to
Ellen that she was 'a good sort.'[21]

While Irving was in Cromer, Ellen went to Winchelsea. She

A photograph of Edy which appeared in the magazine, the *Theatre*, in October, 1895, under her early stage name of Ailsa Craig.

was tired and her letters to Shaw that year constantly mention that she was ill, hadn't the strength to go on stage, was on the verge of a breakdown. Her son, Ted, took a more caustic view of this, writing of his mother, 'Never was any one less actually ill than she.' He attributed her continual references to 'feeling ill' in her letters to Shaw, to being her way of using the Victorian middle-class habit of having vapours when wishing to avoid an unwanted duty. Her general health was really quite good – although she startled Shaw once by complaining of having neuralgia of the palate – but she was frequently exhausted and had discomfort and pain with her eyes.

Shaw had arranged for Edy to go on a tour that summer in *Candida* and *A Doll's House*, in a company run by the actress Janet Achurch and her husband, Charles Charrington. These two pioneered Ibsen's plays in England, in 1889 performing *A Doll's House* for the first time to a dedicated audience of Ibsen followers. Among the non-dedicated critics was Clement Scott, who made one of the milder comments when he called the characters 'an unlovable, unlovely and detestable crew' and it was clear that if Ibsen and others writing the New Drama of social realism were to be seen on stage, it would have to be through a private theatre society. In 1891, the Independent Theatre was created and the 1897 tour organised by the Charringtons, was under its aegis. Edy, a dedicated Ibsenite, was delighted to be included.

Ellen was grateful to Shaw for organising this for Edy, but admitted to him that,

> I miss my Edy every minute of the time. However, I know she is happy; and it is good for her to feel the struggle of life alone for awhile. She has always thought it so easy, and it's time she knew some of the little difficulties. She is splendidly resourceful in *big* happenings and displays great character, but she must make acquaintance with the small worries I suppose.[22]

Although Shaw had offered to sit in on rehearsals and help Edy in any way, he thought her perfectly competent, and told Ellen to stop worrying about her, as he was sure she'd take care of herself and indeed all the rest of the company, very efficiently:

She has inherited your social powers and would be worth
£20 a week in the company even if she didnt act at all. And
she has lots of acting in her, though she has been much
neglected technically by an unnatural mother . . . she is
perfectly easy and unguarded and spontaneous in her ways.
So you may leave her to herself with perfect tranquillity: she's
the only member of the company that needs no looking after.[23]

Ellen went to see Edy in *A Doll's House* at Eastbourne in
August, liked the play and thought all the cast played cleverly.
Edy was enjoying herself immensely and decided to stay with
the Charringtons' company instead of rejoining the Lyceum.
Ellen's despondency at this news was not helped, she told
Shaw, by a friend of hers telling her that if Edy stayed long
with the Independent Theatre Company, 'she will get dull,
heavy, conceited, frowsy, trollopy, and *dirty*! In fact will look
moth-eaten! And *no* one will see her act, because nobody goes
to their Theatre.'[24]

That same month, Ted was in Southwold, staying with the
family of a musician friend, Martin Shaw. Earlier that year he
had produced two plays at Croydon Theatre Royal under his
own management. But there was little profit in it: the money
went on costumes and scenery and printing the special posters
he'd designed.

Ted was now twenty five and although he had been
extravagantly praised for his recent *Hamlet* at the Olympic
Theatre, acting was holding less and less attraction for him.
Watching Irving, he felt he must either content himself with
being a feeble imitation of him or be somebody, do something,
in his own right. But what? This he didn't yet know: he was
dabbling with different ideas, but none yet appealed as a career.

After the Croydon show he wrote to Edy saying, 'I wish I
were dead at the present moment. All seems agoing wrong –
work – affection – position – can't write a note of music – can
do nothing.'[25] That year, 1897, he ended his apprenticeship
with Irving, threw up £8 a week, and had stopped acting
entirely by the end of the year. 'I woke up,' he was to say. This
upset Ellen who felt the stage was losing a talented actor.

Ted was by now the father of three children by May:
Rosemary (three), Robert (two) and Philip (one). But his life
with her had quickly disintegrated into rows: he was bored by

domesticity; she was sick and tired of having no money when she felt he could easily support them all if he signed with an acting company instead of indulging himself by drawing. She also resented his general selfishness: the way he never gave her any money to buy clothes for herself, spending it instead on buying himself hats.

But the real rot in their marriage was Ted's Terry charm. This, and his striking, girlish good looks, bowled over the women he met. He in turn regarded them as so many rows of sweets laid out on the counter for his gratification. Every touring company he had joined since marriage to May seemed to contain an old girlfriend, with whom he took up again. May, at home, bringing up three children on her own, inevitably heard the rumours and relations between them deteriorated further.

Ted was worrying Ellen greatly by drifting around, doing sketches for journals, and designing book-plates and posters. May wrote complaining letters to Ellen about him; and Ellen had to send May £3 a week on which to manage. He saw May occasionally – resulting in the arrival of their fourth child, Peter, in the autumn of 1897, and in yet more rows over money.

That autumn Ellen went on a provincial tour with the Lyceum company. These constant tours not only brought in much-needed profits but also made Irving and Ellen well-known and popular figures throughout Britain. Ellen, however, was in poor spirits. 'I dread feeling "dull," "blue," and I do believe it's coming on!' she wrote to Shaw from Leeds in October, asking him if he was doing anything new in the way of a play. 'Never a play for your Ellen, oh no,' she chided him. 'I'm rather hating everything just at present and have had quite enough of doing without Edy.'[26]

The next month, while she was in Edinburgh, Shaw wrote asking if the rumour about her marrying a Scottish admirer was true. Although dismissing the idea as ludicrous, she admitted that with Henry concentrating on his work, Ted busy with his own life and Edy being away,

I feel as if I'd like to go to one who would be full enough of me, if it only lasted for five minutes. But the feeling of loneliness (for that's what it is, *loneliness* mixed up with

jealousy, ugh! detestably!) passes directly Edy turns up. I
think she is the only one I was ever jealous about. Folk think
she cares for me. I dont. I never plague her with my love, but
oh, how she cuts my heart to ribbons sometimes, and very
likely she doesnt intend to be unkind!'[27]

The correspondence between Ellen and Shaw was edited by
Christopher St John, with whom Edy was to live, and in the
note to this particular letter, she came to Edy's defence, saying
those who thought Edy cared for her mother were right.

To one as ebulliently expressive as Ellen Terry, her
daughter's Cordelia-like abstention from the demonstrations
of admiration and affection lavished on her by adoring
friends of both sexes must often have caused pain. Later in
their lives that shyness which often exists between parents
and children disappeared and the friendship between Ellen
Terry and Edy became more intimate. It outlasted all Ellen
Terry's other friendships and was the chief consolation of her
old age. "Edy" was the last name her lips pronounced in the
hour of her death.

This particular tour was mainly memorable because of the
death of Irving's dog, Fussie, who fell through an open trap in
the stage. Ellen rushed round to Irving that evening to see if he
was all right. 'Henry was almost as fond of him as of one of his
rehearsals,' she said. She was tired enough of rehearsals at the
time. *Peter the Great* was the next production at the Lyceum
and the company was having to rehearse it between performances of *Madame Sans-Gêne* (a comedy, first staged at the
Lyceum in April that year).

Ellen wrote to Bertha Bramley from Hull on 30 October,
however, to say *Peter the Great* was coming on well and that
Laurence was a wonderful stage director.

Unfortunately I have a *horrid* part – a vulgar very short part
– I've promised Laurence to play it, but I'm almost sorry I've
done so. Henry keeps well thank God – it's wonderful when
he is *always* at work. I've begged him to drop Friday
rehearsals (as he acts morning and evening on Saturdays) and
go for a drive with me and he has promised he will – no fresh
air!! how can he live like it – I drive every day or I'd die.[28]

While they were on tour in Bradford, on 16 December 1897, both were appalled to hear of the murder of the actor William Terriss who was stabbed outside the stage door of the Adelphi Theatre in London, by a half crazy actor with an imagined grievance. Terriss was one of the oldest members of the Lyceum company: nicknamed 'Breezy Bill,' he was praised by reviewers for his 'manly presence' on stage. Irving, full of anger at the murder of a lifelong friend, said in bitterness: 'They will find some excuse to get him off – mad or something. Terriss was an actor – his murderer will not be executed.' Terriss had died in the arms of the actress Jessie Millward, his mistress of some fifteen years. Society's conventions at the time forbade her – as they had forbidden Ellen with Godwin – to attend the funeral alone, thereby admitting her true position in his life. On the morning of the funeral, Irving went to her flat and offered himself as her escort. She gratefully accepted.

The company spent December in London on final rehearsals of *Peter the Great*. Ellen survived by planning to buy herself a small house in the country, where she and Edy could share a bedroom and living room, but have a latchkey each. Shaw wrote to say that he and Henry might be taking opposing sides in a debate and he intended to 'blight the traitor's oratory' and Ellen loyally replied that she would end their friendship if he worried Irving when he was ill.

The next month, January 1898, saw the first publication of a shilling monthly magazine called *The Page*, designed and produced by Ted, who sometimes coloured the woodcuts by hand. Ellen's friends as well as his own generously contributed to his first edition. They included Burne-Jones; Max Beerbohm; Irving (with a unique sketch); Walt Whitman; and James Pryde. The magazine lasted about three years and Ellen, at first worried about the money Ted might owe, became overwhelmed with pride and sent out copies to all her friends – anxiously asking Shaw on one occasion if he thought Edy's poem in it, addressed to Robert (Ted's eldest son), was any good.

Peter the Great opened at the Lyceum the same month and was praised for being impressive and unconventional, but there were few bright touches to relieve the gloom of this tragedy. Ellen's part in it as the Empress Catherine was, as she said, almost too negligible to notice. Laurence had just got engaged to Ethel Barrymore, but this lasted little longer than his play, which was replaced in February by standard repertory pieces. Irving consoled himself by driving out most Sundays with Mrs Aria.

The play had lost money but there was a far more crippling financial disaster on the 18th of that month. The Lyceum's entire and vast stock of scenery and properties, kept under railway arches in Southwark, went up in flames. Irving was relying upon using these for revivals of plays in the future: instead he found himself stripped of resources at a time when he needed them most. But he took the loss quietly, coolly remarking that perhaps the fire had been caused by a spark of moral indignation from new drama supporters, who preferred plays without scenery.

Ellen, in her memoirs, made no mention of the fire. She was preoccupied with Edy, who was now, she wrote to her friend May Webster on 2 March, 'book making' in Paris and having a good time there. 'Meanwhile she has no engagement – so think of her please May if you hear of anything which *you* would despise – I can't bear her to come back to *no* work!'[29]

The Medicine Man, Irving's next production at the Lyceum on 4 May, was no help financially. Ellen wrote in her diary that it was rubbish, the only production at the Lyceum that was quite unworthy of them, and that if that kind of play was to be put on, she would really have to do something else. When the play opened the critics confirmed Ellen's judgment and it was replaced by stock pieces for the rest of the season.

Edy had been asked to go to South Africa with a touring company, an idea Ellen – who disliked her being away for long – was far from happy about. 'I *do* wish someone would hasten and offer her (Edy) a *London* engagement,' she wrote to Shaw. 'It is *so* bad for her to be far from me for a long time.' She explained why in another letter to him two days later:

> The difference between Edy in Manchester and Edy in Africa (oh, my heart is in my boots as I realize it) is this. If she is in any real difficulty she always sends to me, or comes to me, and we pick up her ends together. But when she is in Africa! Oh Lord, whom will she go to? And if she is ill too, she gets better quicker with me than with anybody. It's not jealous thought, all this. (I'm 'made that way,' with no inside Hell) and if someone would go to her and forgetting self for ever

so short a time (as I'm able to do, just because I love her)
then she would be healed, but there is not very much love
wasting about, and folk like Edy dont get it just at the right
moment. However, I know I am too anxious. I shall let her
go. She is only sorry to leave me; else she delights in going. I
wish I were going with her.[30]

In the end, Edy's plans fell through. Ellen and Edy went off
for a short break to Boulogne in July, Ellen mourning the death
of her friend Edward Burne-Jones on 17 June 1898. A
memorial service for him was held on 23 June at Westminster
Abbey, the first ever held there for an artist, and a distinguished
audience attended.

Ellen was fretting that summer at having no interesting parts
to look forward to. Her son was no less depressed. In August
he moved into a new cottage in Hackbridge, Surrey, and
redecorated it, Godwin style, with brown packing paper up to
the wainscoting – in between producing *The Page* and
designing book-plates. Nevertheless, he was out of spirits and
restless. He went down to Southwold then meandered along the
coast.

Feeling lonely – his wife and children possibly having slipped
his memory – he wrote to his actress friend, Jess Dorynne, to
ask if she'd like to join him. She arrived the next day. Ted
claimed in his memoirs that it was Jess who surprised him by
climbing into his bed: whichever way it was, their east coast
village idyll was quickly shattered by the arrival of an enquiry
agent sent by May. Jess decided to stay with Ted, and although
he claimed that she was no more in love with him than he with
her, they returned to live together at Hackbridge.

To recoup the losses of the season, the Lyceum company set
out on a further tour. It began rather wretchedly in the suburbs
of London, amid intense heat and a tram strike, and ended far
more seriously for Irving in Edinburgh, in the October, where
he went down with pneumonia and pleurisy and nearly died.

'I am still fearfully anxious about H.,' Ellen wrote to Edy.

It will be a long time at best before he regains strength. . . .
All he wants is for me to keep my health – not my *head*! He
knows I'm doing that! Last night I did three acts of *Sans-
Gêne*, with *Nance Oldfield* thrown in! That is a bit too much

– awful work – and I cant risk it again. . . . A telegram just come: 'Steadily improving'.[31]

To offset debts, Irving had to sell most of his theatrical books and prints – his lifelong interest. He had become an old man; ill and depressed about the future. Then, in January 1899, Joe Comyns Carr made him a financial proposition. A syndicate (made up of himself and his two brothers) would relieve Irving of all his financial responsibility, taking over the remaining eight years of the Lyceum's lease – in return for Irving's services and interests in the Lyceum. He would have to play at least one hundred performances at the Lyceum and guarantee to tour Britain or America for at least four months in every year – in both cases sharing profits with the company. Against Bram Stoker's advice, Irving signed.

Ellen's extensive diary entry for January 1899 gives an insight into her own feelings about Irving at the time and his plans:

Poor old King H. is at his downest. . . . We have all (his friends) helped him a little. No word from him, however! Is it shyness? Indifference? Anger? *What?* I rather think self-consciousness by indifference out of conceit! It sounds hard, but I think this is just true.

He wrote and asked me to go down and see him at Bournemouth. I went, and found him looking much better. He wanted to tell me that not only was he broken in health but he was what is called 'ruined.' At which word I refused to shed tears, for, said I: 'As long as you and I have health, we have means of wealth. We can pack a bag, each of us, and trot round the Provinces. Yes, and go to America, Australia, India, Japan, and pick up money by the bushel, even were we to take just the magic book of Shakespeare alone with us.'

I then asked his plans, and he astonished me by saying: 'That's why I asked you to come down to Bournemouth. (He might have written, but no; he'd not *write* that.) I propose – have in fact written to the managers – going round the English provinces with a very small company, and playing *The Bells, Louis XI, Waterloo* and perhaps another play.' Long pause. I didn't think it *possible* I heard aright. '*What*

plays?' said I. '*Bells, Louis, Waterloo*,' he said irritably.
'Well, and where do *I* come in?' said I. 'Oh well, for the
present, at all events, there's no chance of acting at the
Lyceum.' (He looked exceedingly silly.) 'For the present, you
can, of course, er, *do as you like!*'

I felt – a good many feelings! At top of all came
amusement to save the situation. 'Then,' said I, 'I have in
plain terms what Ted would call "the dirty kick out?" '

'Well – er – for the present I don't see what can be done,
and I daresay you –' I cut him short. 'Oh, I daresay I shall get
along somehow. Have I your permission to shift for myself,
and make up a tour for myself?' 'Yes.' 'For how long?' 'Well,
I can scarcely say.' 'Until Christmas next?' 'Yes.'[32]

Ellen returned to London and at once arranged a six-week
tour with Frank Cooper from 30 January. That was all she
would have time for, with the syndicate's insistence that she
and Irving play at the Lyceum every season, from April to July,
before going on tour.

Recovering slowly, Irving staged Sardou's play *Robespierre*
on 15 April 1899. Ellen, who told Shaw that if Irving were not
in the dumps just then, she'd 'see him further' before appearing
in it, thought it a wonderfully showy play, even if a bad one,
and was cheerful at its first night success. What really pleased
her was that Irving employed Edy to redesign the costumes and
she told Shaw that Edy had made crowds of excellent dresses
for nothing: 'She is a tremendous organiser, and a first-rate
worker. She's a duck!'

The success of the costumes was a breakthrough for Edy,
making her decide to be a theatrical costumier. She was now
nearly thirty and this was her first chance of a really
independent job. Although she had toured successfully with the
Charringtons' company for a year or so, she had then returned
to the Lyceum where, as a walk-on actress, she had little chance
of distinguishing herself. Fortunately, Irving knew of her flair
for costume design and that, since childhood, she had amassed
a reference collection of pictures of fashion, people and places.
He also remembered how, in America, she had devised the
costumes for *Godefroi and Yolande*, including Ellen's spectacular scarlet gown, out of next to nothing.

Edy's flair with costume on that tour was recalled by another

actress, May Whitty, who replaced her as Jessica in *The
Merchant of Venice* one night.

> When I was tremblingly making up, and asked for my dress,
> the dresser produced many scarves and bits and pieces and
> said Miss Edy always fixed these herself! By the aid of the
> dresser and many safety-pins I managed to adjust these
> strange, shapeless materials into some semblance of a dress,
> and I decided I must watch Edy at work another time.[33]

After her success with the *Robespierre* costumes, Edy started
up business as a theatrical costumier in Henrietta Street,
Covent Garden. She was still not economically independent of
Ellen, who financed her business initially and continued to
support it, for Edy's success was artistic rather than financial.
Both children had been spoiled by Ellen and grew up to look on
her as an unlimited source of money. Her letters to Ted
frequently contained money and, just as frequently, a scolding.
One of these, which enclosed £100, is headed, 'This makes
£500,' and continues: 'Do you understand that *as yet* I am not
out of debt . . . I am pencilling in autumn tours of 20 weeks,
for *I must go on* or what will become of us?' Another says,
'You must be careful dear not to lose cheques – it gives *such* a
lot of trouble – to the bank I mean – not to me.' A third ends:
'PS – Gas cut off – I had that once, it don't hurt much. I give
Edy nothing in the way of either money, work, nor position –
she earns it by serving to the best of her ability in the way I
want to be *served* – and she does not worry the life out of me
beyond my bearing powers.'[34] Despite her frustrations over
Ted's constant begging, Ellen was too soft-hearted to stop
sending money whenever he asked for it.

Irving remained in *Robespierre*, despite an infected lung, and
planned to tour America in the autumn. Ellen was concerned at
the idea, as he was having bad coughing fits, but the Lyceum's
losses had to be recouped somehow. She showed him Shaw's
Caesar and Cleopatra, but wrote to Shaw in May that year to
say that she was now certain that Irving would never produce
anything of his. Shaw was uncaring, replying that he didn't
want Ellen to do Cleopatra: 'She is an animal – a bad lot.
Yours is a beneficent personality.'

That summer of 1899 saw Ted involved in working again
with his old friend Martin Shaw. Martin Shaw had recently

started the Purcell Operatic Society and, wanting to put on *Dido and Aeneas*, asked Ted for new ideas on staging this. For almost a year the production of the opera preoccupied Ted, who left his cottage in Hackbridge and moved up to London with Jess, to be nearer to Shaw in Hampstead. The following year, Ted's production of *Dido and Aeneas* marked his emergence as a stage director.

CHAPTER 12

EDY: TWICE LOVED

The year 1899 was also a crucial one for Edy, for she met Christopher St John again.

Christopher St John was born Christabel Marshall, but took part of St John The Baptist's name on converting to Catholicism. She had met Edy only briefly three years before, in Ellen's dressing room at the Lyceum. She had 'fallen in love' with Ellen after seeing her act in *Ravenswood* and, like the rest of the band of Ellen's young women worshippers, had sent her presents, letters, poems and flowers.

Her reward was the occasional letter from Ellen and, finally, an invitation to the dressing room during the run of *King Arthur*. Chris St John remembered it in detail: Ellen scrubbing her face at the washstand before she made up, telling Chris that her clever letters always made Ellen wish she had been better educated. They met Edy in the corridor, and Ellen explained that Edy always stood in for her during the vision in the prologue, because she could never stand still as long as that: 'Fidgeting is one of my worst faults.'

Edy couldn't remember this meeting: her mother was always accompanied by one or other of her satellites and Edy had little time for them. For the next three years, Chris, now at Oxford, had no further contact with Ellen. Then she sent her a poem and got a further invitation to join Ellen at Fulham, during her tour of surburban theatres with Frank Cooper early in 1899.

Edy recalled Chris arriving in a red coat and small black three-cornered hat, and being told by Ellen to look after her, as she knew nothing about the theatre. This was no new task and Chris was aware of getting a reluctant welcome. Edy was mending a mitten at the time and accidentally pricked Chris with the needle. 'Cupid's dart,' said Chris later, 'for I loved Edy from that moment.'

The feeling was to become mutual. Edy admitted to Chris that she had felt antagonistic at first as her mother's girl adorers were apt to become a nuisance if encouraged. 'But I liked you at once, all the same,' she said. 'How pleased I was when mother asked you to come home to supper with us that night at Fulham. You didn't seem like a stranger. You "fitted in," as mother said after you had gone.'[1]

Chris remembered it all vividly: Ellen grilling kidneys over the dining-room fire; the creamed rice that Edy preferred; the light-hearted conversation between mother and daughter. The next day she and Edy had lunch, Edy calling for her at Great Cumberland Place where Chris worked each morning as secretary to Lady Randolph Churchill, and occasionally for her son, Winston. They lunched near the Lyceum, so that Edy could get back quickly to her work making the costumes for *Robespierre*.

Although she was not quite thirty, Edy's near black hair already had one white lock in it. Chris, smitten, recalled that her brown eyes, set wide apart, were her most beautiful feature.

> The nose was rather too long, though its upward tilt deceived one about that. The straight lips were a fault in her mouth, which otherwise was very like her mother's. She had a lovely slender figure in those days, and looked taller than she was (about 5 foot 8 inches) owing to her elevation. Her carriage was perfect in its grace . . . warm, mellow, deep, resonant give only faint clues to what Edy's voice was like. It had a penetrating timbre, rather like that of an oboe.[2]

Edy spoke vigorously and unaffectedly, and expressed herself concisely, but she didn't regard talking as an occupation in itself: she would disconcert Chris by always doing some small job at the same time, like sketching costumes, or sorting programmes and press-cuttings.

In the autumn of 1899, Ellen left for her last tour of America with Irving. She welcomed Edy's plan to join Chris while she was away, and the two of them took a Queen Anne house in Smith Square, Westminster. It was recklessly beyond their means, but they were to live there for six years.

Their style of living was decidedly casual, according to Irene

Cooper Willis, a friend of both women:

> The atmosphere was quite undomestic, the telephone rang
> incessantly, Edy and Chris shouted commands from different
> headquarters, and all the things that I had been brought up
> to believe should be done first, bed-making, dusting and
> washing up, were done last or, quite likely, not done at all.[3]

Nicknamed 'The Squares,' Edy and Chris, in striking hats
adorned with drooping cocks' feathers, lunched and dined
constantly at the Gourmets Restaurant with artists, painters
and actresses. For Edy, living away from home for the first
time, it was all enthrallingly independent. Chris, too, was
exceptionally happy, having had no previous serious relationship. She was a very plain woman, heavily built with a slight
limp, and a speech impediment (a taxi driver, unable to
understand her attempt to say 'Smith Square', had once told
her to go to hell)[4], and Edy's deepening friendship meant a
great deal to her.

When Ellen returned from America, Chris claimed she
accused her of having enticed Edy away from her house in
Barkston Gardens and of coming between the two of them. In
Hungerheart, an anonymous autobiography, with disguised
names, published in 1915, Chris writes of Louise's [Ellen's]
jealousy on finding that her daughter is not coming back to live
with her. She describes Sally's [Edy's] reaction to this:

> It's nothing to do with you, and mother knows it. When I
> was a little girl I made up my mind I would leave home when
> I was twenty-eight. I think women ought to, whether they
> marry or not.
>   You don't know mother. She wants me because I have
> gone away. When I lived at home I hardly ever saw her . . .
> partly because she was never there and partly because she
> can never bear to be with any one for long at a time. Please
> don't think she doesn't love me. Of course she does –
> tremendously; at the same time she has all sorts of ideas and
> sentiments that she doesn't wish realised. One of them is my
> living with her and looking after her. No one can look after
> my mother.[5]

Ellen, despite her admiring coterie of young women, had
relied on Edy's help for years. She was miserable if Edy went

off on tour or was away for long and, as Edy was now thirty, had taken it for granted that she would always live at home. It was a selfish hope, perhaps, but a jealous reaction to Chris would have been understandable. In *Hungerheart*, however, Chris observed that 'Louise' in a very short time,

> overcame her dislike to me, and ceased to treat me as an interloper. . . . I found myself treated as a son-in-law might have been treated. Louise and I discussed 'Sally's' health, Sally's talents, Sally's looks, Sally's clothes. I became the willing slave of both mother and daughter.[6]

The letters Ellen wrote to Edy shortly after her return from America bear this out, as they show no hint of strain. She mentioned Chris St John frequently, in a casual, friendly way, asking how her story for the *Daily Mail* was getting on, or thanking both 'girls' for their birthday presents:

> The bag was lovely and as for the head wrap – it makes me long to go out to 'a damned party in a parlour.' How beautifully it was done. . . . Thank you my minx. Just the sort of present I like. Chris was naughty (but nice) to spend her money on me. You must make her understand I don't very much like to have presents – and costly ones – 'rich gifts' positively pain me – I can't tell her this, but you will know how – I wouldn't hurt her for the world.[7]

Ellen had stayed in America for eight months, from October 1899 to June 1900. Before going, she had unsuccessfully tried to persuade Irving to include *Captain Brassbound's Conversion* in the repertory over there, though she dared not tell Irving that Shaw was the author. Shaw in fact had based the part of Lady Cicely Waynflete in the play on the picture he had of Ellen through her letters, though Edy said that, unlike Ellen, Lady Cicely was not clever, humorous or vital and lacked humanity. Ellen herself was rather disappointed with the play.

But she enjoyed her American tour, writing to a friend to say that amazing New York was more amazing than ever. She was amused to hear about a man being held up in the street for a mere ten cents, and a society column's announcement that 'Mrs Otis will hold a *Welsh Rarebit* in honor of her niece.' Only the Boer War in South Africa, which had started that year over the treatment of British subjects in the Transvaal, upset her. 'The war – and the disgrace of it (beef-headed Buller's doings) – this is the only subject which excites me and makes me want to kill, Kill, KILL!'[8]

But her professional career was also preoccupying Ellen: she was now fifty two and needed to assess her future carefully. She wrote again to Shaw from America in January 1900 to say she would return to the Lyceum for a few months, then never again act with Irving. Instead, she would do *Captain Brassbound's Conversion* in London, then a two year farewell tour around England and America, and then retire 'as a dear old Frump in an arm chair in one of my pretty cottages, and teach Ted's youngest babes to be rather useful and not to trouble about little things.'

Her plans then changed twice. Irving offered her a tour of America beginning that autumn, which Ellen thought it practical and more profitable to take, apologised to Shaw and asked him to cast *Brassbound* without her. Irving then about-turned and postponed the tour for a year and Ellen told Shaw that she was disgusted not at her weakness, but her strength in 'sticking on with folk who wont "play fair" ' and that she was 'deeply furious (inwardly) that all my desire for Brassbound is all of no use!'

Yet despite her exasperation with Irving, Ellen's notes during the tour praised as well as criticised him. Just before their return, she wrote: 'April, 1900. H. has sciatica badly. Really he has a very dull time of it, it seems to me, and I believe for the first time begins to appreciate my very long service, to know I am valuable.'[9]

Public interest in Britain that year was fixed on the Boer War. On 17, 18 and 19 May, after seven months of preparation, Ted and Martin Shaw staged performances of Purcell's *Dido and Aeneas*. At the time, the country was waiting to hear if the British garrison in Mafeking had been saved and half way through the last performance, when newsboys could be heard shouting that Mafeking had been relieved, half the audience rushed out to buy a paper.

Ted's production was highly praised, but it still had a deficit of £180, and Ted asked his mother for help. She sent him £2, with the promise of a further £2 weekly to come, and a note saying, 'I enclose the first £2, *not* for trying to pay off any futile debt, but for *necessaries*. A chop – a toothbrush – a Boot – A Bed.'

After their return from America, the company opened at the Lyceum in yet another revival of *Olivia*. 'Too bad!' wrote Ellen in her notes. 'Every one, but H., is about half my age. I'm angry at having to do it, but patience!'[10]

Irving spent his holidays that summer, as usual now, with Mrs Aria, who was impressed by the almost royal way he travelled – with the station master preceding him up the platform, carrying his top hat. But the Lyceum company's extended winter tour proved too much for him and he became ill again. Ellen, though admitting that she was terrified by his exhaustion and feebleness, found him icy and indifferent as soon as he recovered.

Writing to Shaw in November, she said:

> Ah, I feel so certain Henry just hates me! I can only *guess* at it, for he is exactly the same sweet-mannered person he was when 'I felt so certain' Henry loved me! We have not met for years now, except before other people, where my conduct exactly matches his of course. All my own fault. It is *I* am changed, not he. It's all right, but it has squeezed me up dreadfully.[11]

She became ill and told Shaw that she only wished she could use this as an excuse to retire to her farmhouse in Smallhythe, Kent.

Ellen had bought this timbered, sixteenth century farmhouse two months previously. She had first seen it by chance some years before, when driving around the marshlands between Rye and Tenterden with Irving, and promptly decided this was where she would like to live and die. She asked the old shepherd living there if it was a nice house ('No,' he said) and if he'd tell her should it ever be for sale. In the autumn of 1900 she got an unsigned postcard, with a Tenterden postmark, saying merely 'House for sale,' and sent Edy to have a look around. Edy went down with Chris St John, and was immediately enthusiastic – deciding at once that one room, into which she could hardly see as it was filled with fleeces, would be her mother's bedroom. Two adjacent cottages and a large barn went with the farmhouse and Ellen, on buying the property, let Edy and Chris live in the Priest's House, one of the cottages.

Ellen Terry's Cottage, Small Hythe.

Ellen Terry's house at Smallhythe, near Tenterden, Kent in 1906. Now belonging to the National Trust.

On 30 November, Oscar Wilde died in Paris from cerebral meningitis. His plays – which he dubbed 'those modern drawing room plays with pink lampshades' – had been phenomenally successful. They were commissioned and staged by George Alexander, the young manager of the St James's Theatre, or Beerbohm Tree, who managed the Haymarket Theatre, both of whom – unlike Irving – recognised that Wilde's plays caught the mood of the public.

The Christmas of 1900 saw the first production of *Captain Brassbound's Conversion*, at the Old Strand Theatre. Ellen was delighted that Laurence Irving was to play Captain Brassbound, though less so that Janet Achurch was to be Lady Cicely Waynflete ('It is too, too bad that I am not Lady C,' she said).

But the most memorable thing about the performance was that Ellen met Shaw for the first time. Their belief that a meeting might spoil their paper courtship seemed oddly borne out: fifteen months were to pass before their correspondence resumed and, for the next twenty or so years, they wrote only some three or four letters a year to each other. She was to tell him, 'They say you could not bear me, when we met, that one time, under the stage.'

In fact the drastic reduction in the number of letters, and the gradual change from flirtation to friendship, had already begun before their meeting and was a natural result of Shaw finding a new confidante in Charlotte Payne Townshend, whom he had married in 1898; and of his lessening need to attack Irving, as Irving's partnership with Ellen was breaking up of its own accord.

In late January 1901, the streets of London were hung with crepe, in mourning for Queen Victoria, who had died on the twenty second of that month. Irving was busy working on designs for a production of *Coriolanus*, with Ellen as Volumnia, as yet unseeing that for the Lyceum, too, it was the end of an era.

When Irving and Ellen began their partnership, there were only three main theatres housing permanent companies: now high quality plays throughout the West End were attracting audiences – plays by Oscar Wilde, Bernard Shaw, Arthur Pinero, J.M. Barrie and Henry Arthur Jones. Despite the obvious popularity of such plays, Irving stuck firmly to Shakespeare, sentimental comedies by the French playwright,

Victorien Sardou (which Shaw referred to dismissively as Sardoodledum), historical plays or melodramas. Pressed to produce Ibsen's *The Pretenders*, Ellen recalls him reading it, full of hope, then 'was left staring before him all through the night wondering was he or all his friends stark staring raving mad!'

The old spark was not revived for *Coriolanus*, which opened at the Lyceum on 15 April 1901 and was a failure. Irving wore a disfiguring beard, which made it difficult to see his face or hear him; Ellen was politely admired as 'a stately figure.' It was a dull affair.

In the autumn, she and Irving once more set out for America. They were spending more time there than in England. It was an exhausting seven month tour: Irving was now sixty three, Ellen ten years younger. But she was being paid £300 a week and as she virtually had to support her son and daughter, other dependents, her homes in London and the country – and the sixty or so requests a week from the public for financial help, some of which she responded to – the money was too good to refuse.

When they returned in March 1902, it was to find that the London County Council was insisting on stringent fire precautions at the Lyceum that would cost £20,000. There was not enough capital to pay this: at the end of the coming season, the Receiver would have to be called in.

Irving decided to re-stage *Faust*. Ellen at her age could hardly play the virginal Marguerite, and it was given to Cecilia Loftus. It left Ellen depressed about the future. Shaw wrote to say he had rejected Lily Langtry's offer of putting on *Brassbound* at the new theatre she had built at Westminster, the Imperial, and that he had been forced into this ungentlemanly and unbusinesslike course 'by an angry desire to seize Miss Ellen Terry by the hair and make her play Lady Cicely.' But Ellen was unsure the play would appeal.

She went down to Stratford to play Queen Katherine during the Shakespeare Birthday Festival which made her feel, she said, that 'there was life in this old 'un yet.' Herbert Tree obviously thought so too, asking her if she would play Mrs Page in *The Merry Wives of Windsor* at Her Majesty's. Ellen delighted in the rollicking production of *The Merry Wives*, which was just her style. One night she put a pin in the padding worn by Falstaff and delightedly watched his whole stomach slowly collapse.

Ellen hurrying to rehearsal in Philadelphia, during her tour of America in 1901.

The hundreds of letters – many of them love letters – from the public cheered her enormously and she was also pleased that Edy was the costumier for the production, writing in her diary, 'Edy has a real genius for dresses for the stage.' She had reason to thank her: when Ellen's dress was burnt during a fire in her dressing room, Edy had produced a new one by the same night.

In June, London prepared for the coronation of Edward VII, and Irving decided to hold a last, memorable reception at the Lyceum in honour of the king, who was his patron and friend. Although the king's illness caused the coronation to be postponed, the reception went ahead. According to Mrs Aria, the Lyceum Theatre was an Arabian Nights scene, with the stage hung in crimson velvet, huge palms covering the footlights and an enormous Union Jack made up of red, white and blue lights, stretching across the front of the dress circle. Irving played host to a procession of Eastern highnesses, wearing blazing jewelled turbans.[12]

The season ended with a matinee on 19 July, with Ellen acting Portia to Irving's Shylock. 'I shall never be in this theatre again. I feel it . . . I know it,' she said to him after their last curtain call. Her prophecy was right. Within a few months the Lyceum theatre company had gone into liquidation and the dimming lights had gone out.

Irving was planning to produce *Dante* by Sardou, at the Theatre Royal Drury Lane in April of the following year, 1903, then take it to America. He offered Ellen a large sum to accompany him to America, but she read the play, saw no part in it for herself, and turned him down. Later that year she wrote to Shaw to say that 'Henry is pretending he is not furious with me, and that makes me feel a guilty wretch for refusing to speak a few lines in his old *Dante*.' She and Irving were never to act together again.

Ellen was, for the first time in some twenty years, now faced with having to decide her own future. She told Shaw she was nervous about renting a theatre herself, then changed her mind and leased the Imperial Theatre. Her intention was to form a company of her own and produce plays in conjunction with her son, Ted. Although it meant risking her savings – and Ellen was very conscious that she relied on these for her old age – she thought the venture might help not just her own career, but her children's too.

Edy, for instance, undoubtedly had a high reputation among the few as a theatrical costumier. But her *atelier* in Covent Garden never made money and Ellen always had to support it. With her own company, she could commission Edy to make the costumes from Ted's designs and get her work more widely known.

The same applied to Ted. Ellen thought him a brilliant designer and producer and had been stunned by his production of *The Masque of Love* in March the previous year, with its beautiful movements and colour effects; and delighted by the critical acclaim he received for this and *Dido and Aeneas*. But his audiences had been small. And despite his shiningly creative talent, no one offered him a post as producer or stage manager. At the Imperial, Ellen could let all London see his worth.

She also hoped that it would stop Ted losing so much money on his productions. She had sent yet another angry letter to him earlier that year, when he had asked for money for his new venture, *Acis and Galatea*, a two-act pastoral opera by Handel, saying

> You have strength and talents and opportunities, and you must finish this bill paying by yourself. Sixty pounds just before I came away – Thirty afterwards – Two hundred I stand for, in honour to Saunders for you, & now Sixty-three Pounds – it is in all about upon £400 – & you say in your letter 'these pin pricks worry me' – Good Lord! *Pin Pricks*!! my patience is fast going.[13]

Ted's personal life at the time was in no better shape. After producing *Dido and Aeneas*, he and Jess Dorynne went to relax in the country, where Jess broke it to him that she was expecting their child. Ted always believed, when wife or mistress became pregnant, that it was a deliberate move to trap him. He thought himself sophisticated; and professionally he was. But personally, he was still immature and self-absorbed, swinging from enthusiasm to enthusiasm: from woman to woman; from acting to graphic artist to music. Faced yet again with fatherhood, he reacted irresponsibly, running away from Jess and returning to London.

Back in Hampstead, he threw his energy into collaborating with Martin Shaw on *The Masque of Love*. Martin's friend and neighbour was the artist, Signor Gaetano Meo; and Meo had a daughter, Elena, twenty two years old and a violinist. Susceptible as ever, within seventeen days of meeting her Ted was writing of her magnificent black eyes, noble brow and clear white skin.[14] Elena was a Roman Catholic and, Jess and the new baby apart, Ted was still married to May. Three months later, in March 1902, to the fury of Elena's father, Ted and Elena ran away together.

They returned to live in Kensington – Elena soon becoming pregnant – and in the December of that year, Ted produced Laurence Housman's musical nativity play, *Bethlehem*. Ellen at the time was trying to decide which play she should open with at the Imperial Theatre and Ted advised her to put on Ibsen's *The Vikings of Helgeland*, a tragedy based on an Icelandic saga. Ellen agreed, 'not thinking so much of the play's suitability for me, as of its suitability for my son.'

She also consciously broke away from the constrictions of choice she had experienced at the Lyceum, writing in her memoirs that

> I hope it will be remembered, when I am spoken of after my death as a 'Victorian' actress, lacking in enterprise, an actress belonging to the 'old school' that I produced a spectacular play of Ibsen's in a manner which possibly anticipated the scenic ideas of the future by a century.[15]

Ted asked Martin Shaw to compose the music and the play opened on 15 April 1903, with Ellen playing Hiordis, a fierce warrior queen – not a part that came naturally to her. Martin Shaw considered the play the real beginning of Ted's work – but after the first night, Ellen wrote in her diary: 'All played well and all went well until 3rd Act when I forgot most of my words and the whole thing went to pieces.' Although the audience applauded, she was right in her prediction that it would prove an artistic success only. It was further handicapped by the theatre being out of the West End and the play being insufficiently advertised. Within a month it was taken off. Needing to put on another play quickly, Ellen played safe with *Much Ado About Nothing*. Bernard Shaw praised the way Ted produced it, but it, too, closed for lack of audiences. To replace the money she had lost, Ellen was forced to go on a provincial tour.

During the season, Edy, as costumier, and Martin Shaw, as

composer, were naturally together a great deal. In June, after the season was over, Ted wrote in his diary:

> About this time (1903) my friend Martin Shaw seems to have proposed to my sister Edy. E.T. was greatly disturbed and came to see me about it, as though it was any of my business. She said it was to be prevented and I must help her to prevent it. Well, all I could do was to do nothing except agree dutifully with E.T. – but the matter seems to have been pretty soon forgotten. For they did not elope – and real lovers always do that if any obstruction is encountered. So E.T. was right after all.[16]

Ted's calm assertion that real lovers always elope was based on his own behaviour and that of his parents. But his remark about the love affair coming to nothing, and Ellen being right after all, clearly implies that Ellen believed Edy and Martin were not really in love.

It's not clear why Ellen should have been so disturbed about the projected marriage. She had already 'lost' Edy to Chris: would marriage make so much difference? Had her dominant feelings of possessiveness been triggered by there being a man involved? True, Martin had a disfiguring birthmark on his face, but Edy was unconcerned by this. Ted, though admitting Martin was a bit gruff in manner, said he was also immensely kind, and played the piano with intense brilliance.

Chris St John mentions Martin's disfigurement in *Hunger-heart*. Her description is not an attractive one; but then she was naturally biased against him.

> He was sickly, stunted, and had a disfigurement which made sensitive people avert their eyes quickly from his face. But he was not sensitive about his affliction. He seemed to be proud of it, to brazen it out, to wear it as a *panache*, which made compassion for him difficult.[17]

A letter Ellen wrote to Ted at this time shows that Ellen was relatively unperturbed by Martin's disfigurement, or his lack of funds:

> Edy there tonight at the play with the Hildermans . . . and crew you introduced to her – oh, I feel so wild with you when I see her with them. Poor Chris seems to be having an

awful time of it. . . . They all and others went round to Smith Square afterwards. I took Chris round there for they had left her behind at the theatre. . . . M.S. was not there – anyway I suppose I want you to tell me what there is against him except his misfortunate personal appearance, his poverty. The Hildermans are backing E. up and saying 'How fine' etc – *Wait!* – Poor Edy is absolutely naughty to me . . . her attitude to me I mean – I'm sick at heart and cry my eyes out all through the night – I don't think the affair will come off somehow – with no gilt on the gingerbread they will get sick of each other I believe – oh I am just *mad* with Edy this moment.[18]

If, according to this letter, Ellen had little against Martin Shaw, even if she thought the affair wouldn't last, why (according to Ted) was she then so 'greatly disturbed' about Edy and Martin? Was it just possessiveness? Chris St John in *Hungerheart* claims Ellen felt far more strongly than Ted realised

I found out that Louise [Ellen] hated him as much as I did. This gave me hope, a hope of which I was ashamed. As Robin [Martin Shaw] had no money, and Sally [Edy] was dependent on her mother, they could hardly leave Louise out of their reckoning. Would Louise stop Sally's allowance if they married? This seemed to me unlikely, but I thought it quite likely that she would reduce it.[19]

Edy might have ignored Ellen's opposition to the marriage. What she found it impossible to do was fight against the double pressure of both Ellen and Chris. Chris became hysterical at the idea of Edy marrying. Her account of the episode in *Hungerheart*, is full of purple passion:

One horrible moment. . . . A bomb hurtling through the serene air of my paradise, exploding with a noise of devils' laughter, tearing up immemorial trees by the roots, laying waste the greenery of hope and faith – then filth, stench, corruption – then nothing, no suffering even – nothing.
    'Yes, I care for him,' said Sally. 'I want to marry him.'
    'That deformity,' I cried . . . behind my hot forehead my brain felt like ice. I remembered clearly a bottle of cocaine lotion in the bathroom, which had been prescribed for my

ear-ache. I went in and drank it without a moment's hesitation.[20]

Chris nearly killed herself by doing this. Edy looked after her until she recovered. She may have realised Chris's action was emotional blackmail: in any event, she didn't give up seeing Martin. Yet nothing was to come of their relationship. Chris in *Hungerheart* wrote:

How it ended I never knew. Sally did not marry Robin. Her love affair fizzled out. She never spoke of it, she never explained. Her heart was not broken. Perhaps the hearts of people who have work don't break. At this time Sally threw herself with immense energy into arranging a long tour for her mother.[21]

The broken romance contributed to a rift between Edy and Ted, however. In the December of 1903, Ellen wrote to Ted to say:

You and Edy quarrelling has finished me nearly . . . and shown me we are all standing on the brink of a height from which we shall assuredly topple and be useless any of us *to help the other* – unless something is done at once to avert the catastrophe.

Another letter at that time read:

I hear you rushed into my little house the other day when Edy was there and took no notice of her! I do wish you wd be *better mannered* at least in the new year.[22]

Recalling the trauma years later, Chris wrote: 'I think our life together subsequently was all the happier, because we did not break open the grave of the thing past which had threatened to separate us.'[23] They never separated again, Chris being with Edy when she died at Smallhythe in 1947.

It was never clear whether Ellen realised the close nature of Edy and Chris's relationship – that they were living together as lovers – or whether she thought they were just casual flatmates. There is certainly no hint of awareness in any of her letters; but then so many of these were destroyed – first by Ellen, then on her death, by Edy and, on Edy's death, by Chris and Tony. Because of the destruction of such evidence, it also cannot

Relaxing in the garden at Smallhythe: left to right, Christopher St John, Edy and Ellen.

be proved whether Edy and Chris were sexual lovers. In *Hungerheart*, Chris portrays herself as a congenital lesbian, but says that Sally (Edy) liked men 'if they behaved well.' She implies that 'Sally' was sexually reserved and that their physical contact was confined to hand-holding. But she writes of their relationship as being one of warmth:

> We fought sometimes, but we loved – that was the great point. Even our fights were interesting, and our reconciliations bound us together more closely. . . . Did she love me because I was a waif and stray? What attracted her to me? She never told me. The foundation of our happiness together was a harmony of taste rather than a harmony of character. . . . We were as happy as a newly-married pair, perhaps happier; and we certainly disproved the tradition that women were incapable of friendship.

It was possible that there could have been some kind of sexual element in their friendship: certainly Chris, in later years, spent a night with Vita Sackville West.

Ellen may have deliberately not faced up to the truth about Edy and Chris, even in her own mind: or possibly, despite open relationships among theatrical people, she simply didn't know about female homosexuality: Queen Victoria, after all, was meant to have refused to sign an act that would have made female homosexuality illegal on the grounds that it didn't, couldn't possibly, exist: a 'good woman' in those times was expected to be sexually passive towards all-comers.

Victorians might have castigated Oscar Wilde for his homosexuality, but the sentimental, so-called 'romantic friendships' among women were accepted less emotionally and not discouraged until around the turn of the century, when the theories of the sexologists, like Freud, began to be more widely known. The hostility that Wilde's homosexuality evoked was not publicly paraded against female homosexuals until 1928, when Radclyffe Hall's lesbian novel, *The Well of Loneliness* was banned as obscene in a sensational court case.

Ellen had shown herself to be sympathetic to Oscar Wilde: homosexuality as such didn't worry her. But if she did not realise the closeness of her daughter's relationship with Chris, it was because Edy, aware that she would have resented this, didn't tell her. Mother and daughter might have been close, but there were no sexual confidences or understanding between them.

Children often find it difficult to confide in a parent, and Edy must have found it particularly hard with a mother who was out and away a lot, tired through overwork, and invariably had a host of people surrounding her. Despite her mother's affectionate pride in her, and dependence on her, Edy had had to become self-reliant. She successfully developed her own rather acerbic character, despite Ellen's strong, dominating personality, and viewed the world drily and caustically from an early age. Ellen might not have had time for private confidences: Edy was to have no inclination for them.

Ellen, as her letters to Edy and Bernard Shaw show, also tended to try to manage her daughter's life, believing that mother knows best. A professional herself, she put her energies into helping Edy's career rather than providing a comforting shoulder for her private anxieties. In Ellen's defence, Edy, an essentially private person, never gave the impression that she had any.

Edy's career took a new direction after the failure of *The Vikings*; in the provincial tour Ellen went on afterwards, she acted as stage director. From then on, her workshop in Covent Garden foundering, play production became her main interest. It was already Ted's main preoccupation, but after *The Vikings*, he could find no one interested in backing him further to produce plays, and rather sourly commented:

> So when it became obvious to me that E.T. could only carry on with one of her children, I decided to get along to Germany and to Russia and other lands where my notions were regarded without prejudice, and progress was preferred to argumentative retrogression.[24]

Irving meanwhile sailed for New York alone at the start of his American tour. 'It will be strange and somewhat sad without Nell,' he was to write to his friend, the critic William Winter, before he left, 'poor dear, she has been absolutely under the influence and spell of her two children – who have launched her on a sea of troubles.'[25]

He was not just referring to the money Ellen had lost over *The Vikings*; but the disagreement the play had caused between

Ted, Ellen and Edy – which contributed to the iciness between Edy and Ted, initiated by the Martin Shaw episode. Ted criticised Ellen for lacking strength and experience as an actor manager, having always relied on Irving. And he criticised Edy for tolerating what he called a female 'obstructionist' in her costume department who, he claimed, upset Ellen and played off people against one another. Ellen should have sacked her immediately, he said:

> She would flare up, for no reason, about the cut of a cloak or
> the colour of a cloth, and anathematize me and all the male
> members of the company. . . I think she is not to be held
> entirely responsible for her devilry – for she had become one
> of the suffragettes.[26]

It is hardly surprising that Ted was appalled by the feminist outlook of the suffragettes. His attitude to women is summed up by his remark to Isadora Duncan, with whom he had a later affair: 'Why do you want to go on the stage and wave your arms about? Why don't you stay at home and sharpen my pencils?'[27] But though Ted did what he could to help women busy themselves at home – having ten children in all, five being illegitimate – he couldn't stem changes in society. The year 1903 saw the founding of The Women's Social and Political Union, by Mrs Emmeline Pankhurst and two of her daughters, Christabel and Sylvia – a militant organisation, campaigning for women's enfranchisement to have the vote.

It was not the first organisation in the field: the National Union of Women's Suffrage Societies had been active since 1861. But the intellectual approach of the NUWSS had not achieved any concessions, and many felt it was time to take a stronger line. Middle-class women at the start of the Edwardian era were better educated and less able to tolerate the constant child-bearing and management of large households that had totally occupied their mothers. Living was also becoming simpler then – clothes were less ornate, etiquette less demanding. This gave women more free time – which was welcomed until they found they could do little with it. Their activities were still strictly limited to those considered 'acceptable': they were certainly not allowed entry into the all-male world of politics.

Ellen was fortunate in that she could hardly visualise a life frustrated by the lack of a responsible job. She had worked all her life in one of the few professions where there was equality: and for many years, she earned more money than most men in Britain. Cicely Hamilton, the actress and suffragette campaigner, recalls in her autobiography that it was through 'the movement' that she first met Ellen, 'whom her daughter, Edy Craig, had stirred up to interest. Not, I think, that she needed much stirring; Ellen, who had worked, and worked hard, all her life, probably took it for granted that women had a right to citizenship.'[28]

The attitude of the times hardly encouraged other women to follow suit. An article in the *Daily Express* in 1906 summed this up:

> To a woman with any stimulus of ambition the stage must offer a life replete with exaltation and triumph – so full of satisfaction, in short, as to afford perhaps half the pleasure which comes from a marriage of affection and a happy home. If any women today are disposed to envy Miss Terry her fifty years of success, they may take consultation from this reflection.

Such attitudes fed the growing anger among women. At the time Ellen was hardly aware of women's changing attitudes, being busy touring and relaxing at Smallhythe. 'Edy is here,' she wrote to Shaw in the summer of 1904,

> Did I tell you she is my right hand, and still growing to be my left hand, and happy as a sandboy all the while? I fear to be too happy in her – I try to be very quiet with it all. She has a cottage of her own here and we visit each other every day![29]

Later that year, Ellen moved from Barkston Gardens to 215 King's Road, Chelsea, a small early Georgian panelled house, where she lived until 1921.

The suffragettes' hard work was to be rather wasted on her. Writing some fifteen years later to Ted, she said:

> Folk want me to vote – *I won't* – a dangerous thing to do without knowledge . . . *in my heart* I am a *good* democrat – but oh, I see *this* way and *that* way – and a *wobbler* like that does mischief. I'm not clever. I'm a fool. – So knowing Fools

are very dangerous in times like these, I shall leave it to old Edy and Co. who will plump of course for Labour.[30]

She also made the point, when in later years she toured, lecturing on Shakespeare's heroines, that even the 'clever *women* of the present day ... appear quite unconscious that the burning questions that they are discussing now are as old as the hills.' She argued that there had been a regular women's movement back in the fifteenth and sixteenth centuries, when women often successfully filled the places of men in the council chamber, and that although Shakespeare gave Katherine of Aragon a tutor

> who worked heart & soul for the higher education of Englishwomen – it was not so much *emancipation* that he preached as *self-improvement* – Perhaps he knew that whenever women have improved themselves, they have without any definite declaration of independence immediately attained a great deal of freedom.[31]

But the WSPU had been formed in 1903 because its members wanted action, not more words – though the first militant move did not occur until 13 October 1905, when two women disrupted a Liberal meeting at which Sir Edward Grey and Winston Churchill were speakers by standing on their chairs and waving banners which said 'Votes for Women.'

On that same evening, Irving died. He had been touring in Britain since his return from his American tour in the spring of 1904, and his health had been worsening. When Ellen heard the tour had been stopped because of his illness, she came to see him. It was the first time they had been alone together for several years and he looked, she said, 'like some beautiful grey tree she had seen in the Savannah.' Irving welcomed her. 'Two Queens have been kind to me this morning,' he said. 'Queen Alexandra telegraphed to say how sorry she was I was ill, and now you.' She asked him how he would like the end to come. 'Like that,' he replied, snapping his fingers. He was to get his wish. He never recovered his health and while on tour in Bradford, after a performance of *Becket*, he collapsed in the hall of his hotel and died.

Ellen was playing in J.M. Barrie's *Alice Sit-By-the-Fire* at the time. In her diary, she wrote,

'Henry died today – "and now there is nothing left
remarkable beneath the visiting moon" – Cleopatra.'

The next night, when she came to the lines; 'It's summer
done, autumn begun . . . I had a beautiful husband once . . .
black as raven was his hair . . .' she broke down, and the
curtain was lowered.[32] Writing of him in a magazine some
months later, she said:

> Irving always put the theatre first. He lived in it, he died in it.
> He had none of my bourgeois qualities – the love of being in
> love, the love of a home, the dislike of solitude. I have always
> thought it hard to find my inferiors; he was sure of his high
> place. In some ways he was far simpler than I. He would
> talk, for instance, in such an ignorant way to painters and
> musicians that I blushed for him. But was not my blush far
> more unworthy than his freedom from all pretentiousness in
> matters of art?[33]

Irving was buried at Westminster Abbey on 20 October,
despite the Dean of Westminster's sister protesting that no
actors should be allowed in Poet's Corner. Flags were at half
mast throughout the country and the Lyceum was hung with
crepe. Ellen's chief thought as she saw the coffin carried up the
aisle under its pall of laurel leaves – made by Mrs Aria – was
'How Henry would have liked it!' She was to send an annual
wreath. Her note to the florist one year read:

> 'Please prepare for me the usual (delicate) *Rosemary wreath*
> for the grave at Westminster of Sir Henry Irving . . . and
> please attach the enclosed paper tying it loosely on the
> wreath – with *very* narrow white soft *silk* ribbon.'[34]

Outside the Abbey, police were controlling a suffragette
demonstration – which was likely to happen now at any public
event. Seeing the police outside the Abbey made Chris wonder
if the suffragettes were not also her concern. Both she and Edy
were soon converted to the cause and their flat – they were now
living at 31-32 Bedford Street, off the Strand – became a safe
house for women who had just left prison, or were being
sought by the police. Neither of them went to prison themselves, though Chris once seized the bridle of a police horse
and was arrested, but successfully appealed on a point of law.

Some thirty years later, Edy wrote in the *Glasgow Herald* that she still could not speak calmly of that terrible time, but tried instead to remember the lighter side. The first thing, for instance, that the suffragettes had asked her to do was to meet a woman near Downing Street, and carry a letter from her to another woman further up Downing Street. The next day she discovered that all those concerned had been arrested, save herself. 'It was rather a blow to me that I never was arrested.' Chris was the more active campaigner:

> I distributed handbills announcing meetings, chalked 'Votes for Women' on pavements, heckled cabinet ministers when they addressed their public, and knew what it was to be flung into the street by six or seven stewards, who tore my clothes and thumped me on the back with a mad-dog violence that astonished me.[35]

On 20 March 1906, Ellen opened in *Captain Brassbound's Conversion* at the Court Theatre. Edy accompanied her to each performance, looking after her costume, making sure she arrived on time, seeing she got as much rest as she could. Allan Wade, the actor, recalled Ellen chatting to everyone backstage until she heard Edy's voice calling 'Come *on*, Mother.' He found Edy 'genial, a little brusque in speech, somewhat impatient, and certainly a very dominant personality.'[36]

Shaw had been meeting Ellen daily during the rehearsals, and in the introduction to the published letters between them, says he speculated about filling the empty place in Ellen's heart after Irving's death. As a married man, his intentions were unclear; but whatever he intended, he was beaten to the post. While Shaw was talking to Ellen at the theatre one day, in walked a young American actor called James Carew, who was cast as Captain Hamlin Kearney in *Captain Brassbound's Conversion* and played the part 'fairly strongly,' according to *The Stage*.

Ellen, Shaw recalled, looked at Carew with interest and asked who he was. Then, 'without an instant's hesitation she sailed across the room; put Mr Carew in her pocket (so to speak); and married him.'[37] He confessed to marvelling at such a swift decision by so fastidious a huntress.

CHAPTER 13

MARRIAGE TO JAMES CAREW

In June 1906, Ellen celebrated her fifty years on stage. The *Staffordshire Sentinel* reported that when Ellen mentioned her Jubilee to Edy, she said, 'Don't you say a word about it and nobody else will remember.' It was a naive hope: there was a celebratory banquet, and a Jubilee matinee at Drury Lane – the queues for which started forming nearly twenty four hours beforehand. At midnight, Ellen visited the enthusiasts camping out in front of the theatre, shook their hands and ordered coffee for them.

An almost entirely all-male executive committee was set up to organise the Jubilee matinee and Ellen, when shown the draft programme, was shocked to find no actresses were included. The executive hastily added a series of tableaux for London's leading actresses, to which Ellen replied:

An amusing notion this, of women of talent appearing in *tableaux* only, but if that has been decided upon by the Committee, I elect, if you please, to appear only in a tableau myself. I couldnt, I couldnt, I *couldnt* do anything else![1]

She was finally persuaded to appear in a scene from *Much Ado about Nothing*, supported by every available member of her family. The rest of the programme was made up of a vast number of celebrities: Caruso sang, accompanied by Tosti; W.S. Gilbert presented *Trial by Jury*; Mrs Patrick Campbell recited; Eleonora Duse, the actress, came over from Italy; the *tableaux vivants* included fifty actresses, among whom were Lily Langtry, Ellaline Terriss, Violet and Irene Vanbrugh; the 'Leading Comedians of London' gave a minstrel show and Ellen's friend, music hall player Gertie Millar, also sang; there was a scene from *The Beauty of Bath*, starring 'Mr Seymour

Hicks and *all* the Bath Buns' and a masked dance arranged by
Ted – who remained abroad, apparently in dudgeon that
Godwin's name was not mentioned in the entertainment.

The matinee was a great success, lasting nearly five hours,
and bringing in over £6,000 benefit to Ellen. An Ellen Terry
Jubilee Celebration Fund was also set up by the *Tribune* and
shillings from the public poured in, finally totalling £3,000.
Ellen was very moved by this and the number of celebration
dinners and events she was asked to, but rehearsals for *The
Winter's Tale*, in which she was playing Hermione (fifty years
after she had first played the child Mamillius in the same play)
started on 7 August and she told Shaw she wished she was not
acting it, as the jubilations had nearly killed her.

Carew, meanwhile, was visiting her constantly at her King's
Road House and at Smallhythe. Ted got a letter from her in the
October of that year referring, he presumed, to Carew, saying,

> Yesterday I went to the River in a motor and then *on* the
> river – with a very nice man – I am so sick of being eternally
> with crowds of women – they just *bore* me – and always
> want something being done for them.[2]

She told Charles Frohman, who had engaged her to go on a
winter American tour with *Captain Brassbound*, that she
wanted James Carew as her leading man. Carew, born in
Indiana, was of German-Jewish parentage, his real name being
Usselman. He had been on the stage in America, and made his
first appearance in London at the Lyric, in *Her Own Way*, the
previous year. Later on, in the 1930s, he was to become one of
the best known actors on the London stage, famous for his
famous black-face cross talk act, 'Alexander and Mose.'

James and Ellen married, with much secrecy, on 22 March
1907 at Pittsburg. Ellen did not announce the marriage until
the tour was over and the company were embarking for
England, not even confiding her secret marriage to Edy. She
may have been aware that Edy would disapprove of her choice,
yet again, of a man who, though amiable, had little to offer
apart from his ruggedly handsome looks. At thirty four, Carew
was four years younger than Ted, and twenty five years
younger than Ellen. ('I give it two years,' Edy was to say,
acidly.) Chris St John went to Ellen in her cabin to reproach her
for her heartlessness in not telling Edy,[3] which made Ellen

PUNCH, OR THE LONDON CHARIVARI.—March 28, 1906.

FIFTY YEARS A QUEEN.

(An Author's Tribute.)

[A scheme is on foot for presenting a National Tribute to Miss Ellen Terry on April 28, the fiftieth anniversary of her first appearance on the stage.]

A Bernard Partridge cartoon, which appeared in *Punch*, celebrating Ellen's stage jubilee in 1906.

regard her for some time, said Chris, as if she was infectious.

Ellen, having been gossiped about when she was conducting her flirtation with Frank Cooper, and recalling how her family had ostracised her when she lived with Godwin, was anxious to behave respectably. She had considered the idea of marriage before the tour. America would decide her.

> If I was coldly received, in other words plainly told I was too old and ugly to remain upon the stage, I had determined to give up all thought of the marriage, to put away 'all foolish fond records,' and leave the stage quietly at the end of the tour. But they opened their arms to me, flattered and spoiled me delightfully to the top of my bent, and I was married.[4]

Carew was happy to oblige his goddess. He was a kind protective man, remaining admiringly devoted to Ellen throughout the last part of her life: even after her death he always referred to her as 'My lady.' Ellen needed this admiration and protection. Carew gave her the confidence she lacked now that Irving was dead, the Lyceum partnership over, her paper courtship with Shaw all but ended, and her professional future looking gloomy.

She had written to Shaw two weeks after her marriage – though not revealing this – saying, 'James Carew goes on trying and striving and acts better and better every week. He is a splendid fellow and adores you, *and me!*.'

After her return to England, she and Carew spent the summer touring around the provinces in *Brassbound*. Shaw, who now knew about the marriage, sent Ellen a teasing letter, telling her not to play Carew off the stage with her tricks, or she'd lose him, but Ellen replied, 'No, James hasnt jilted me yet. He bosses me nicely instead!'

Far from playing Carew off the stage, Ellen was very thoughtful when they acted together. Shortly after the marriage, for instance, she played Portia at a Shakespeare Festival to James Carew's Shylock. When she came to say, 'Here's thy money offered thee,' she laid her hand on his arm, shocking the purists by this unexpected action. Explaining her gesture, she said she did not put her hand on Shylock's arm, but on her husband's, sensing his fear and tension and wanting to reassure him.[5]

But problems soon started. The first was finding work, any

Ellen and Edy departing in style for America, 1906.

work but *Brassbound*, as Carew was sick of playing in it month after month, even though Ellen had elevated him to the main part. That spring, she had written to Shaw from America to ask if he could find work for Edy on their return: in the October, a month after the tour ended, she was asking for herself and her husband:

> He is not tied to my apron strings (nor is 'his mother' [Ellen] tied to his) and if one of us is at work I shall be satisfied and so will he. I'd like you (for he loves you) to make him an offer. Oh, do be quick and ask him to play a fine part with a fair salary, or a mere good part with an unfair salary! Will you? Quick quick, oh, Shaw, and save us from the 'Halls' or the Hells. (Not that I am going 'on the 'alls' anyhow, but save me from rushing about the land when we both want to settle down in our country home to do nice work.)

Ellen may have implied that she was all set for retirement, but she certainly didn't behave like it. Around this time, she went over to pay a call on Mrs Hodgson Burnett, who was her neighbour at Smallhythe and lived in Maytham Hall. This was a large country seat, with a lake, cedar trees, and a paved terrace from which a steep slope of grass led to the lawn. In her autobiography, Ella Hepworth Dixon recalled that all this opulence meant nothing to Mrs James Carew:

> She simply saw an opportunity to break the horrid formality of a bridal 'call.' 'What a lovely place to roll down,' cried Ellen and proceeded to do so. She was dressed in a brown gown and brown cloak and when her amused hostess rescued her at the bottom, she resembled a long brown German cigar.[6]

Shaw had responded to Ellen's pleas for work for Edy by giving her the part of the bishop's wife in his new play, *Getting Married*, produced at the Haymarket on 12 May 1908. This opportunity for Edy had actually arisen by chance. She and Chris had moved almost next door to Shaw, and Shaw, hearing her call up to Chris to throw down the latchkey, decided she had the right voice for the part.

Ellen was also asking Shaw, rather desperately now, for any part in a play of his for herself. 'Am I too old? I *must* act,' she said. A year later, she had given up the idea of work in England

Two sketches of Ellen: left, as Beatrice in *Much Ado*; right as Lady Cicely
Waynflete in *Captain Brassbound's Conversion*, 1906.

and wrote to say that she was booking an autumn tour in America. Despite the depressing thought of 'the filthy heat of an American winter,' she was remarkably cheerful when she met Lena Ashwell, an ex-Lyceum actress, over there. 'Almost blind, alone, stripped of all the luxury and care which had for so long been hers, courageous, undefeated, young,' Lena Ashwell recalled, 'she hugged me and said "What do you think of me Lena? Sixty-three, and on one-night stands." '[7]

When she had left for the tour, she told Shaw she hoped that James would not be with her as she thought he would become a lunatic if he played Captain B. much longer. 'We are both extraordinarily happy together,' she ended, 'and it seems a pity to go different ways for a while.'

Despite the protestations, it was to be the beginning of a longer parting. In another couple of years, they were to separate, though informally. It was a leading man, an escort, that Ellen had wanted, not a husband. For this reason the marriage was never consummated – which may well have been the case with both Watts and Kelly. Ellen, exuding love and warmth to all around her – family, friends and audiences – couldn't and wouldn't narrow it down to one man.

Her son's claim that she was 'unmarriable,' however, was based on what he thought marriage entailed: loving obedience from the wife. Ellen did not need or want a managing husband. She was a strong, dominant woman, used to managing her own life: the flat in the Kings Road, and the farm at Smallhythe were hers: so were the fame, the stage contacts, the visitors, the friends from the theatre, the grandchildren. Everything seemed to revolve around her. Carew, overwhelmed, recognised this, telling Edy after Ellen's death, 'I should never have quarrelled with Nell. The only way to get on with her was not to live in the same house.'[8]

However, she still saw Carew and remained on friendly terms with him for the rest of her life. She wrote to Shaw in the January of 1910 to say, 'Remember James Carew is a very good actor of some parts, & give him one if you can. *It would do me such a good turn*.' The next year, she was asking Shaw for copies of two of his plays, so that Carew could read these to her and save her eyesight and in June 1912, she was writing to a friend, Mrs Dorothy Alhusen, in reply to an invitation, saying she would like to come 'and so would Jim – my good man.'

Top: Ellen and James at Smallhythe. Bottom: Ellen as Elizabeth of York and Carew as Henry VII, in *Henry of Lancaster*, 1908.

A key factor in the marriage break-up was Edy's resentment and jealousy of Carew. She and her mother obviously cared deeply for each other, and, to a remarkable extent, relied on each other both personally and professionally. But the possessiveness underlying their relationship immediately erupted if the other had a serious emotional relationship with someone else. It obviously posed, to both of them, an unacceptable threat to their own relationship. When Edy fell in love with Joe Evans and then with Martin Shaw, Ellen simply rode over Edy's feelings in the conviction that she, Ellen, knew what was best for her daughter. When Ellen married James Carew, Edy upset Ellen just as much by reacting with equal selfishness.

Ted, on the other hand, said of James Carew that he did not know of a jollier, better fellow. And on hearing the news of his mother's marriage, said he

> felt delighted that our mother should have the pluck to face that daunting phase of life once more, and I wished her very, very well on her new course; but my sister was, I remember, utterly distraught. She seems to have thought that others have a say in these matters: she was inexperienced and, I think, ignorant of most things to do with life as it is – and somehow or other, prejudiced in some odd way against the male sex, though always kind to me.[9]

At the time of the marriage, Edy and Chris, when not in their London flat, spent their spare time at the Priest's House in Smallhythe, the next door cottage Ellen had given them. But Edy refused to visit Ellen if Carew was with her and locked the connecting gate between the houses. In June, 1908, Ellen wrote to Edy, saying 'I hope it's not *we* are keeping you away from the cottage! That wd be too absurd – if you don't want to see us, there is *space* between the houses you know!'[10] She went on to say that she had fallen down and bruised herself black and blue, but apart from that she was very well and very, very happy – 'except for *one* thing.' She underlined the word 'one' four times.

But Edy's refusal to visit the two of them continued, despite a further sad note from Ellen saying, 'I don't go to the cottage because I can't go anywhere where Jim can't go – and is not welcomed – never mind.'[11] Arrangements were made for there to be separate 'service' between the farm and the cottage, which

Ellen thought was much better, as it had never worked well 'and of course now it wd never do. I am your most loving old mother.' Another letter to Edy expressed her feelings more forcibly:

> I consider you are a very badly behaved young person but that I love you most dearly and trust you will see your way to leave off being a cruel and belligerent young woman as soon as you conveniently can, for it is a foolish behaviour which is commonly adopted by common girls and I can never class you with them in my mind.[12]

But only at Ellen's unofficial separation from James Carew did Edy unlock the garden gate between their two houses in Smallhythe.

CHAPTER 14

PAGEANTS AND PIONEERS: A BLOW FOR WOMEN

In December 1908, the Actresses Franchise League was formed. Its first public meeting was rather like a theatrical premiere, with West End stars, like Ellen, Madge Kendall and Violet Vanbrugh attending, and telegrams of support from writers like Arthur Pinero and Jerome K. Jerome. Speeches were made supporting the women's cause, though the League was neither for nor against the militant suffragettes, maintaining a careful balance. Its members wrote and distributed literature; held meetings at which they sang, danced and recited poetry; and took part in deputations and rallies. But its main aim was to produce propaganda shows for suffrage societies.

Cicely Hamilton, the actress and a founder of the Women Writers' Suffrage League, remembered being one of Edy's helpers in these shows and, being friendly with her, was puzzled by always receiving stiff typewritten notes that were obviously written by a secretary. When questioned, Edy admitted shamefacedly that she couldn't spell. Chris St John respected Cicely's work, but was nevertheless jealously alert to a rival. 'I'm sorry C. thinks Cicely H. a humbug,' wrote Ellen to Edy, 'I thought she liked her!'[1]

With Edy now constantly busy on producing shows and pageants for the League, Ellen no longer worried about getting work for her through friends like Shaw and could concentrate on getting parts for herself and James. During the Christmas of 1908, Ellen had appeared in Graham Robertson's *Pinkie and the Fairies*, a musical play for children – mostly as a favour to Robertson. She had not been on the West End stage for several years and was greeted by a lengthy outburst of applause.

Ellen was much loved by the theatrical public but her serious career as an actress was over. She was now sixty two, had a cataract on one eye, and her memory for lines, always bad, now let her down completely. On stage she was rather a sad figure, but in any case little work was on offer.

During the summer of 1909, she wrote to a friend to say she couldn't afford certain items, 'until Jim or I get some work – or sell a house, or *sell each other*!! or something.' To another, she wrote, 'Did you say anything about James as "James Hook" (Capt Hook)? I'm sure he wd be *very* good in the part.'[2] For a couple who were informally separated, they were together a lot, either building a workroom for James at the bottom of Ellen's tiny garden in Chelsea, or relaxing at Smallhythe. When Carew finally left, he forgot to take his large country boots and Ellen was always to wear them.

That autumn, Carew finally managed to get a touring job and Ellen joined him in Edinburgh. In November, she appeared as Nance Oldfield in *A Pageant of Great Women*, which she called 'the finest practical piece of political propaganda.' Written by Cicily Hamilton, it showed Woman, longing to be free, pleading with Justice for social and political liberty, while Prejudice in the form of a man argues against her. To fight his objections, she calls on women who are famous in various spheres. Edy played Rosa Bonheur, the famous French painter of animals, and the first woman to receive the Legion of Honour, and Marion Terry was Florence Nightingale. *The Times* praised its idealistic view of the cause of women's suffrage.

The pageant was put on at the Scala Theatre by the Actresses' Franchise League and the Women Writers' Suffrage League, and Edy produced it as well as taking part. She also suggested what characters were to be included among the main groups of famous women rulers, artists and saints; cast the parts; arranged the music; gave expert advice on lighting; and designed and made the costumes. She did have help. A by-product of the League was that members not acting would, without any experience, organise performances, stage manage them, run the box office and the accounts, and manage the publicity.

The pageant was Edy's second production for the League. Her first had been in May: a one-act comedy called *How the Vote was Won*, written by Cicily Hamilton – who remembered Edy coming to her full of the idea of having a pageant of great women, which she suggested Cicily wrote: '"Suggested" perhaps is the wrong word to use; if I remember aright her suggestion was more like an order.'[3]

When Edy arranged costumes for her pageants and plays, she was obsessed with every detail – wanting the correct underclothes to be worn, like stays and petticoats. The actress Sybil Thorndike once got a specially designed dress for a play Edy was producing. 'She looked at it and said, "Well, I don't so much mind, provided you wear it in rehearsal so that it is part of the woman and not this dreadful cleanliness you all seem to like so much – and Sybil, never have clothes cleaned for the theatre – it takes all the bloom off – the dirt has got something in it which you'll miss if you send it to cleaners".'[4]

Sybil Thorndike also remembered how Edy never wanted new designs, but simply turned over a lot of old junk in the theatrical clothes basket, picked out certain bits, and made a whole costume from it. She did the same with scenery and furniture, transforming old curtains and chair covers into something quite different.

The Pageant of Great Women was a great success. Edy had a gift of combining pictorial effect with drama, and there were repeated requests for it from the provinces. Edy took brisk charge there, too, bringing with her the three actresses with speaking parts, and rehearsing and dressing the thirty or forty players from the local suffragette society, who would make up the rest of the company.

Edy was now totally and enthusiastically involved in political theatre, and her production of propaganda plays was of immense value to the women's cause: admittedly the audiences were mostly enthusiastic suffragettes, but the plays were reviewed, and for once the publicity was good instead of the constant knocking the suffragettes got in the press.

She had immense energy and concentration; combined this with her own experience as an actress and a good eye for the pseudo. She once said to Sybil Thorndike, 'Don't say God in that reverent, holy way, as if you were an atheist.' Her knowledge of stage technique, learned at the Lyceum and in Paris, where Irving once sent her to take production notes of *Cyrano de Bergerac*, gave her an assured confidence and she loved tackling plays which needed ingenious treatment.

Her reputation at rehearsals was an alarming one, as she

Edy as the French painter, Rosa Bonheur – a part she played many times in her productions of the Pageants of Great Women.

insisted that everyone worked to her own high standard. Eleanor Adlard remembers helping to set a stage and being told to fling a drapery 'carelessly' over a throne – which she had to do more times than she could count until Edy was satisfied. She was icy if anyone was late. 'What guarantee have I that she will appear?' she once said coldly about an actress who had failed to turn up and was replaced. And she once hung a sign on the callboard saying, 'Any member of the company who forgets their lines will be fined for each offence.'

The actresses working under her, however, though smarting under her criticism, admitted she got the very best out of them. Sybil Thorndike remembered being delighted at working with Edith Evans for the first time,

> but honestly, Edy gave us such a lashing, we'd come away from rehearsals bruised beyond words – but with a feeling that there was something we *might* be able to achieve if we went down to the nethermost hell and then struggled back and up. Edy used to get something with atmosphere that was quite unique . . . the mysterious quality none of us can put a name to – but when we meet it in a producer we call genius.[5]

Edy's originality worked well on stage, but not so well off it. Cicely Hamilton remembered arriving at the office for a meeting of the Actresses Franchise League, only to find her fellow members heatedly discussing a recent disagreement with Edy who, according to them, was 'behaving most unreasonably and, despite objection on the part of the majority, insisting on her own way.'[6] Edy's dictatorial manner and individualism prevented her from ever being part of a team.

The Pioneer Players was founded by Edy in 1911, as by then it was clear to both her and the League that it would be best for her to work independently. Ellen Terry was president, Edy the managing/stage director and Chris St John the secretary. Two members of the advisory committee were men (Bernard Shaw and Laurence Housman) and seven were women (including Olive Terry and Mrs Bernard Shaw, the latter having recovered from the shock of Actresses' Franchise League writing 'Votes for Women' on the Shaws' doorstep in an indelible smear of butter and blacklead). All other positions – from auditing the books to scene shifting – were held by women.

The annual subscription of thirty one shillings and sixpence,

twenty one shillings and ten shillings and sixpence respectively
allowed members a single seat at performances and a minimum
of five plays were to be presented annually; more if funds
permitted. Small London theatres were chosen for performances – which were single matinees only, usually on a Sunday.

There was almost no capital backing the venture: just a small
amount guaranteed in case of loss. The money coming in from
subscribers paid for the hire of the theatre. Other expenses
were kept low: casts were small in the often one-act plays; the
actresses, producer and writer were unpaid, and Edy conjured
up costumes from nothing. But the lack of any additional
money made production difficult and there was a constant call
for more subscribers. To everyone's surprised relief, the first
season made a profit of nearly £40.

The stated aim of the Pioneer Players was 'to present the type
of play which is known as the "play of ideas," and particularly
that variety which deals with current ideas, social, political and
moral.'[7] It did so with gusto. So far, Elizabeth Robins's play,
Votes for Women!, staged at the Court Theatre in 1907, had
been one of the most effective, realistic pieces of feminist
propaganda yet seen, but the Pioneers had a wider brief. The
plays put on were strongly feminist, airing the attitudes of, and
towards, women of that time. They were preaching to the
converted, as audiences were 99 per cent cheering women, but
it was a radical move in the theatre and the plays were widely
reviewed.

Chris St John, writing in the newspaper *Votes for Women*
back in 1909, had shown the need for such plays when she
wrote:

> There is not one play on the London stage at the present time
> which takes any account of women except on the level of
> housekeeping machines or bridge players – the actual or
> potential property of some man valuable or worthless as the
> case may be. It is strange to go out of the world, where
> women are fighting for freedom and showing unparalleled
> courage when most despised and rejected, into the theatre
> where the dramatist appears unaffected by this new
> Renaissance.[8]

The Pioneer Players opened with a treble bill showing on
8 May 1911 at the Kingsway Theatre. The theatre already had

a feminist link, being leased to Lena Ashwell, an active member of the Actresses' Franchise League and the only woman then in theatre management.

The first one-act play was Cicely Hamilton's comedy, *Jack and Jill and a Friend*, about the rivalry of an engaged couple for the same prize in a competition for the best novel. Jill, who wins the prize, was played by Athene Seyler. The second was Margaret Wynne Nevinson's *In the Workhouse*, a biting satire on a husband's legal right to detain his wife in a workhouse.

The last part of the bill was *The First Actress* by Chris St John and Cicely Hamilton. The subject was sex discrimination in the theatre in Restoration England – a time when actresses were having to fight against actors wanting to play all the female parts as well as the male and were rebuked for invading 'a sphere where woman is totally unfitted to shine.' It allowed Edy – as Chris intended – to show off her talents as a costumier as well as producer. In a final tableau of successful actresses, past and present, Ellen appeared as Nell Gwyn.

A later production was Shaw's *Mrs Warren's Profession*, still banned from public performance, about attitudes to prostitution and the economic independence of women; and *Macrena* by Chris St John, about a nineteenth century Russian nun who faced death rather than give up her Catholic faith – an example of women's courage when a principle is at stake.

The shock of the first season, however, was a play called *The Surprise of His Life*, a drama about a pregnant woman refusing to marry the father of her child – ironically by Jess Dorynne, the woman Ted had made pregnant and then deserted. The unnerved critics claimed disgustedly that it was a 'brief for bastardy'; and though some praised what the Pioneers were doing – 'That brave society,' said the *Sketch* – the general press reaction was that the Pioneers had been formed solely for the purpose of suffragist propaganda. There was paranoia about the militant suffragettes by then, because of their stone throwing, mass window smashing, arson, and attacks on property.

The first annual report of the Pioneer Players refuted the press's views.

It has more than once been suggested in the Press that we are a Society formed for the purpose of suffragist propaganda only; but this suggestion is a misleading one.

It is obviously quite impossible nowadays to produce thoughtful plays written by thoughtful people who do not bear some traces of the influence of the feminist movement – an influence which no modern writer, however much he may wish it, can entirely escape. But those responsible for the selection of the plays that we have performed have never had either the wish or the intention of narrowing their choice to works dealing with one phase only of modern thought. All we ask of a play is that it shall be interesting; and if many of those who have sent us plays have found inspiration in various aspects of the feminist movement, we must conclude that it is because the feminist movement is, in itself, not without dramatic interest.[9]

For a small fee, the Pioneer Players would arrange productions for other societies. During the first year of its existence, these included *A Modern Crusader*, a food reform play at the King's Hall for the Agenda Club, and Shaw's *Man of Destiny* at the Savoy Theatre for the International Suffrage Shop. Edy was also staging pageants, including a big one that year at the Albert Hall. Ellen wrote apologising for not being able to come, and added:

> Good luck to you and strength to your elbow. Take care what you eat just at this important time and *try* to get food *regularly* – if you break down it would be just the wrong moment with Mrs Warren ahead – by the way keep me 2 seats.[10]

Apart from playing Nell Gwyn in *The First Actress*, Ellen was rarely on stage that year, though she recited Wordsworth's *Daffodils* at a couple of matinees at the St James's Theatre, in aid of the newly founded (feminist) Three Arts Club. At the Kingsway Theatre, for the Pioneers, she also gave one of her lectures of Shakespeare's heroines.

The idea of such lectures had come from the literary agents, Curtis Brown, who approached Ellen to do a lecture tour in America. The request came at a time when she was dispirited and puzzled at her failure to maintain her position; but the lecture tour, lasting from November 1910 to the spring of 1911, proved strikingly successful. She gave lively, evocative impersonations of the characters; her penetrating comment being based on a lifelong study.

After the success of the lectures in America, Ellen decided to try them out in England and, in the autumn of 1911, went off on a lecture tour around the provinces. It was thought that the word 'lecture' would frighten off the unacademic English, and the tour was billed, more enticingly, as 'A Shakespearean Discourse With Illustrative Acting.' Edy was in charge of the stage design. Ellen wore flowing robes of crimson, white or grey, against dark green curtains, with bunches of flowers and ingenious lighting. The lectern she used was one of Irving's decorative desks, and because her eyesight was so poor she had a copy of each lecture printed in very large bold type. It must still have been difficult to read, however, as she scribbled comments all over it.

Before the tour started, Ellen had a summer break at Smallhythe with Elena and Ted and their two children, Nellie and Teddy. Ted made only rare trips to England these days, having left the country in 1904 for Berlin. When he went, he had intended to stay only four months, to design a production of *Venice Preserved*, and had left Elena, who was pregnant again, at home with their young baby, Nellie (the first child, also a girl, had died). To their surprised delight, May had at last agreed to file for a divorce. But in December 1904, in Berlin, Ted had sat 'still and speechless,' on seeing Isadora Duncan dance and, before long, they were lovers.

Early the next year, Elena wrote to tell him they now had a son. He paid her a brief visit that autumn, but didn't get back to England again until the following summer and by then Isadora, too, was pregnant. Tragically, Deirdre, the baby girl she had, died in 1913 at the age of seven, together with her half brother Patrick, when the car they were in plunged into the Seine. But Ted and Isadora had split up long before then, within only a year of Deirdre's birth.

Ted went to live in Florence, working on his magazine, *The Mask* and in 1908 he was joined by Elena with four year old Nellie and three year old Ted. They all made occasional trips to England, and in 1912 Elena and the children stayed on in England with Ellen. It thrilled Ellen, who felt it was like the old days in Harpenden with her own two small children, and she found herself calling Nellie 'Edy.' She was delighted when they both had a walk-on part with her in a charity matinee, and was later to write in her diary,

> Elena and her two wonderful children, my most beloved grandchildren, have lived with me for four years and I am most happy, and not alone. Ted comes and goes from his work in Italy, and this must soon fix them all there. Meanwhile, they are my joys.[11]

They were to stay nearly five years. Despite being divorced from May, Ted was never to marry Elena.

Edy was rather hostile about Ted's occasional visits, resenting the way he charmed money from Ellen and her obvious adoration of her laughing, handsome son. Currently, however, the Pioneer Players was taking up all her time. The second season, beginning 1912, included three translations of foreign plays and produced a higher profit than the first, helped by the proceeds of a fancy dress ball and fifty new members. The annual report commented:

> We do not intend to be cast down by any depressing queries as to whether there is room for us. . . . If our plays are good enough to make our audiences think and feel, we have no fear of their not being good enough to entertain.[12]

Despite these brave words, many of the old members did not rejoin for the third season. This time, there were two foreign plays: *Paphnutius*, a play by a Benedictine nun, translated by Chris; and *Daughters of Ishmael*, a play about social evil, translated from the Latin. Affording plays that contained a stirring message for the audience was proving difficult. The end of season report read: 'Harassed and hampered by financial considerations in choice of plays for production. But we face the fourth season with confidence.'[13]

The fourth season was also full of stern stuff, including *Sisyphus and the Wandering Jew* by a young Belgian poet; *The Theatre of the Soul* by a Russian writer noted for his boldness; a premiere of a French play by Paul Claudel; and a paper on 'The Drama as a Factor in Social Progress.'

But though the Pioneers continued to make a small profit or break even for the next year or so, it was proving to be a tenacious struggle rather than a triumphant progress.

With the start of the First World War in 1914, many former

subscribers wrote to say they could no longer afford the luxury of belonging to the Pioneers: even if they had the money they felt obliged to spend it on other things. A few said they had patriotic scruples. Plays became difficult to cast, because actors were signing up for military service, and The Little Theatre, one of the most suitable theatres for their performances, was transformed into a YMCA hostel for soldiers and they had a harassing search for other venues.

As the report on the season said: 'Literature, art, music, and the drama all appeared to be submerged by the high tide of that most violent of human activities which men call war.'[14] A meeting was called and the fourth season was formally closed. Financial disaster was averted because Lady Randolph Churchill held a charity matinee to raise funds for the Soldiers and Sailors Free Buffets; and for the Pioneer Players. The proceeds enabled the Players to continue, one of only two theatre societies – the other was the Incorporated Stage Society – to survive the war.

CHAPTER 15

DOWN UNDER: SUFFRAGETTES AND SHAKESPEARE

When war broke out, Ellen wanted to work in the theatre, but found she was in demand only for her Shakespearean lectures. These were so highly praised that she had an offer of a world lecture tour, beginning in 1914 in Australia. She wanted to take it, needing the money. Her doctor advised her against it: her heart, he said, was in poor condition. Her lawyer pointed out that if she would only reduce her allowances to certain dependents and stop trying to leave a large sum of money to her children, she wouldn't have to go on working.

Shaw wrote anxiously to ask what had become of the Jubilee money, or was she supporting one of Ted's families in every European capital? It was almost true. Ellen was paying Ted's ex-wife May's alimony; supporting Charles Kelly's wife's sisters; paying for Godwin's son (by his second wife) to go to Canada; and giving Edy an allowance on which Chris also lived. Ellen was now aged sixty seven, too old for an exhausting tour. Nevertheless, she decided to go to Australia directly.

She arrived in Melbourne in late April, 1914, unwell after the heat in the Red Sea. But she had had one bonus on the way there: the boat had stopped at Naples on 4 April and Ted had unexpectedly come on board. 'Red Letter Day,' she wrote in her diary, and went off happily with him on a long drive.

Interviewed before she left London by an Australian magazine, *Table Talk*, Ellen was portrayed as almost a royal presence, living in an atmosphere of lavender and old lace:

> There is a step – a rustle of draperies – a faint sweet
> something that suggests an atmosphere of indescribable
> charm – and another slave is added to Ellen Terry's

The Women of Shakspere =
The Women of Shakspere! As I read
out the title of my lecture, I
am frightened at the hardihood of
my undertaking — I remember the
great host of Shaksperian com —
-mentators who for generations have
made these fascinating figures
their study, +, going to Shakspere
himself, for an expression which
fits the occasion (a favourite custom
of mine when I am travelled or
for want of words!) I am

1 —

inclined to say —
" If there be nothing new, but that which is
Hath been before, how are our brains beguiled,
Which, labouring for invention, bear amiss
The second burden of a former child "!
Even the most patient student,

Ellen toured England, Australia and America with her lectures on Shakespeare's
heroines. Above, a handwritten excerpt.

numberless retinue. . . . 'Now you want to know what I am going to do. Well, in the first place, I am not going to lecture. . . . Just imagine me lecturing – it is really too funny. . . . I am told, too, that I shall be expected to make speeches. I do hope not. I hate making speeches: in fact, I can't make them.'

When Ellen arrived in Melbourne, the Australian press descended on her. They wrote effusive reports of her looks ('Her hair is grey but her eyes are bright and forever twinkling and her cheeks are clear and rosy as a girl's'); asked about her husband, James Carew ('He is often down [at Smallhythe] when the children are there, but he always wants to alter the old place and make it new – just like an American, isn't it'); and if she'd ever, like Sarah Bernhardt, appeared at a music hall ('I have never appeared myself at a music hall and am not likely to now. One reason is that Sir Henry Irving did not care about the idea. They have come on a great deal even since his death. There are splendid music halls in London').

But when she calmly admitted her age the *Sun* called her 'certainly the most unwomanly woman and surely the most frank artist that has visited these shores for some time.' It was further startled when she said, with a mixture of pride and defiance: 'Of course you all know I'm a suffragette. Of course I am, and so is my daughter, Edith Craig.'

It was one of the few occasions that Ellen admitted publicly to being a suffragette. Although she had supported the Actresses Franchise League and Edy's Pioneer Players, and was an example herself of a liberated woman, she never appeared at any suffragette meetings or spoke out about women and the vote. She hated making speeches. When, for instance, she was asked at her Jubilee if her acting had improved during her time in the theatre, she replied: 'I don't want to express opinions. I don't allow myself to form any – not for publication at any rate.'

In Australia, she responded more confidently, saying emphatically, in reply to questions about suffrage, that women should have the vote, and ridiculing the attitudes of those who spoke against it. ' "You should hear some English men talk," she exclaimed,' reported the Melbourne paper, the *Age*, 'You will hear them say in a tragedy voice, "I love my wife and I love my mother and sooner than see them turned into one of those political creatures." ' Here Ellen broke off with a shrug and a laugh.

She was quick to disassociate herself from activities like window smashing. 'I'm an ardent suffragette, but I don't believe in all their militancy,' she told the *Age*.

> It antagonises people and women never do any good that way. The suffragettes are a magnificent lot of women, but I think, perhaps, their ardour carries them away at times. And it shouldn't, it shouldn't. It makes them lose their poise and poise is everything.

It is rather hard to remain poised when you are being force fed. But although Edy and Chris sympathised with the belief that militant tactics were necessary to advance the women's cause, Ellen still preferred the approach to be feminine rather than feminist: she jumped up, during one interview in her tour, to give the only *Votes for Women* reporter present a bunch of roses. Perhaps it's as well she never appeared on the same platform as the more militant Pankhursts if she was to argue that the battle's spearhead should be poise. Not even the fact that, as the *Age* pointed out, 'Miss Terry has been brought up in the grand school of manners' would have excused her.

Indeed, Ellen seemed, at times, to regard the suffragettes as part of some splendid theatrical production, which failed to adhere to conventional rules. When asked by another paper if she had ever walked in a procession, for instance, she replied that she wouldn't walk ten yards, much less in a procession:

> But I remember the procession the suffragettes organised after the King's death. His procession was quite a farce, you know. A little tin pot band here and there, and really nothing at all; and then, a few weeks later, came the suffragettes; and it was just wonderful. One glorious band after another, and hundreds of women and girls looking as fresh as spring buds. You see, they had been having a bad time with people making remarks aboout their untidy dress, and so they determined to pay special attention to all those details this time. And so they should – so they should. I hate to see girls untidy. I always am myself, but then I can be excused. You see, I'm 66.

She refused however to tell the Australian papers what she thought about modern women. 'Why should I?' she said. 'I'm both modern and old-fashioned myself. I'm not going to give up my old ideals, and I don't say either that some of the modern ideals aren't good, too.'

Her tour in Australia went well, and she wrote to Edy to say 'houses good, notices splendid.' Her health suddenly deteriorated, however, and though she then visited New Zealand, she had to spend time there recuperating.

On 4 August that year, England declared war on Germany and back in Australia in the October, Ellen wrote to Edy to say that everyone was talking of nothing but the war and the drought ('they pronounce it "draut" '). Her own thoughts were also all about the war, often jotted down in her copy of Shakespeare, which she used as if it were a diary: 'The "break-promise Kaiser" ... I think he is a *madman* ... the war is a nightmare.'[1] She wrote to Edy about the Germans, saying,

> Maybe they are in Kent by now, perhaps inhabiting *our cottages!* And perhaps you may be giving them some tea! Or toko! The horrors of this war for a few minutes now and again make me crazy, when I dare think, but I *darent*, and only pray that no harm comes near you, and that somehow or another we meet at home before Christmas.[2]

She was further devastated by the news that Laurence Irving had drowned when the passenger ship *Empress of Ireland* was sunk by the Germans. Ellen had always been close to him and wrote in her diary, 'Laurence Irving died in the St Lawrence River – Canada. Remember thee! Ay, thou poor ghost, while memory holds a seat in this distracted globe.'[3]

Ellen was advised to go home via America, as the Mediterranean was not considered safe. She arranged to continue her Shakespearean lectures there, and visited some twenty towns, sending a review of one of her performances to a friend with a note saying, 'Do you know Allentown, Pa? A onehosse place & the cuties I'm told never notice the theatre.' But her worsening eyesight and headaches stopped the tour. A New York oculist found the cause: the cataract on her left eye needed immediate removal. The operation was carried out in February 1915, shortly before her sixty seventh birthday and, according to Ellen, 'hurt like hell.' She was recuperating when she heard that Sarah Bernhardt was in worse trouble, having had a leg amputated. 'The mere idea seems grotesque when a reporter asks you to say *"what you think of it,"* ' Ellen wrote in her diary. 'Well if any bit of her is left, it is precious.'[4]

Ellen's lecture tour was her last appearance abroad. She left New York at the end of April, refusing Charles Frohman's offer of a suite on the doomed *Lusitania* only because she had promised Edy to return on an English ship. There was little for her to do in England: on 10 July she wrote to her friend, Mrs Dorothy Alhusen to send her two shillings and sixpence for stamps for her hospital, saying,

> Remember *something* is better than *nothing* and spare me!! I am so unhappy at *not being able* for the first time, to pay my bills monthly – and it seems as if I'll not be able to pay at all soon!! I've travelled round the world to keep up my one good habit, but now!!! . . . I don't in the least mind being laughed at but oh, I *do* mind being unable to send you a cheque. I *just cannot*, at present at least – but perhaps – later on – Oh! – I do feel it so – the Music Hall will have to be my refuge! I do appear (tho'*not for money for myself*) at the Palladium tomorrow week (18th) for the Wounded Allies Relief Fund – of course I am doing something or other every week – but became so ill.[5]

Ellen's main work during the war was for war charities. She also appeared at the Coliseum in scenes from *The Merry Wives of Windsor* and then went on tour with the production around the Stoll music halls in the provinces. In 1916, she took part in her first film, called *Her Greatest Performance* – about a mother whose son is wrongly convicted. She was to appear in several other films, but she did not take to the medium ('She's just past taking direction,' said one producer) and they show no real glimpse of her skills as an actress.

Although several theatres were hit by bombs during the war, Ellen acted on, whenever she had the chance, seemingly unperturbed. There was a sudden air raid whilst she was on stage at the Coliseum in 1918, in the trial scene of *The Merchant of Venice*. The manager told two young artists, who were screaming in their dressing rooms and too panic-stricken to appear, that they should be ashamed of themselves: 'Think of Ellen Terry! She's an old woman, and she's as cool as a cucumber. If she dont mind the bombs, why on earth should you?"[6] Despite the danger, Edy was equally unconcerned. The actress Margaret Webster was once with her in an air raid shelter in Covent Garden, where they played charades to keep their minds off the bombs and Edy, wrapped in an eiderdown, gave a marvellous imitation of an elephant.

CHAPTER 16

MÉNAGE À TROIS

Although the Pioneer Players survived the war, no one would have gone to see their plays for light relief. The 1916-17 season, for instance, opened with *Mancha que Limpia*, a story of revenge, by the Spanish dramatist Jose Echegaray, and continued with Chris St John's translation of *The Hired Girl* by Herman Heijermans, about social conditions; *The Luck of War* by Gwen John, on a supposedly dead husband returning from the war; a monologue from the Russo-Israelite author, Rabinowitz, on the difficulty facing a Jewish parent in Russian Poland to get his son into a government school; and a four hour play by Paul Claudel, *The Tidings Brought to Mary*.

The *Westminster Gazette* spoke of the Pioneers' courage in staging the Claudel play, though its critic added, 'I almost wish they had had the audacity to cut it a little.' It would have been a pity: there could have been few stories like it. Set in the time of Joan of Arc, a beautiful girl near Rheims becomes a leper through kissing a leprous mason out of sheer kindness of heart. Her name is Violaine and she has a jealous sister named Mara. Mara immediately marries Violaine's lover and they have a baby girl who dies. Mara takes the dead baby to Violaine's cave on Christmas Eve and on being nursed in the leper's bosom, the child comes to life again, but with blue eyes like Violaine's instead of brown, like Mara's. Such is Mara's ingratitude that she tries to murder Violaine by throwing her into a sandpit. Violaine is brought home dying, but is afterwards apparently raised up to heaven.

The critic Desmond McCarthy, wrote in the *New Statesman*, that the public owed a debt to the Pioneers for having produced this play and that the whole season was 'A real contribution to the liveableness of life in London. In their choice of plays the

Pioneers have been enterprising and judicious. The acting has been excellent.' The committee's annual report also paid tribute to Edy, claiming that her art as a producer had been one of the most notable features of the sixth season and that the quality and beauty of her design for *The Tidings* was universally admired.

But despite the tributes and the growing reputation and influence of the Pioneers, the season brought in less than £100 profit and matters did not improve. The annual report for the 1917-18 season warned that the Pioneers 'must beware of allowing their courage to degenerate into foolhardiness. The wiser course would seem to be to keep the venture honourably alive by giving one or two performances of high quality.'[1]

Edy was particularly hit by the constant struggle for money: for the first six years, she was paid nothing for her work; and only after that did she receive a small fee for each production. There was no money for an office and, at the beginning of the war, she had to loan a room in her flat for one – remaining unperturbed by the entire cast turning up to rehearse there.

Despite the lack of money, everyone working on the performances was exhilarated. The actress Margaret Webster recalls Edy sitting by a gasfire in a brightly coloured dressing gown, 'just talking – telling stories, discussing, recalling, planning, prophesying, throwing out splinters of ideas with every sentence, sparks flying from her words . . . making herself a channel for the age-old "life-force" of the theatre.'[2]

One of those helping on set designs was Clare Atwood, an artist who had painted portraits of the Terry family. Clare, known as Tony, was a calm, gentle woman, who was a member of the New English Art Club, had exhibited paintings at the Royal Academy, and was one of the few artists to be given official painting commissions during the First World War. Edy got on with her very well and in 1916 asked Tony if she would like to come and live with her and Chris. Aware, however, of Chris's easily roused jealousy, she warned Tony while the move was still being arranged, 'that if Chris does not like your being here, and feels you are interfering with our friendship, out you go!'[3]

But Chris did like her being there, admitting that 'the bond between Edy and me was strengthened not weakened by Tony's association with us.' Tony was a born peacemaker and her tact and humour smoothed the relations between the other two. The arrangement worked so well that all three remained together throughout Edy's lifetime, at their various London flats and then permanently at their cottage, the Priest's House, at Smallhythe. Shaw wrote to Chris, after Edy's death, to say that she should write a history of their *ménage à trois* as, in his experience, it was unique.

The relationship worked because, apart from Tony being a great leavener of tension, all were busy in their own areas. Sheila Kaye-Smith, the writer, remembers the scene with the three of them: 'Edy would perhaps be producing a pageant, with Chris at work on the literary side and Tony busy with the dresses and "props." They would discuss it all eagerly.'[4] They were all deeply interested and involved in each other's work and moved in the same artistic world. They would go off to the theatre, cinema, concert or gallery together, or play Mahjong or Bezique.

They spent hours discussing books and politics, teasing each other, joking, quarrelling, very much attuned. Sybil Thorndike recalled a conversation during a rehearsal at Edy's flat after someone asked the meaning of an acting instruction and Edy replied:

> 'I can't keep explaining all these simple fundamental
> questions – it's probably all in the Apostle's Creed – you get
> most rules for acting there, don't you Chris?' – this last
> shouted to Chris who, with Tony, was concocting some food
> on the kitchen stove. 'What's that' yelled back Chris.
> 'Apostle's Creed rules for acting – yes, better than the
> Athanasian – simpler on the surface'.[5]

Sybil Thorndike thought this mysterious conversation made more sense than many a producer would believe.

In London the three gave teaparties in their flat, which was full of oriental objects, blue Chinese porcelain, silk embroidery, red lacquer chairs and a Japanese teapot in a lined basket. Irene Cooper Willis, Treasurer for the Pioneers, often dropped in because no one at Bedford Street knew anything about accounts. Edy had no bank account – putting her mother's weekly allowance straight into her purse – and took such fright at the sight of a business communication that she would summon Irene to relieve her fears. Irene was called to

Smallhythe, too, and remembered the familiar scene years later: 'Lame, heavy Chris is wedged into a chair at the table, writing; sprite-like Tony is flitting about.... They are dressed immemorially in coats and trousers, woolly caps on their heads if it is cold.'[6] The three would go hop-picking, but spent most of their time in their much-loved garden at Smallhythe – Edy in her sandals and hand-loomed linen smock, Tony in a man's hat and coat. Irene once turned up in smart clothes and Edy dismissed her with, 'Irene, never let me see you in that get-up again.'

The American actress, Florence Locke, recalls once visiting the cottage during one of Edy's organising days, to find her the centre of activity:

> Every question was directed towards her – her ringing voice was calling to everyone within earshot – Edy planning a pageant with one group, promising to costume a play for a second group, Edy stopping suddenly to do a crossword puzzle in a newly arrived magazine and demanding to know the name of a one-horned gazelle from South Africa.[7]

They would all go off round the countryside for rides in Edy's motor car, Belinda, with Edy sitting in the front seat next to the chauffeur, who doubled up as gardener and maintenance man, while 'the serfs' – the nickname friends had given to Chris and Tony – sat meekly in the dicky. They in turn called Edy 'Boney' because of the way she ordered them around. After supper, they usually sat amicably around the lamp, with Tony sketching, Chris reading aloud and Edy pasting yet more cuttings of places and people, flowers and furniture, costumes and buildings, reproductions of Old Masters, anything that she thought theatrically useful, into her scrapbooks. Her passion for collecting objects never tired. Tony recalled one moonlit night when the Tenterden fire-engine roared past and burst a new, rubber tyre and Edy promptly called out, 'Tony! Go and pick up as much as you can of that rubber!'[8]

There were disagreements among the three of them at times, but they rarely lasted long. They worked together too closely. In the 1918-19 season of the Pioneers, for instance, Edy acted as producer; one of the plays put on was translated from the Dutch by Chris; and Tony, who was play secretary, was praised in the annual report for a beautifully-made figure on a crucifix – constructed in two days out of the materials Edy had given her: a sack of paper and cardboard, some wood, a large pot of glue and an even larger ball of string.

Tony was particularly impressed by Edy's unexpected accomplishments: her ability to arrange stage fights to perfection; the way her crowd scenes had such a sense of design; the ease with which, as a good dancer herself, she had no difficulty in directing any kind of dance. All these skills were of immense advantage to her as a producer; but they were still not enough to save the Pioneer Players.

By 1920, the costs of the performances were no longer covered by members' subscriptions. Yet, artistically, the reviews were good, the *Arts Gazette* reviewer writing of the 1919-20 season that 'I have no hesitation in saying that Miss Craig has proved that she is second to none of the producers in this country, that she promises to vie with the great producers abroad . . . she inspired the actors.'

One of the plays in that season was Susan Glaspell's *Trifles*, which continued the strong feminist tradition of the Pioneers. In it, a man has been found strangled in bed. His wife, 'the downtrodden partner of his hearth and couch,' can offer no explanation. She is arrested, and the crime reconstructed in her home by the Attorney and Sheriff's wives, who build up a portrait of the woman. They find a dead canary in a painted box and, say the programme notes, 'we see in a moment the tragedy of the silent neglected wife, goaded to desperation after years of loveless, songless life, by the brutal murder of her little pet.' James Carew, in the part of the energetic attorney, gave a masterly performance, but the magazine, *Ladies Field*, commented that 'Unless the society can find a few lively writers, they will gain the name of the Pioneers of Pain.'

Two other plays put on during that season demonstrated the truth of this comment. One was *The Children's Carnival*, about a woman coping with the machinations of a half crazy brother, which one critic called 'A brutal assault on one's feelings and nerves.' The other was *The Higher Court*, dealing with divorce and Catholicism.

Virginia Woolf, writing in the *New Statesman* in April 1920, expertly summed up the expectations of the audience as she waited to see this latter play:

Pioneers – a subscription performance – Sunday evening –
the very name of the play – all conspire to colour one's
preconceptions. We are not going to enjoy ourselves
comfortably all over (that is the shade of it); we are going to
be wrought into a sharp nervous point. . . . In short, we are
going to be scraped and harrowed and precipitated into some
surprising outburst of bitterness against – probably the
Divorce Laws. On the other hand, there is the new Bastardy
Bill, and Dr Freud may very well have discovered something
entirely new and completely devastating about children's
toys.

The financial situation worsened, and an extraordinary
general meeting was called for the May of that year. But only
one hundred people attended out of a possible four hundred,
and it was recorded that 'the threat of its dissolution was
regarded with apathetic indifference.'
In the following year, 1921, the Pioneer Players was brought
to a formal end. The last annual report read:

Miss Craig was obliged to work in circumstances which
crippled her greatly. It was quite impossible to get a theatre
for rehearsals and the dress rehearsals had become a farce.
Although she had made the Pioneer Players famous by the
work she had done, it was impossible for her to be expected
to go on working under such conditions.[9]

CHAPTER 17

ELLEN IN OLD AGE: 'ALL IS PUZZLEDOM'

In the early 1920s, Ellen's grip on reality began to fade. On 26 April that year, she wrote in her diary, 'I am unhinged (*not* unhappy) and uncomfortable. I wonder where everything is. Cannot remember new things. All is changed. Change at 73 puzzles the will. I live in puzzledom.'[1] Having spent most of her life on the stage, she was at a loss without it. John Gielgud who had seen her as the Nurse in *Romeo and Juliet* the year before, found she still had the power to enchant the audience even though the actors playing Romeo and Mercutio had to whisper every word in her ear. She then spoke the line herself, as if she had just thought of it.[2]

Ellen couldn't come to terms with age and nor, indeed, could her associates, as they listened to her holding forth on every subject, even though disconnectedly, with flashes of her old vitality. Once, when a waiter told Chris St John, who had gone to get her coat after lunching with Ellen, that 'the old lady' had gone on ahead, Chris was shocked at the description. Yet Ellen at this time was white haired, almost blind, rather deaf, faltering in step and unable to concentrate on anything for long. Clemence Dane described her as 'Ariel in the tree.'

More immediately serious than the problem of increasing fragility was the state of Ellen's finances. There had been one crisis over money before she left on her Australian tour; now, to her bewilderment, there was another. Spending little on herself in the way of clothes and luxuries, aware of having earned a fortune on the stage, she couldn't see that her generosity towards dependents and the expenses of keeping up both a town and a country house, was causing her to live above her means. There had been crises before. Irene Cooper Willis remembered a funereal day when Edy heard news that Ellen had to cut down her allowance; 'The flat felt as if the bell of St Paul's Covent Garden were tolling.'[3]

Tony Atwood, who was a good businesswoman, came to Ellen's rescue, along with the lawyer Gilbert Samuel, and H.A. Gwynne, the editor of the *Morning Post*. Ellen had to hand over financial control to them, and follow the budget they drew up. On their advice, she sold her Georgian house in Chelsea and most of her belongings, and stopped allowances to dependents. Edy voluntarily gave up hers. Together with the money from two film appearances – in *The Pillars of Society* (1920) and *The Bohemian Girl* (1921) – she now had a small income, on which she could live.

Ellen first rented, then bought, a tiny flat in St Martin's Lane, which Ted, far away in Italy and believing all these economies unnecessary, described as 'most un-Terrylike.' But though he and other admirers of Ellen felt she should be presiding over dinner parties, in the old Lyceum style, in reality, too many people around her confused her. Her doctor was to say: 'It is very important that she should lead a very quiet life. Indeed it is wiser for her not to see more than one or two persons at a time.'[4] Ellen was fortunate in that James Carew was living in a flat above her and did all he could to help her.

Edy, needing to earn money, began working for the Everyman Theatre in Hampstead. It was not the first time she had worked there. In 1920, when the Pioneer Players started to lose its struggle for existence, she had acted as assistant producer for a performance there of *Romeo and Juliet* and had successfully organised crowd movements and fights. She had acted as assistant on the same play two years previously at the Lyric, when Ellen played the nurse, and her coloured sketches of the costumes and tiny drawings of each scene on three inch square pieces of paper, still survive.[5]

The newly-opened Everyman was the first popular London theatre that had a director-producer – Norman MacDermott – who controlled both policy and production. This type of theatre management first developed in the years after the First World War, when it was realised that more than just stage management was needed. The Everyman theatre itself was also modern in its design, having a projecting forestage.

Edy was an enthusiastic supporter of the Everyman. She, Chris and Tony were jocularly known there as 'The Three

Edy in the garden at Smallhythe, which she retrieved from being a potato patch, in 1925.

Musketeers,' because after a visit to Italy they had come back wearing large floppy black hats and the voluminous black capes worn by Italian police officers. In 1921, Norman MacDermott decided to run a Shaw season – rather a risky project as Shaw had seriously upset patriots with his proclaimed pacifism during the 1914-18 war. MacDermott asked Edy if she would take over the entire season's productions, but under his general direction. He would cast the plays, but only after consultation with her; and, as he put it in his history of the Everyman, 'have general supervision on important matters.'

The idea worked surprisingly well, given Edy's experience and preference for running the whole show herself. MacDermott said,

> Miss Craig not only accepted this very unusual arrangement, but most loyally carried it into practice during the course of our association. I found her delightful to work with, easy, good-humoured and loyal. The Everyman, and even more myself, owe her a deep gratitude for the richness of spirit that she brought to this difficult assignment.[6]

Ellen came to the premiere of Shaw's *The Shewing-up of Blanco Posnet*, which got good reviews, as did the entire season.

Despite her success at the Everyman and with the Pioneer Players, and to her friends' disbelief and anger, Edy was offered no work as a stage director in the West End in the 1920s. The only offer was to produce two plays at the Kingsway Theatre, during Anthony Ellis's brief management there. Ellen felt this as deeply as Edy, saying about friends who were lobbying for her to receive some kind of official honour, in recognition of her services to the theatre, 'Let them instead do something for my children who, talented as they are, lack advancement.' Ted's work, now being acclaimed in Germany and France, had received little encouragement in Britain.

Like her brother, Edy worked creatively: she was both innovator and interpreter. As the actor Ernest Milton said, 'She avoided the worn-out formulae, the too consciously over-drilled effect of expertness, and gave to her productions an element of surprise achieved by a guarded nonchalance, an air of improvisation.'[7]

Another actor, Harcourt Williams, rightly considered that

Edy's fastidiousness, demand for perfection, and need for complete control, could never suit the commercial theatre. Certainly West End theatre managements preferred conventional plays, conventionally produced, which could be assured of a long run. Successes in the early 1920s, for instance, included Conan Doyle's *The Speckled Band*, the American comedy, *His Lady Friends* with James Carew, and J.M. Barrie's *Peter Pan*.

Edy was a born director, but her perfectionism, conviction that she was always right, and brusque manner was disliked by too many of the theatrical establishment. Ernest Milton was one of many who found their first meeting with her disconcerting: 'Her manner was so direct, her handclasp so athletic. Her voice seemed gruff. An abrupt scorn for fools was at once apparent.'[8] Those who got to know her admired the honesty under the ruthlessness; others backed away. Lilian Baylis, when asked to give Edy the job of stage director at the Old Vic, said: 'We don't want another woman here. And anyhow we don't want Edy. She would upset the staff.'[9]

With no openings for her in London, Edy had to turn to the provinces to earn some money and for a time became stage director of the Leeds Art Theatre. She spent much of her time over the next few years working in York, Letchworth and Hampstead with amateur groups who either owned theatres or rented them – known as the Little Theatre Movement. She also continued to organise pageants, one being at Mount Grace Priory, in Yorkshire, where she ordered round the locals in her usual brisk way. Warned that amongst them was one of the biggest ironmasters in Yorkshire, Edy retorted that she didn't care: he would still have to do what she told him.

In the February of 1922, Edy went off to Egypt for about six weeks and Ellen wrote to her friend Marguerite Steen to say she was 'rather in the depths' about it, and wished she were going herself. Her spirits were low:

> I do nothing from day to day, and it is an AWFUL waste of time – and of course I am *bored* – think of that!! My memory frayed to smithereens and 'there is no health in me.' I feel rather like *hating* everything – a bad state of things – CIRCULATION IS LACKING – I feel sure that is the trouble.[10]

Ellen acted at some charity matinees that year and unveiled a memorial tablet to Sarah Siddons at Bath — where she briefly regained some of her lost exuberance. Her old friend, Squire Bancroft was one of the reception party at the station and as he and Ellen drove in an open carriage through the city, they pretended to be minstrels, both singing a music hall song, with Bancroft strumming an imaginary banjo and Ellen shaking a non-existent tambourine.[11] Her critical faculties remained sharp: after seeing Mrs Pat Campbell in *Pygmalion*, she commented that she played well at first, then got careless and lazy.

The same year, Gerald du Maurier was knighted and Genevieve Ward, a tragedienne, was made a Dame. Agitation grew for some kind of public recognition for Ellen. In sympathy with this feeling, Sir James Barrie, who was then Rector of St Andrew's University, presented her with an honorary degree on 5 May.

Ellen saw the year out still depressed. Writing again to Marguerite Steen, she said:

> Old age is not all sweets — but of course I'm just wicked to say I've 'had enough of it' — but — well for one thing all my usefulness is over & to be of *no use to anyone* . . . well . . . that *is Hell* it seems to me.[12]

Her mood was not always unhappy. Her frequent stays at Sandhills, the house in Witley, Surrey, of Graham Robertson, the artist and writer, gave her much needed rest and refuge and she happily took part in local activities. But she was further upset the following year by the death of Sarah Bernhardt, whose last performance in London in *Daniel*, in 1920, Ellen had enthusiastically applauded. Sarah, then aged seventy six, had played thirty year old Daniel. When she heard the actor cast as Daniel's forty year old brother was actually aged fifty, she protested crossly, 'Why the man's too old! He'll look like my father!'[13] A requiem mass was held for her at Westminster Cathedral which Ellen attended.

In the February of 1924, Ellen took great delight in seeing every single performance of the first production of Shaw's 'Pentateuch' at the Court Theatre, then celebrated her seventy seventh birthday that month by seeing a film by Charlie Chaplin, a favourite of hers. She had never particularly liked

Edy (left) and Ellen, taken in York, January 1925, shortly after Ellen was awarded the Dame Grand Cross of the British Empire.

the cinema, but had been won over when she had seen Rudolph Valentino in *Blood and Sand*, saying, 'If I were going to play Romeo, I should come here every night and study that man. *That's* the way to stand under the balcony!' The year was later saddened for her by the death of another actress she greatly admired, Eleonora Duse.

It was not until the 1925 New Year's honours list that she was at last made Dame Grand Cross of the Most Excellent Order of the British Empire. To spare her fatigue, it was decided to invest her in a private room at Buckingham Palace. Edy walked alongside her wheelchair, then watched her stand and give a magnificent curtsey on entry into the room. After the ceremony, Ellen groped for the door, then made the King laugh by exclaiming with horror that she had forgotten to leave the royal presence walking backwards. Queen Mary asked to see her and they had a long talk about the old days of the Lyceum. Queen Alexandra, who died that year, was another royal admirer of Ellen's, always sending her a telegram on her birthday. 'A lovely time,' Ellen wrote in her diary.

Ellen was now a worry to her family and friends. Without someone to watch her, she was quite likely to give away valuable possessions, or wander off, half-blind, into streets busy with traffic. She needed someone to read to her, write her letters for her, see she was dressed warmly enough. At times she could reduce her maid to affectionate laughter by wearing a bedsock on her head; at others she was a fractious employer, going through some twenty five or so maids in five years, and being black-listed by the top London agencies, before finding a good-tempered and sensible Yorkshirewoman called Hilda Barnes, known to all as Barney, who was to look after her for the rest of her life.

Her final performance on stage was in November 1925, in Walter de la Mare's *Crossings*, at the Lyric Theatre, Hammersmith. Chris St John, watching her first entrance at the dress rehearsal, wrote of it:

The vision of this fragile creature, far advanced in years, yet somehow not old, tremulously gliding across the stage with loving arms outstretched, all earthiness purged away by time, the spirit of beauty, rather than beauty itself, filled the spectators with a strange awe. A long sighing 'Oh!' arose from them all.[14]

Ellen herself, more prosaically, complained that when she had asked the producer for instructions over her part, he said, 'Well you see – you – er – well, you come on.' Ellen waited. 'Well, then you – er – well – you come off again.' Not surprisingly, the play didn't last.

That same year, the Pioneer Players came out of their retirement to present *The Verge* by Susan Glaspell, America's leading playwright, about a woman whose attempt to change her lifestyle brings her to the verge of madness. It had a mixed press, though Sybil Thorndike's acting was praised. 'One comes out holding one's head. Oh dear, oh dear,' said the *Yorkshire Post* critic. But the *Time and Tide* critic said that Edy's work was full of style.

Early the next year, Edy went down with pneumonia and Ellen went to stay at Graham Robertson's who wrote to a friend:

> I am a little nervous about the visit, as the Lady is rather a responsibility at her age and without any of her own folk or attendants, but Edy has been very ill lately and wants a quiet time badly – has gone off to her Smallhythe cottage today.[15]

Ellen spent a pleasant summer and autumn down at Smallhythe. Her sister Marion came to stay and Graham Robertson remembered Ellen's wickedly funny description of the visit. Marion, known as 'the perfect lady' in the Terry family, had taken Ellen off to visit 'good houses' with 'really nice people,' watching her carefully in case she committed some social *faux pas*. Ellen told Graham it was as well he was not there, or she would have laughed and disgraced herself.

But later that year she became seriously ill with bronchial pneumonia and Ted was summoned from Italy. Ellen had not seen him for three years and was immediately cheered by his presence. He said he found her 'pretending to be far more ill than she would in secret allow.' This was what he wanted to believe, and further deceived by Ellen's radiance at seeing him, he returned optimistically to Italy. Ellen was to recover slowly. She had set her heart on celebrating Christmas with Edy, but

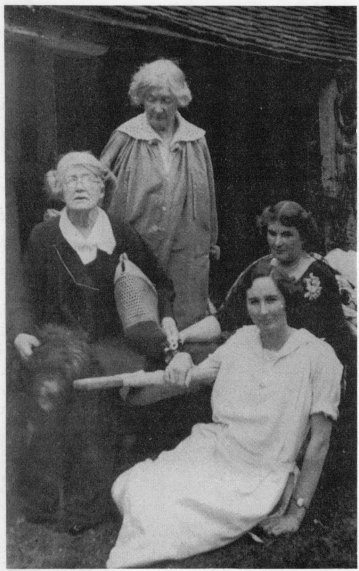

Ellen (left), at eighty, by now nearly blind. Edy stands protectively behind her; two other friends in front. At Smallhythe, 1927.

four ambulancemen had to carry her up the stairs to the London flat.

Visiting her in London early the next year, Graham Robertson had found her comfortable and happy, with Edy dropping in after tea and her grandson, Teddy, over from Italy. Robertson thought him a nice boy: 'Perhaps Pa's and Grandpa's little peculiarities may have skipped a generation.' Only the following month, however, he was to write that Ellen was now 'very sadly,' and was 'drifting away into a strange vague world where nothing is real and people bear no names.' James Carew had told him that he had visited her and, for once, she had recognised him.

'Tell me, Jim,' she had said slowly, 'I can't quite remember – did I kick you out or did you kick me out?' 'Well dear,' said poor Jim cautiously, 'I think we arranged it between us, didn't we?' 'Yes, so we did,' said Nell. Then, after a pause: 'Dam' fools, weren't we?'[16]

Ellen at this point was staying with her friends Alix and Mabel Egerton at Wateringbury who, according to Graham Robertson, were 'having the hell of a time' with Edy, who was quick to react if she felt anyone else was taking Ellen over. Ellen's friends, in turn, felt Edy, backed by Chris and Tony, was dragon-like in her protection.

Even Barney, Ellen's housekeeper, nurse and daily protector, caused Edy a certain amount of angst – a fact she obviously knew, as her tactful letters to Edy show. One of these begins:

Just to say your mother was more than glad to have your card, as long as she has a line from you now and again she is perfectly happy. The only thing that frets her is not hearing from you . . . she just shed a little tear when she got your card and said she had been a wicked woman to ever think you should forget her,

and ends,

Dame Ellen says, my love to my blessed Edy – she knows I want to write but can't.[17]

Another, written from Epsom, reflected family factions:

Your mother is alone with me and we talked of you and she

would have me ask if you are well. . . . My letters are rather
in the hands of any one going out and I feel disturbed you
have not always had mine – that explains Olive [Ellen's
niece] saying, 'Do always tell Edy things' but I cannot
understand her saying, 'Do try to be fond of Edy.'

It has made me think there is something or someone like
an enemy in the camp – my conversations with Olive should
by now have convinced her I am fond of you – or would I
give up Xmas or keep many many worrying things from you
and stick to your mother as I do. Her latest stunt is
undressing in any drawing room she is in – no matter who is
there. At times it is more than embarrassing – and as the
doctor says, she is remarkably strong for a woman of her age
– these last few days she has talked of joining Miss Marion
[Ellen's sister] in Monte Carlo – and she says she will take
good care no one stops her going.[18]

Barney's letters to Edy chronicle the difficulties Ellen
presented in her last years – sometimes confused and vague, at
other times incredibly strong willed. 'Your mother . . . was
terribly naughty the whole night,' said one letter from
Maidstone:

wanting to wander out and look for me – I tried to stay in
bed and let Miss Hassal cope with it, but once I had to go – a
terrific noise was going on and things seemed to be flying
round the room – However in spite of a very hectic night
your mother seems to be as strong as three of me put
together . . . & is now thoroughly turning over the morning
paper – with an occasional mutter of 'Why should I have two
to do for me – God knows one's enough.'[19]

Barney also wrote of Ellen's depression at having none of her
own family around her. It made her believe she was being kept
prisoner and she announced she intended to sneak out in the
middle of the night and escape.

Ellen was away from Smallhythe for so long because the
heating was being repaired. Edy, increasingly perturbed by
Ellen's state of mind, hurried the work along and in the March
of 1928, Ellen was brought back there. Arriving in her
wheelchair, she told the doctor, 'This is my own house, doctor,
bought with my own money.' She improved in spirits once

The last photograph of Ellen, taken at the age of eighty one, down at her farm in Smallhythe.

home, but also said, 'I hate being old. Yes, I just hate it. People are very kind, but that makes it worse. However, it's absurd to cry over spilt milk. I intend to go into my grave smiling.'[20]

The July of 1928 was hot and on the sixteenth of the month Ellen persuaded Barney and the nurse to wheel her outside for the first time since her return. Tired with the exertion, they left her by the road as they rested nearby: when they didn't answer to her call, Ellen peremptorily got their attention by the simple method of throwing her shoes into the road.

Next morning, Barney rushed to Chris and Tony in the cottage to say that Ellen had had a stroke. A message was telephoned to Edy, who had gone to London the day before. By chance, Ted too was over in London from Italy. He hadn't been down to Smallhythe, still not considering Ellen to be that ill, but Edy collected him and they drove straight down. Edy, on arrival, promptly put on her smock, so her mother would see a familiar sight if she rallied.

Ellen didn't. Paralysed by the stroke, she never opened her eyes again, though she tried to speak. The news that she was dying spread quickly: her brothers Fred and Charlie, sister Marion, and niece Olive came down; the King and Queen sent messages of concern; so did hundreds of others. It jolted the memories of thousands in the country.

Edy hardly left Ellen's side, but sat by the bed holding her hand. Once Ellen's voice, thick and indistinct, said the word 'Happy.' At eight thirty on the morning of 21 July, she died. Her son wrote sentimentally,

> She died in the morning sun, which shone warm and yellow on to her. She sat up suddenly – opened her eyes – fell back and threw off fifty old years as she fell. She became twenty five to look at – and in truth she became once more Nelly Terry, back again at Harpenden with little Edy and little Teddy and the one she loved better than all the world.[21]

In her bedroom, Barney found a copy of *The Imitation of Christ*, on the flyleaf of which Ellen had copied out William Allingham's poem:

> No funeral gloom, my dears, when I am gone;
> Corpse-gazings, tears, black raiment, graveyard grimness.
> Think of me as withdrawn into the dimness,

Yours still, you mine. Remember all the best
Of our past moments, and forget the rest.
And so, to where I wait, come gently on.

Under it, in Ellen's handwriting, were the words, 'I should wish my children, relatives and friends to observe this when I die.'

CHAPTER 18

EDY: 'WHO'S PUT OUT THE LIGHT?'

On 24 July 1928, the day of Ellen's funeral, cars filled the miles of roads around Smallhythe, blinds were drawn in Tenterden, the nearest town, and, at the church, haymakers and shepherds from the fields formed an impromptu guard of honour. A copy of William Allingham's poem had been pinned to the gate at Smallhythe and in accordance with Ellen's wishes that there be no funeral gloom, the men in the long, winding funeral procession wore coloured ties, the women bright summer dresses. One person who was plunged in funeral gloom, however, was Mrs Aria – sobbing that Ellen, by dying first, would get to Irving before she did.

After the service, the coffin, designed by Ted, and covered in a gold pall, was taken to the Golders Green crematorium in London. Although the ashes were then brought to St Paul's Church, Covent Garden in a silver casket made by Ted's friend, the silversmith John Paul Cooper, the negotiations for them to remain there permanently were not concluded for over a year. Until then, a special room in Edy's flat was converted into an oratory. It was blessed, and prior to St Paul's the casket remained there with a sanctuary light continuously burning. James Carew sent flowers every week for the oratory.

Chris St John said she noticed a change in Edy after her mother's death. She seemed to gain some of Ellen's authority, and a little of her charm. She began, almost uncannily, to resemble her more physically: her flowing clothes had always been similar. In later years, although she could see perfectly well, she was occasionally to falter and feel her way through doorways, as Ellen, half blind, used to do. Chris and Tony felt at times that Ellen's spirit possessed her. Even a seven-year-old child, when down at Smallhythe being told all about Ellen – the

Ellen's funeral cortege led by Ted and Edy and followed by James Carew and Olive Chaplin (Ellen's niece), with Fred Terry behind Carew. Tuesday 24 July 1928, Smallhythe.

way she would sit cross-legged on the floor, the red combs she wore in her white hair – said in the end, 'But, Mummy, aren't you telling me about Edy?'[1]

Edy threw her energy into a scheme for a memorial to Ellen. The main objects were to raise enough money to turn Ellen's home into a memorial museum; endow it sufficiently to keep it repaired and pay a custodian; and to convert the barn into a theatre and stage dramatic performances there on the anniversary of Ellen's death. The estimated cost was £15,000.

The lack of interest and response shook Edy: only a tiny amount of money trickled in. Under the terms of Ellen's will, she had inherited part of her money, though less than Ted and his family. But Ellen had left her house to her. So, unpaid, she started the work herself. By the summer of 1929, she had filled two of the rooms with theatrical relics, to which visitors were welcome. By organising a benefit at the Palace Theatre, she raised enough to get the barn ready for a performance on the first anniversary of Ellen's death – despite holes in its roof and gaps in its timbered walls and the only seating being rough benches on a beaten earth floor.

Edy was now sixty years old, and in addition to the emotional upset of her mother's death, she was exhausted by the amount of work she was doing to build up Smallhythe as a shrine to Ellen. In the end, the Memorial Committee decided to wind up the appeal for more money and instead give Edy an annual contribution, from the income of the fund as it stood, for general upkeep of the house. She in turn would give the memorial trustees an option to purchase the house within the next ten years.

For the rest of her life, although she continued to stage pageants and produce the occasional play, Edy dedicated herself to preserving the memory of her mother. The house was obviously an important part of this; but she was also anxious to dispel the impression of Ellen that often came through in articles about her, that she was a charming scatterbrain. It struck her that she could do this by publishing a collection of Ellen's letters and Shaw was one of those to whom she wrote to ask if he could contribute some letters. He turned up at her flat with hundreds of them and Edy, on reading them, thought they brought her mother vividly to life. The idea of publishing the correspondence began from there.

Although the copyright of the letters was Edy's, she nevertheless consulted Ted about publication, as his dislike of Shaw was well known and she was anxious to avoid controversy. Ted reluctantly but formally gave his consent in 1930, but on their publication in 1931, spoke indignantly of Shaw's perfidy in allowing his private letters to go public and besmirching the image of his mother. Some other papers, like the *Morning Post*, also reacted with disgust, calling it an insult to Ellen's memory. Ted promptly wrote *Ellen Terry and her Secret Self*, a sentimental portrait of his mother, which included a number of side-swipes at Shaw.

It hardly helped heal the breach between Edy and Ted. Graham Robertson – who was sympathetic to Ted, and disliked Edy – wrote to his friend Kerrison Preston to say that he had been amused at the way Shaw had presented Edy in an article in the *Observer* 'as the sweet, loving sister, flinching from Ted's attacks.'

Edy took refuge at Smallhythe. She and Chris started work on revising and annotating Ellen's memoirs. From then on, Edy's way of life was hardly to change. One of her main interests was organising the annual Shakespearean matinee at the Barn Theatre to commemorate the anniversary of Ellen's death. This meant a lot of hard work. She chose the play, made the costumes, oversaw the set designs, and rehearsed the cast in London. 'No one could ever say no to Edy,' Vita Sackville West wrote, and actors and actresses like John Gielgud, Sybil Thorndike, Peggy Ashcroft and Edith Evans, though acting in the West End, would learn new parts for the Barn Theatre, rehearse them with Edy in London, then cheerfully travel the sixty five miles down to Smallhythe for a single performance.

During the summer months, Edy produced five or six plays for the Barn Theatre Society. She established this society in 1931, running it on the same subscription basis as the Pioneer Players and putting on similarly unknown and quirky plays. There was nothing like it in that area of Kent, and from 1931 to 1939, under Edy's direction, the Barn Theatre became a dramatic centre.

In the middle of July, 1931, Edy invited their Rye neighbours, Radclyffe 'John' Hall, whose novel, *The Well of Loneliness* about lesbian love had caused a sensation in 1928, and her companion Una Troubridge, over to Smallhythe to a pageant in the barn. The Rye couple liked the unworldly atmosphere of Smallhythe and were intrigued with the trio: Tony, called 'The Brat' by the other two, in white duck jacket and trousers and over-large panama hat; Chris, known as 'Master Baby,' with her rollicking laugh (it was the fashion among their group to give everyone lighthearted nicknames); and the strong-willed Edy, to whom both Tony and Chris deferred.

During the 1930s the five women became close friends. The Rye couple enjoyed themselves lounging in Tony's studio, gossiping about mutual friends; and when the Smallhythe trio accepted a dinner engagement with the Rye couple, it was the first time they had gone out for an evening meal since living at the cottage. Chris, to celebrate, wore a black velvet smoking jacket with vast bell-bottom trousers.[2]

The Smallhythe trio were regarded as unconventional and odd: but they didn't arouse the same hostility as the Rye couple, who deliberately made a public statement out of their openly lesbian relationship. Lesbianism was by now attracting antagonism: in 1919, there had been a move to add a new clause to the Criminal Law Amendment Act to prevent 'acts of gross indecency by females,' which was over-ruled by the House of Lords on the grounds that it would only bring such behaviour to the attention of decent women. In 1928, the publication of *The Well of Loneliness* was greeted by the *Sunday Express* headline, 'The Book That Must Be Suppressed.' Such a climate only brought the Smallhythe and Rye women closer together.

Rye at the time was something of a literary centre. Besides Radclyffe Hall and Una Troubridge, E.F. Benson lived there, as did the novelist, Francis Yeats Brown, who had been editor of the *Spectator* and whose autobiography, *Bengal Lancer* had been a best seller. Another novelist, J.D. Beresford and the publisher Vincent Marrot were also local. They would go to each other's houses for dinner, or meet at the Mermaid Inn; and Edy, Chris and Tony would sometimes join them. The writer Sheila Kaye-Smith lived in the surrounding area and so did the painter Paul Nash.

Sheila Kaye-Smith remembered them all having a memorable Christmas dinner at The Black Boy (Radclyffe Hall's High Street house in Rye) and the many return visits to the cottage at

Smallhythe, 'where the family at Priest's House always gave me the impression of activity to the point of urgency.' She admired Edy's gift of being absorbed in each of her visitors. When Sheila wrote a miracle play – for reading only – she was amazed at how Edy transformed it into a stage play and at the sharpness and originality of her interpretation.

Eleanor Adlard, the actress, noticed the same frantic activity when she visited them. 'They all cooked,' she said:

> they all argued (and the house was small enough to carry on animated conversations from room to room) and they all entertained lavishly. Visitors motored from London, neighbours called, the telephone rang, there were exchanges of country gifts of eggs, quince jelly and fruit, people came to see the museum, others to ask about a pageant to be produced, Terry children were always popping up and to each and all, Edy was the perfect hostess, wise adviser and playmate. No one was idle, no one was allowed to be at anything less than high pressure.[3]

The life of all three women at Priest's House during the 1930s was unconventional and energetic fun. Vita Sackville West, a visitor there, wrote of their evenings around the long table in the dining room, with Edy presiding and Chris and Tony sitting in any seat they could find:

> They talk. It is enchanting talk; it ranges widely; it isn't always consecutive; it starts too many hares too quickly to follow up; they argue; they quarrel; they interrupt; it is impossible to have any sequence of conversation. Yet how stimulating it is! and how friendly! how lively! What live wires they all are; what a sense of life one gets from them. Tony may be a peacemaker; but Edy is a pace-maker. She rushes the other two; she has too many ideas for them; ideas that they must put into practice. No wonder that they sometimes say 'Edy has bitten off more than we can chew.' For, let us be honest, Edy is a tyrant, and the other two must obey her commands. Edy sitting in her big chair under the dim mirror, is the dominating character, the matriarch, of this encampment.[4]

The three women continued to enjoy each other's company, as they drove around the lanes in a coster's cart; went hop picking; visited the local pikies [gypsies]; drove to Bodiam in the moonlight; and were an audience to friends' children, whom they allowed solemnly to act their made-up plays in the Barn Theatre.

In 1932, Vita Sackville West was invited to read her poem *The Land* at the Barn Theatre to an audience which included her husband Harold Nicolson, the Woolfs, Stephen Spender, Raymond Mortimer, William Plomer and the painter Eardley Knollys. Afterwards, Vita wrote to her friend Evelyn Irons, describing Edy as a tearing old lesbian, not unlike Radclyffe Hall, who held no charms for her: 'Seeing me trying to sharpen a pencil, she came up and took it away. "Here, give me that," she said, "no woman knows how to sharpen a pencil." You may imagine Orlando's indignation.'[5]

Nevertheless, a return invitation to Vita's Sissinghurst home was given and it was there while Vita was showing the trio her bedroom, that a potentially explosive situation arose. Describing the scene later in her diary, Chris wrote: 'Contemplating a worn piece of green velvet on her dressing-table, I felt my whole being dissolve in love.'[6] Vita went up to Edy's Bedford Street flat in London to see Chris and in November that year they slept together for the first and last time. As Vita was leaving almost immediately for a three month lecture tour of America, she easily dismissed this from her mind: agreeing with Virginia Woolf's description of Chris as a 'mule-faced harridan,' she had no wish to get involved.

But Chris's feelings were seriously aroused. She wrote constantly to Vita while she was in America, addressing her as 'My Lord Orlando,' and, on her return to England in 1933, wrote in her love journal of her disappointment that Vita had not sought her out and developed the relationship. Nevertheless, Chris's infatuation remained. When she asked Vita if they would ever have another night together, she replied, 'Why not?', keeping Chris's hopes marginally alive.[7] But the mere sight of Vita, when she came to the Barn Theatre, together with her husband, to give a joint performance called 'Impressions of America,' upset Chris. She was even more despairing when, by the October of that year, it was evident that Vita had no more interest in her.

Though in the past Chris had praised Edy's calm immunity from jealousy, this came to an abrupt end with Chris's defection and there were tremendous scenes at the cottage until the involvement was over. Radclyffe Hall and Una Troubridge had been seriously considering building a house on some land near the cottage. But they backed away from the idea of being neighbours to the volatile threesome after finding the normally sweet-tempered Tony marching around muttering loudly 'We can't possible have a house out here.'[8]

One of Edy's abiding enthusiasms was mounting pageants on history, the theatre or literature, and she went on producing these in villages and towns round the country for the rest of her life. Because of her passion for historical accuracy, these pageants took much more time and thought than merely rehearsing crowds of local people for the parts. Sheila Kaye-Smith remembers Edy ringing her up to ask for some information about Jane Austen and her sister Cassandra, whose lives came into a pageant she was organising, and remembers how the pageants were never ragged or amateurish, but full of life and colour. Colour was important to Edy: she never liked the 'greenery-yallery Grosvenor Gallery' dresses she had to wear as a child: instead, she preferred smocks of crimson, blue and yellow.

She occasionally acted in pageants and sometimes took small parts in films. But she preferred to spend any spare time she had in tending her wild, but much loved garden – originally a potato patch – and in researching for her valuable collection of scrapbooks and notebooks. Every detail of the plays she produced had to be accurate, down to the right colour of a telephone used in a French play; or the correct period pictures on the walls.

She would jump at any opportunity to further people's understanding of, or interest in, Ellen. In 1933, she gave a plaster cast of her mother's hands to the Shakespeare Memorial Theatre Museum. They were placed in an oak casket, wreathed with rosemary from Ellen's own garden at Smallhythe. She put in months and months of careful work at Ellen's house, arranging the wardrobe room with Ellen's more famous dresses, including the beetle-wing dress she had worn as Lady Macbeth; hanging the family photographs, portraits and posters; laying out the personal gifts and relics from other actors and actresses like Sarah Bernhardt. She left Ellen's bedroom exactly as it had been on the day she died, with its schoolroom double-desk and the crucifix Ellen kept by her bed. Her aim was to create an intimate impression of Ellen; not merely catalogued lists of objects.

In the same year, Virginia Woolf joined the Barn Society and, together with Vita Sackville West, went over to meet the Smallhythe trio. The visit resulted in a graphic picture of Edy, disguised as Miss La Trobe, in Virginia Woolf's posthumously published novel, *Between the Acts*:

> Miss La Trobe was pacing to and fro between the leaning birch trees. One hand was deep stuck in her jacket pocket; the other held a foolscap sheet. She was reading what was written there. She had the look of a commander pacing his deck.
>
> Wet would it be, or fine? Out came the sun; and, shading her eyes in the attitude proper to an Admiral on his quarterdeck, she decided to risk the engagement out of doors. Doubts were over. All stage properties, she commanded, must be moved from the Barn to the bushes. It was done.
>
> 'Bossy' they called her privately. . . . Her abrupt manner and stocky figure; her thick ankles and sturdy shoes; her rapid decisions barked out in guttural accents – all this 'got their goat.' No one liked to be ordered about singly. But in little troops they appealed to her. Someone must lead.[9]

As well as directing, Edy also wrote and lectured about the modern theatre. In one lecture in January 1937, she argued that the picture frame atmosphere of a conventional theatre made both actors and audiences apathetic, and stunned listeners by saying it was much better to perform plays on lorries at street corners with the audience standing round as part of it all. Most of all, she said, she liked working in churches.

Despite this modern outlook, she wrote an article for the *Evening News*, in March 1938, looking back nostalgically on certain aspects of the old-style theatre: the way gaslight made stage effects more striking, even if it sometimes scorched the edges of costumes; the more professional attitude towards acting – she herself being once sacked at a moment's notice from the Adelphi Theatre for laughing on stage.

In October 1938, Sybil Thorndike presided over a dinner at the Savoy to honour Edy's fifty years' connection with the stage. According to press reports, it was a happy occasion.

Cicely Hamilton described how Edy had thrown her into impossible situations in pageants, even making her conduct an orchestra when she had no idea what to do. Lady Maud Warrender's son recalled that when one countryman, in a pageant, was asked how he got on with Edy, he said, 'Oh, I *liked* her. She's rude!' – meaning she had not minced matters when giving instructions. Only one speaker mentioned that Edy's insistence on the highest quality was not always expressed as gently as more sensitive people would have liked.

At the dinner, a message of congratulations from Queen Mary was read out and Edy was presented with a scroll containing the names of all present with a cheque in recognition of her services to the English theatre. The formal recognition was there, but as *The Times* was to say, in her obituary, 'Her devotion to her mother shone out more brightly than the remarkable theatrical talent which never, perhaps, received its due attention.' Bernard Shaw explained it this way: 'Gordon Craig has made himself the most famous producer in Europe by dint of never producing anything, while Edith Craig remains the most obscure by dint of producing everything.'

It was an unfair remark about Ted who had been praised extravagantly abroad for his productions of *Venice Preserved* (1905) in Berlin, *Rosmersholm* (1906) for Eleonora Duse in Florence, and *Hamlet* (1912) at the Moscow Art Theatre. Between Ellen's death in 1928 and the start of the Second World War, he remained busy in Europe and England, even though his most important work for the stage was by then over. He produced one book on Irving, another on his mother; an edition of *Hamlet* with woodcuts; the last number of *The Mask*, his unique magazine on the art of the theatre; and designed the scenes for a New York production of *Macbeth*. He did not think too highly of these, signing them 'C.p.b.', standing for 'Craig pot boiler.' He was to spend the war years in Paris, mainly working on his theatre collection.

For the Smallhythe trio, the war was to put an end to their carefree life, effectively cutting them off from London. Irene Cooper Willis, a long-time friend of Edy's, frequently visited the cottage during the war, when bombs and incendiaries were falling every night and so many farms on the Marshes had been hit that it was quite possible that Smallhythe would be, too. She recalls

Edy (left, sitting), Chris St John (standing) and Clare Atwood, from a photo by the late Antony Marshall, in his garden at Bethersden, Kent.

I remember going down one snowy day in February, with a bag of Cornish oysters and a bottle of wine, and hearing, as we feasted, of all Edy's plans for an exodus, if it should come to that. She was looking out for an old perambulator which she could pack with rations and other necessaries and go forth with on the push. Meanwhile as the planes droned and the bangs and crashes sounded, Edy and Chris ensconced themselves calmly under the dining-room table, the most solid piece of furniture in the house, while Tony prowled along the road as a fire-watcher.[10]

At the end of the war, Edy was seventy five. Her health was now poor: she had a heart condition and was in constant pain from rheumatism and arthritis. She needed a stick to walk with and sometimes used a wheelchair. But friends still found her essentially unchanged, as, white haired, wearing a brightly coloured smock, she would fling up her hands in welcome as they arrived. In July 1946, she produced a spectacularly beautiful pageant at Chilham, Kent, based on the classics of literature. Chris remembered her looking calm and dignified in the friar's habit she always wore at rehearsals and performances of pageants, so that she could go on stage unnoticed if anything went wrong.

In defiance of her doctor who told her to stay at home, and despite the freezing weather, she insisted on attending the 1947 memorial service at St Paul's, Covent Garden, commemorating Ellen's centenary. A few days later, on the morning of 27 March, she and Chris were planning the annual Shakespearean production for the Barn Theatre. Edy's idea was that all the players would be members of the Terry family. But the journey to London had worsened her heart condition. Suddenly calling out, 'It's all dark. Who put out the light?', she died.

POSTSCRIPT

While the casket of Ellen's ashes had remained enshrined for months in a specially blessed oratory in Edy's flat before being taken to St Paul's Church, Edy was not to receive the same treatment. Some twelve years after she died, Olive Chaplin, Ellen's niece, happened to come across a tin box with a puzzling amount of dust inside. 'Then I remembered – it was Edy Craig's ashes. When she died she had asked for her ashes to be buried with Kit and Tony . . . I'll nip across one day and scatter them on the grave.'[1] In holding on to the ashes waiting for Chris and Tony to die – and Tony was in her early nineties before she died – Olive Chaplin had forgotten all about them.

James Carew's ashes fared no better. Chris St John told actor Donald Sinden[2] that a long time after Ellen had died, Carew's representatives had arrived at the Priest's House because he had requested that his ashes be scattered on the farm at Smallhythe:

> and there they were in the nasty little box . . . I told them to be off. . . . The next morning I went out into the garden and do you know what they had done – they had thrown the box over the hedge. . . . I buried it in the rubbish dump over by the hedge.

According to Margaret Steen, however, it had been a gardener who tried to dispose of them this way, and Ellen's niece, Olive Chaplin, had stopped him and buried them at the end of the garden.[3]

Although the Smallhythe property was left to the National Trust, Chris and Tony were given the right to live there during their lifetime. They became reclusive: the chain on the door was permanently on and visitors heard only shuffling from within. In her nineties, Clare Atwood went into a nursing home, while

Chris went into Tenterden hospital. On visiting her there, Donald Sinden was greeted by a frazzled matron who informed him that Chris was a terrible woman: she'd been insufferably rude to the other patients and thrown her lunch tray at a nurse. But when he started to speak to Chris about Ellen, she became a different person, happy and talkative.

Chris and Tony Atwood were buried side by side in the little graveyard at Smallhythe.

Writing of Edy's death, Ted said 'our friendship (E & I) was an ideal thing from year 1 to year 20 or so – then a large gap – and it became ideal about 2 months ago – and we both looked forward to ending as we began.'[4]

He was not to return to England, moving instead to the south of France, where he became a well-known figure in his straw hat, brandishing Irving's walking stick. In 1957, he was shocked by the death of his faithful love, Elena; and then again by that of his friend, Martin Shaw, the following year. In 1966, at the age of ninety four, while still working on his manuscripts, Ted himself died. The influence of that small family – Ellen and Godwin, Ted and Edy – had been remarkable. To their friends and followers, the world was a greyer place.

MAIN EVENTS 1847-1947
AND KEY PARTS PLAYED
BY ELLEN TERRY

1847   Ellen Terry born 27 February in Coventry.

1856   Appeared as Mamillius in *The Winter's Tale*, 28 April, Princesses Theatre.
       Puck, *Midsummer Night's Dream*, 15 October, Princesses.

1857   Fairy Goldenstar, *The White Cat*, 26 December, Princesses.

1858   Fairy Dragonetta, *The White Cat*, 26 January, Princesses.
       Prince Arthur, *King John*, 18 October, Princesses.

1860   *Drawing Room Entertainment* tour of Britain.

1861   Clementine, *Attar Gull*, 12 November, Royalty Theatre.

1862   Gertrude, *The Little Treasure*, 27 November, Theatre Royal Bristol.

1863   Titania, *Midsummer Night's Dream*, 4 March, Theatre Royal Bath.
       Gertrude, *The Little Treasure*, 19 March, Haymarket Theatre.
       Mary Meredith, *Our American Cousin*, 26 December, Haymarket.

1864   20 February, Ellen marries G.F. Watts.

1864   Winter, separation from G.F. Watts.

1866   *The Hunchback*, 20 June (benefit performance for elder sister, Kate).

1867   Katherine, *Katherine and Petruchio*, 26 December, Queen's Theatre. First appearance with Henry Irving.

1868   Kitty, *A Household Fairy*, 24 February, Queens.
       10 October, eloped with Edward Godwin.

1869   9 December, birth of a daughter, Edith.

1872   16 January, birth of a son, Edward (known as Gordon Craig).

1874   Returned to stage as Philippa Chester, in *The Wandering Heir*, 28 February, New Queens.

1875   Portia, *Merchant of Venice*, 17 April, Prince of Wales. Separation from Godwin.

1877   G.F. Watts files for divorce.
        In spring, Ellen marries Charles Wardell (stage name, Charles Kelly).

1878   Olivia, *Olivia*, 30 March.

1878   Ophelia, *Hamlet*, 30 December, Lyceum Theatre. Beginning of stage partnership with Henry Irving.

1879   Portia, *The Merchant of Venice*, 1 November, Lyceum.

1880   Beatrice, *Much Ado About Nothing*, Lyceum.

1881   Separation from Charles Wardell.
        Desdemona, *Othello*, 2 May, Lyceum.

1882   Juliet, *Romeo and Juliet*, 8 March, Lyceum.

1883   First of six tours of America.

1884   Viola, *Twelfth Night*, 8 July, Lyceum.

1885   Margaret, *Faust*, 19 December, Lyceum.
        17 April, Charles Wardell dies.

1886   6 October, Edward Godwin dies.

1888   Lady Macbeth, *Macbeth*, 17 November, Lyceum.

1890   Lucy Ashton, *Ravenswood*, 20 September, Lyceum.

1891   Nance Oldfield, *Nance Oldfield*, 12 May, Lyceum.

1892   Correspondence with George Bernard Shaw begins.
        Cordelia, *King Lear*, 10 November, Lyceum.
        Katherine, *Henry VIII*, 5 January, Lyceum.

1893   Rosamund, *Becket*, 6 February, Lyceum.
        27 March, Ellen's son Ted marries May Gibson.

1895   Guinevere, *King Arthur*, 12 January, Lyceum.
        Brief involvement of Edy and Sydney Valentine during American tour.

1896   Imogen, *Cymbeline*, 22 September, Lyceum.

1897   Catharine, *Madame Sans-Gêne*, 10 April, Lyceum.

1898   Empress Catherine, *Peter the Great*, 1 January, Lyceum.

1899   Clarisse, *Robespierre*, 15 April, Lyceum.
        Edy meets Christabel Marshall, known as Christopher St John, with whom she lives for the rest of her life.

1901   Volumnia, *Coriolanus*, 15 April, Lyceum.
        End of Ellen's Lyceum partnership with Irving.

1902   March, Ted elopes with Elena Meo.
       Mistress Page, *Merry Wives of Windsor*, 10 June, His Majesty's Theatre.

1903   Hiordis, *The Vikings*, 15 April, Imperial Theatre.
       Martin Shaw proposes to Edy.

1905   Alice Gray, *Alice-sit-by-the-Fire*, 5 April, Duke of York Theatre.
       13 October, Henry Irving dies.

1906   Ellen celebrates her stage jubilee.
       Lady Cecily Waynflete, *Captain Brassbound's Conversion*, 20 March, Court Theatre.
       Hermione, *A Winter's Tale*, 1 September, His Majesty's.

1907   22 March, Ellen marries James Carew in Pittsburg.

1910   Ellen tours America lecturing on Shakespeare's heroines.
       Informal separation from James Carew.

1911   Pioneer Players founded by Edy.

1914   Ellen tours Australia lecturing on Shakespeare's heroines.

1921   Pioneer Players dissolved.

1925   Ellen made Dame Grand Cross of the Most Excellent Order of the British Empire.

1928   21 July, Ellen dies at Smallhythe.

1947   27 March, Edy dies at Smallhythe, a century after Ellen's birth.

NOTES

CHAPTER 1

1 Ellen Terry, *Ellen Terry's Memoirs* with preface, notes and additional biographical chapters by Edith Craig and Christopher St John (Victor Gollancz, 1933).

2 T. Edgar Pemberton, *Ellen Terry and Her Sisters* (Arthur Pearson, 1902).

3 *Ellen Terry's Memoirs* op. cit.

4 Notes in *Ellen Terry's Memoirs* op. cit.

5 Ellen Terry, 'Stray Memories' in *The New Review* Nos 23, 24 and 25, 1891.

6 *Ellen Terry's Memoirs* op. cit.

7 Ellen Terry, 'Stray Memories' op. cit.

8 *Ellen Terry's Memoirs* op. cit.

9 Ibid.

10 Ibid.

11 Clement Scott, *Ellen Terry* (New York, Frederick A. Stokes Company, 1900).

CHAPTER 2

1 John Ruskin to Margaret Bell in *The Winnington Letters*, edited by Van Akin Burd (Allen & Unwin, 1969).

2 Ronald Chapman, *The Laurel and the Thorn: a study of G.F. Watts* (Faber & Faber, 1945).

3 Wilfrid Blunt, *England's Michelangelo: a biography of George Frederic Watts* (Hamish Hamilton, 1975).

4 Ronald Chapman, *The Laurel and the Thorn* op. cit.

5 Wilfrid Blunt, *England's Michelangelo* op. cit.

6 A.M.W. Stirling, *Life's Little Day* (Butterworth, 1924).

7 A typewritten version, Watts' Gallery, Compton, Surrey.

8 Kerrison Preston (ed.), *Letters from Graham Robertson* (Hamish Hamilton, 1953).

9 Daphne du Maurier, *The Young George du Maurier* (Peter Davies, 1951).

10 Henry Silver's Diary, MSS, *Punch* Publications.
11 Violet Hunt, typewritten record, Watts' Gallery, Compton, Surrey.
12 Christopher St John (ed.), *Ellen Terry and Bernard Shaw: a correspondence* (Constable, 1931).
13 Ellen Terry, *Ellen Terry's Memoirs* with preface, notes and additional biographical chapters by Edith Craig and Christopher St John (Victor Gollancz, 1933).
14 Marguerite Steen, *A Pride of Terrys* (Longmans, 1962).
15 Ellen Terry, *Ellen Terry's Memoirs* op. cit.
16 Wilfrid Blunt, *England's Michelangelo* op. cit.
17 David Loshak, 'G.F. Watts and Ellen Terry' in *The Burlington Magazine* November 1963.
18 A.M.W. Stirling, *Life's Little Day* op. cit.
19 Ibid.
20 Wilfrid Blunt, *England's Michelangelo* op. cit.
21 Ellen Terry, *Ellen Terry's Memoirs* op. cit.
22 *Munsey's* magazine, February 1907.
23 Lady Duff Gordon, *Discretions and Indiscretions* (Jarrolds, 1932).
24 Edward Godwin, MSS, Ellen Terry Memorial Museum, Smallhythe.
25 Ellen Terry, ibid.
26 Lewis Carroll, *The Diaries of Lewis Carroll* edited by Roger Lancelyn Green (Cassell, 1930).
27 *The Heart of Ellen Terry*: collection of letters to Stephen Coleridge (Mills & Boon, 1928).
28 G.K. Chesterton, *G.F. Watts* (Duckworth, 1904).

CHAPTER 3
1 Dudley Harbron, *The Conscious Stone* (Latimer House, 1949).
2 Notes in *Ellen Terry's Memoirs* with preface, notes and additional biographical chapters by Edith Craig and Christopher St John (Victor Gollancz, 1933).
3 Graham Robertson, *Time Was* (Hamish Hamilton, 1931).
4 Christopher St John (ed.), *Ellen Terry and Bernard Shaw: a correspondence* (Constable, 1931).
5 Edward Godwin, MSS, Ellen Terry Memorial Museum, Smallhythe.

CHAPTER 4
1 Christopher St John (ed.), *Ellen Terry and Bernard Shaw: a correspondence* (Constable, 1931).
2 Ellen Terry, *Ellen Terry's Memoirs* with preface, notes and additional biographical chapters by Edith Craig and Christopher St John (Victor Gollancz, 1933).

3 Ibid.
4 Edward Gordon Craig, *Index to the Story of My Days* (Hulton Press, 1957).
5 Ibid.
6 Edward Gordon Craig, *Ellen Terry and Her Secret Self* (Sampson Low, Marston & Co. Ltd, 1931).
7 Sir Johnston Forbes-Robertson, *A Player Under Three Reigns* (T. Fisher Unwin, 1925).

CHAPTER 5
1 Ellen Terry, *Ellen Terry's Memoirs* with preface, notes and additional biographical chapters by Edith Craig and Christopher St John (Victor Gollancz, 1933).
2 Charles L. Reade and the Reverend Compton Reade, *Charles Reade* (Chapman & Hall, 1887)
3 Malcolm Elwin, *Charles Reade* (Jonathan Cape, 1931).
4 Edward Gordon Craig, *Ellen Terry and Her Secret Self* (Sampson Low, Marston & Co. Ltd, 1931).
5 Sir Johnston Forbes-Robertson, *A Player Under Three Reigns* (T. Fisher Unwin, 1925).
6 Ellen Terry, *Ellen Terry's Memoirs* op. cit.
7 Ibid.
8 The Bancrofts, *Recollections of 60 Years* (John Murray, 1909).
9 Ellen Terry, *Ellen Terry's Memoirs* op. cit.
10 Ibid.
11 Edward Godwin, MSS, Ellen Terry Memorial Museum, Smallhythe.
12 Edward Gordon Craig, *Index to the Story of My Days* (Hulton Press, 1957).
13 Notes in *Ellen Terry's Memoirs* op. cit.
14 Edward Craig, *Gordon Craig* (Victor Gollancz, 1968).
15 Kerrison Preston (ed.), *Letters from Graham Robertson* (Hamish Hamilton, 1953).
16 T. Edgar Pemberton, *Ellen Terry and Her Sisters* (Arthur Pearson, 1902).

CHAPTER 6
1 Clement Scott, *Ellen Terry* (New York, Frederick A. Stokes Company, 1900).
2 Ellen Terry, *Ellen Terry's Memoirs* with preface, notes and additional biographical chapters by Edith Craig and Christopher St John (Victor Gollancz, 1933).
3 Charles L. Reade and the Reverend Compton Reade, *Charles Reade* (Chapman & Hall, 1887).
4 Notes in *Ellen Terry's Memoirs* op. cit.

5   Edward Gordon Craig, *Index to the Story of My Days* (Hulton Press, 1957).
6   Ibid.
7   Ibid.
8   Clement Scott, *Ellen Terry* op. cit.
9   Ibid.
10 Notes in *Ellen Terry's Memoirs* op. cit.
11 Ibid.
12 Ellen Terry, *Ellen Terry's Memoirs* op. cit.
13 Ibid.
14 Ibid.
15 Christopher St John (ed.), *Ellen Terry and Bernard Shaw: a correspondence* (Constable, 1931).
16 Edward Gordon Craig, *Ellen Terry and Her Secret Self* (Sampson Low, Marston & Co. Ltd, 1931).
17 Notes in *Ellen Terry's Memoirs* op. cit.

CHAPTER 7

1   Laurence Irving, *Henry Irving* (Faber & Faber, 1951).
2   Ellen Terry, *Ellen Terry's Memoirs* with preface, notes and additional biographical chapters by Edith Craig and Christopher St John (Victor Gollancz, 1933).
3   Ibid.
4   Edward Gordon Craig, *Index to the Story of My Days* (Hulton Press, 1957).
5   Ibid.
6   Henry Irving, MSS, Ellen Terry Memorial Museum, Smallhythe.
7   Ibid.
8   Edward Gordon Craig, *Index to the Story of My Days* op. cit.
9   Ibid.
10 Margaret Webster, *The Same Only Different* (Victor Gollancz, 1969).
11 Marguerite Steen, *A Pride of Terrys* (Longmans, 1962).
12 Lady Duff Gordon, *Discretions and Indiscretions* (Jarrolds, 1932).
13 Violet Hunt, typewritten record, Watts' Gallery, Compton, Surrey.
14 Sir Frank Benson, *My Memoirs* (Ernest Benn, 1930).
15 Ellen Terry, *Ellen Terry's Memoirs* op. cit.
16 Max Beerbohm, *Around Theatres* (Rupert Hart-Davies, 1953).
17 Ellen Terry, *Ellen Terry's Memoirs* op. cit.
18 Clement Scott, *Ellen Terry* (New York, Frederick A. Stokes Company, 1900).
19 Kerrison Preston (ed.), *Letters from Graham Robertson* (Hamish Hamilton, 1953).

20 'Shakespeare's Heroines', lecture notes, Ellen Terry Memorial Museum, Smallhythe.
21 Ellen Terry, *Ellen Terry's Memoirs* op. cit.
22 Ibid.
23 Edward Gordon Craig, *Index to the Story of My Days* op. cit.
24 Laurence Irving, *Henry Irving* op. cit.
25 Ellen Terry, *Ellen Terry's Memoirs* op. cit.
26 'Shakespeare's Heroines', lecture notes, Ellen Terry Memorial Museum, Smallhythe.
27 Ellen Terry, *Ellen Terry's Memoirs* op. cit.
28 Edward Gordon Craig, *Index to the Story of My Days* op. cit.
29 Ibid.
30 Ellen Terry, *Ellen Terry's Memoirs* op. cit.

CHAPTER 8

1 Ellen Terry, *Ellen Terry's Memoirs* with preface, notes and additional biographical chapters by Edith Craig and Christopher St John (Victor Gollancz, 1933).
2 Ibid.
3 Eve Adam (ed.), *Mrs J. Comyns Carr's Reminiscences* (Hutchinson, 1928).
4 Ibid.
5 Blanche Patch, *Thirty Years with G.B.S.* (Victor Gollancz, 1951).
6 Laurence Irving, *Henry Irving* (Faber & Faber, 1951).
7 Ellen Terry, MSS, Ellen Terry Memorial Museum, Smallhythe.
8 Ellen Terry, *Ellen Terry's Memoirs*, op. cit.
9 Eve Adam (ed.), *Mrs J. Comyns Carr's Reminiscences* op. cit.
10 H. Chance Newton, *Cues and Curtain Calls* (Bodley Head, 1927).
11 Edward Gordon Craig, *Index to the Story of My Days* (Hulton Press, 1957).
12 Ellen Terry Memorial Museum, Smallhythe.
13 Irene Vanbrugh, *To Tell My Story* (Hutchinson, 1948).
14 Violet Vanbrugh, *Dare to be Wise* (Hodder & Stoughton, 1925).
15 Marguerite Steen, *Looking Glass* (Longmans, 1966).
16 Lady Duff Gordon, *Discretions and Indiscretions* (Jarrolds, 1932).
17 Ibid.
18 Ibid.
19 Ellen Terry Memorial Museum, Smallhythe.
20 Ellen Terry, *Ellen Terry's Memoirs* op. cit.
21 Edward Gordon Craig, *Index to the Story of My Days* op. cit.

CHAPTER 9

1 Ellen Terry Memorial Museum, Smallhythe.
2 Ibid.

3   Dudley Harbron, *The Conscious Stone* (Latimer House, 1949).
4   Ellen Terry Memorial Museum, Smallhythe.
5   Gordon Craig Collection, Bibliothèque Nationale, Paris.
6   Edward Gordon Craig, *Ellen Terry and her Secret Self* (Sampson Low, Marston & Co. Ltd, 1931).
7   Ellen Terry, *Ellen Terry's Memoirs* with preface, notes and additional biographical chapters by Edith Craig and Christopher St John (Victor Gollancz, 1933).
8   Eve Adam (ed.), *Mrs J. Comyns Carr's Reminiscences* (Hutchinson, 1928).
9   Notes to *Ellen Terry's Memoirs* op. cit.
10 Ibid.
11 Charles Hiatt, *Ellen Terry* (Chiswick Press, 1899).
12 Irene Vanbrugh, *To Tell My Story* (Hutchinson, 1948).
13 Ellen Terry Memorial Museum, Smallhythe.
14 Charles Hiatt, *Ellen Terry* op. cit.
15 Clement Scott, *Ellen Terry* (New York, Frederick A. Stokes Company, 1900).
16 Ellen Terry Memorial Museum, Smallhythe.
17 Ellen Terry, *Ellen Terry's Memoirs* op. cit.
18 Ibid.
19 Ibid.
20 Ibid.
21 Edward Gordon Craig, *Index to the Story of My Days* (Hulton Press, 1957).
22 Ibid.
23 Florence Locke, in *Edy* ed. Eleanor Adlard (Muller, 1949).
24 Ellen Terry, *Ellen Terry's Memoirs* op. cit.
25 W. Graham Robertson, *Time Was* (Hamish Hamilton, 1931).
26 Ellen Terry Memorial Museum, Smallhythe.
27 Ellen Terry, *Ellen Terry's Memoirs* op. cit.
28 Ibid.
29 Ibid.

CHAPTER 10

1   Ellen Terry, *Ellen Terry's Memoirs* with preface, notes and additional biographical chapters by Edith Craig and Christopher St John (Victor Gollancz, 1933).
2   Christopher St John (ed.), *Ellen Terry and Bernard Shaw: a correspondence* (Constable, 1931).
3   Laurence Irving, *Henry Irving* (Faber & Faber, 1951).
4   Ellen Terry Memorial Museum, Smallhythe.
5   Ibid.

CHAPTER 11

1 Ellen Terry, *Ellen Terry's Memoirs* with preface, notes and additional biographical chapters by Edith Craig and Christopher St John (Victor Gollancz, 1933).
2 Ibid.
3 Ellen Terry Memorial Museum, Smallhythe.
4 Margaret Webster, *The Same Only Different* (Victor Gollancz, 1969).
5 Ibid.
6 Ibid.
7 Amy Leslie, *Some Players* (New York, Herbert S. Stone & Co, 1899).
8 Christopher St John (ed.), *Ellen Terry and Bernard Shaw: a correspondence* (Constable, 1931).
9 Laurence Irving, *Henry Irving* (Faber & Faber, 1951).
10 Ellen Terry Memorial Museum, Smallhythe.
11 Christopher St John (ed.), *Ellen Terry and Bernard Shaw: a correspondence* op. cit.
12 Ellen Terry, *Ellen Terry's Memoirs* op. cit.
13 Christopher St John (ed.), *Ellen Terry and Bernard Shaw: a correspondence* op. cit.
14 Ibid.
15 Ibid.
16 Laurence Irving, *Henry Irving* op. cit.
17 Christopher St John (ed.), *Ellen Terry and Bernard Shaw: a correspondence* op. cit.
18 Ellen Terry Memorial Museum, Smallhythe.
19 Mrs Aria, *My Sentimental Self* (Chapman & Hall, 1922).
20 Marguerite Steen, *A Pride of Terrys* (Longmans, 1962).
21 Christopher St John (ed.), *Ellen Terry and Bernard Shaw: a correspondence* op. cit.
22 Ibid.
23 Ibid.
24 Ibid.
25 Edward Gordon Craig, *Index to the Story of My Days* (Hulton Press, 1957).
26 Christopher St John (ed.), *Ellen Terry and Bernard Shaw: a correspondence* op. cit.
27 Ibid.
28 Ellen Terry Memorial Museum, Smallhythe.
29 Ibid.
30 Christopher St John (ed.), *Ellen Terry and Bernard Shaw: a correspondence* op. cit.
31 Ellen Terry, *Ellen Terry's Memoirs* op. cit.
32 Notes in *Ellen Terry's Memoirs* op. cit.

33   May Whitty, *Edy* ed. Eleanor Adlard (Muller, 1949).
34   Gordon Craig Collection, Bibliothèque Nationale, Paris.

CHAPTER 12
1   Christopher St John, in *Edy* ed. Eleanor Adlard (Muller, 1949).
2   Ibid.
3   Irene Cooper Willis, in *Edy* op. cit.
4   Marguerite Steen, *Pride of Terrys* (Longmans, 1962).
5   Christopher St John, *Hungerheart: the story of a soul* (Methuen, 1915).
6   Ibid.
7   Ellen Terry Memorial Museum, Smallhythe.
8   Christopher St John (ed.), *Ellen Terry and Bernard Shaw: a correspondence* (Constable, 1931).
9   Ellen Terry, *Ellen Terry's Memoirs* with preface, notes and additional biographical chapters by Edith Craig and Christopher St John (Victor Gollancz, 1933).
10   Ibid.
11   Christopher St John (ed.), *Ellen Terry and Bernard Shaw: a correspondence* op. cit.
12   Mrs Aria, *My Sentimental Self* (Chapman & Hall, 1922).
13   Edward Craig, *Gordon Craig: the story of his life* (Victor Gollancz, 1968).
14   Edward Gordon Craig, *Index to the Story of My Days* (Hulton Press, 1957).
15   Ellen Terry, *Ellen Terry's Memoirs* op. cit.
16   Edward Gordon Craig, *Index to the Story of My Days* op. cit.
17   Christopher St John, *Hungerheart* op. cit.
18   Gordon Craig Collection, Bibliothèque Nationale, Paris.
19   Christopher St John, *Hungerheart* op. cit.
20   Ibid.
21   Ibid.
22   Gordon Craig Collection, Bibliothèque Nationale, Paris.
23   Christopher St John, in *Edy* op. cit.
24   Edward Gordon Craig, *Index to the Story of My Days* op. cit.
25   Laurence Irving, *Henry Irving* (Faber & Faber, 1951).
26   Edward Gordon Craig, *Index to the Story of My Days* op. cit.
27   Isadora Duncan, *My Life* (Victor Gollancz, 1928).
28   Cicely Hamilton, *Life Errant* (J.M. Dent, 1935).
29   Christopher St John (ed.), *Ellen Terry and Bernard Shaw: a correspondence* op. cit.
30   Notes in *Ellen Terry's Memoirs* op. cit.
31   Ellen Terry Memorial Museum, Smallhythe.
32   James Agate, *Those Were the Nights* (Fleet Street Press, 1946).
33   *McClures Magazine*.

34 Ellen Terry Memorial Museum, Smallhythe.
35 Christopher St John, *Hungerheart* op. cit.
36 Allan Wade, in *Edy* op. cit.
37 Christopher St John (ed.), *Ellen Terry and Bernard Shaw: a correspondence* op. cit.

CHAPTER 13
1   Ellen Terry, *Ellen Terry's Memoirs* with preface, notes and additional biographical chapters by Edith Craig and Christopher St John (Victor Gollancz, 1933).
2   Edward Gordon Craig, *Index to the Story of My Days* (Hulton Press, 1957)
3   Margot Peters, *Bernard Shaw and the Actresses* (Doubleday, 1980).
4   Ellen Terry, *Ellen Terry's Memoirs* op. cit.
5   W. Macqueen Pope, *Ladies First* (W.H. Allen, 1952).
6   Ella Hepworth Dixon, *As I Knew Them* (Hutchinson, 1930).
7   Margot Peters, *Bernard Shaw and the Actresses* op. cit.
8   Notes in *Ellen Terry's Memoirs* op. cit.
9   Edward Gordon Craig, *Index to the Story of My Days* op. cit.
10 Ellen Terry Memorial Museum, Smallhythe.
11 Ibid.
12 Ibid.

CHAPTER 14
1   Ellen Terry Memorial Museum, Smallhythe.
2   Ibid.
3   Cecily Hamilton, in *Edy* ed. Eleanor Adlard (Muller, 1949).
4   Sybil Thorndike, in *Edy* op. cit.
5   Ibid.
6   Cecily Hamilton, in *Edy* op. cit.
7   Pioneer Players' Reports, 1911, Ellen Terry Memorial Museum, Smallhythe.
8   *Votes for Women* 12 November 1909.
9   Pioneer Players' Reports, 1911, Ellen Terry Memorial Museum, Smallhythe.
10 Ellen Terry Memorial Museum, Smallhythe.
11 Ellen Terry, *Ellen Terry's Memoirs* with preface, notes and additional biographical chapters by Edith Craig and Christopher St John (Victor Gollancz, 1933).
12 Pioneer Players' Reports, 1912, Ellen Terry Memorial Museum, Smallhythe.
13 Ibid.
14 Ibid.

CHAPTER 15
1   Ellen Terry Memorial Museum, Smallhythe.
2   Ellen Terry, *Ellen Terry's Memoirs* with preface, notes and additional biographical chapters by Edith Craig and Christopher St John (Victor Gollancz, 1933).
3   Ibid.
4   Ibid.
5   Ellen Terry Memorial Museum, Smallhythe.
6   Ellen Terry, *Ellen Terry's Memoirs* op. cit.

CHAPTER 16
1   Pioneer Players' Reports, 1917, Ellen Terry Memorial Museum, Smallhythe.
2   Margaret Webster, in *Edy* ed. Eleanor Adlard (Muller, 1949).
3   Christopher St John, in *Edy* op. cit.
4   Sheila Kaye Smith, in *Edy* op. cit.
5   Sybil Thorndike, in *Edy* op. cit.
6   Irene Cooper Willis, in *Edy* op. cit.
7   Florence Locke, in *Edy* op. cit.
8   Clare Atwood, in *Edy* op. cit.
9   Pioneer Players' Reports, 1921, Ellen Terry Memorial Museum, Smallhythe.

CHAPTER 17
1   Ellen Terry, *Ellen Terry's Memoirs* with preface, notes and additional biographical chapters by Edith Craig and Christopher St John (Victor Gollancz, 1933).
2   John Gielgud, *An Actor and His Time* (Sidgwick & Jackson, 1900).
3   Ellen Terry Memorial Museum, Smallhythe.
4   Ellen Terry, *Ellen Terry's Memoirs* op. cit.
5   Ellen Terry Memorial Museum, Smallhythe.
6   Norman MacDermott, *Everymania* (Society for Theatre Research 1975).
7   Ernest Milton, in *Edy* ed. Eleanor Adlard (Muller, 1949).
8   Ibid.
9   Richard Findlater, *Lilian Baylis* (Allen Lane, 1975).
10   Theatre Museum.
11   Marguerite Steen, *Looking Glass* (Longmans, 1966).
12   Theatre Museum.
13   Cornelia Otis Skinner, *Madam Sarah* (Michael Joseph, 1967).
14   Notes in *Ellen Terry's Memoirs* op. cit.
15   Kerrison Preston, *Letters from Graham Robertson* (Hamish Hamilton, 1953).
16   Ibid.

17   Ellen Terry Memorial Museum, Smallhythe.
18   Ibid.
19   Ibid.
20   Theatre Museum.
21   Edward Gordon Craig, *Index to the Story of My Days* (Hulton Press, 1957).

CHAPTER 18
 1   Violet Pym, in *Edy* ed. Eleanor Adlard (Muller, 1949).
 2   Michael Baker, *Our Three Selves: a life of Radclyffe Hall* (Hamish Hamilton, 1985).
 3   Eleanor Adlard, in *Edy* op. cit.
 4   Vita Sackville West, in *Edy* op. cit.
 5   Ibid.
 6   Victoria Glendinning, *Vita* (Penguin, 1983).
 7   Ibid.
 8   Michael Baker, *Our Three Selves* op. cit.
 9   Virginia Woolf, *Between the Acts* (The Hogarth Press, 1941).
10   Irene Cooper Willis, in *Edy* op. cit.

POSTSCRIPT
 1   Donald Sinden, *Laughter in the Second Act* (Hodder & Stoughton, 1985).
 2   Ibid.
 3   Marguerite Steen, *A Pride of Terrys* (Longmans, 1961).
 4   Edward Craig, *Gordon Craig* (Victor Gollancz, 1968).

SECONDARY SOURCES

Lena Ashwell, *Myself a Player* (Michael Joseph, 1936).
Denis Bablet, *Edward Gordon Craig* (Heinemann Educational Books, 1966).
Mrs Russell Barrington, *G.F. Watts: reminiscences* (George Allen, 1905).
Madeleine Bingham, *Henry Irving and the Victorian Theatre* (George Allen & Unwin, 1978).
Edward Gordon Craig, *Henry Irving* (J.M. Dent, 1930).
Alan Dent, *Mrs Patrick Campbell* (Museum Press, 1961).
Frances Donaldson, *The Actor Managers* (Weidenfeld & Nicholson, 1970).
C.G.L. Du Cann, *The Loves of George Bernard Shaw* (Arthur Barker, 1948).
Malcolm Elwin, *Charles Reade* (Jonathan Cape, 1931).
St John Ervine, *Bernard Shaw: his life, work and friends* (Constable, 1956).
Meredith Etherington-Smith and Jeremy Pilcher, *The IT Girls* (Hamish Hamilton, 1986).
Lilliam Faderman, *Surpassing the Love of Men* (The Women's Press, 1985).
Kate Terry Gielgud, *An Autobiography* (Max Reinhardt, 1953).
Ronald Hayman, *Gielgud* (Heinemann, 1971).
Julie Holledge, *Innocent Flowers: women in the Edwardian Theatre* (Virago, 1981).
Amanda Hopkinson, *Julia Margaret Cameron* (Virago, 1986).
C.D. Innes, *Edward Gordon Craig* (Cambridge University Press, 1983).
Laurence Irving, *The Successors* (Rupert-Hart Davis, 1967).
Laurence Irving, *The Precarious Crust* (Chatto & Windus, 1971).
Elizabeth Longford, *Eminent Victorian Women* (Papermac, 1982).
Roger Manvell, *Ellen Terry* (William Heinemann, 1968).
Jeremy Mass, *The Victorian Art World* (Barrie & Jenkins 1984).
C.C. Hoyer Millar, *George du Maurier and others* (Cassell, 1937).

Tom Prideaux, *Love or Nothing: the life and times of Ellen Terry* (Millington, 1975).

Enid Rose, *Gordon Craig and the Theatre* (Sampson Low, Marston & Co Ltd, 1931).

Christopher St John, *Ellen Terry* (John Lane, The Bodley Head, 1907).

Mrs Clement Scott, *Old Days in Bohemian London* (New York, Frederick A. Stokes Company).

Ernest Short, *Introducing the Theatre* (Eyre & Spottiswoode, 1949).

Cornelia Otis Skinner, *Madame Sarah* (Cedric Chivers, 1967).

Elizabeth Sprigge, *Sybil Thorndike Casson* (Victor Gollancz, 1971).

Ellaline Terriss, *Just a Little Bit of String* (Hutchinson, 1955).

Lady Maud Warrender, *My First Sixty Years* (Cassell, 1933).

A.A.E. Wilson, *The Lyceum* (Dennis Yates, 1952).

Silver urn, designed by John Paul Cooper, containing Ellen's ashes at St Paul's Church, Covent Garden.

INDEX